Enhancing Student Support and Learning Through Conversational AI

Suha Khalil Assayed
The British University in Dubai, UAE

IGI Global
Scientific Publishing
Publishing Tomorrow's Research Today

Vice President of Editorial | Melissa Wagner
Director of Acquisitions | Mikaela Felty
Director of Book Development | Jocelynn Hessler
Production Manager | Mike Brehm
Cover Design | Jose Rosado

Published in the United States of America by
IGI Global Scientific Publishing
701 East Chocolate Avenue
Hershey, PA, 17033, USA
Tel: 717-533-8845
Fax: 717-533-7115
Website: https://www.igi-global.com E-mail: cust@igi-global.com

Library of Congress Cataloging-in-Publication Data

Names: Assayed, Suha Khalil, 1973- editor
http://id.loc.gov/authorities/names/n2025026714
http://id.loc.gov/rwo/agents/n2025026714
Title: Enhancing student support and learning through conversational AI /
[edited by] Suha Khalil Assayed.
Description: Hershey, PA : IGI Global Scientific Publishing, [2026] |
Includes bibliographical references and index. | Summary: "This book
aims to provide novel research and models for deploying Conversational
AI and chatbots in education, covering both K-12 and higher education"--
Provided by publisher.
Identifiers: LCCN 2025019847 (print) | LCCN 2025019848 (ebook) | ISBN
9798337333168 hardcover | ISBN 9798337333175 paperback | ISBN
9798337333182 ebook
Subjects: LCSH: Artificial intelligence--Educational applications
http://id.loc.gov/authorities/subjects/sh87006783 | Education--Effect of
technological innovations on
http://id.loc.gov/authorities/subjects/sh97007113
Classification: LCC LB1028.43 .E488 2026 (print) | LCC LB1028.43 (ebook)
| DDC 370.285/63--dc23/eng/20250620
LC record available at https://lccn.loc.gov/2025019847
LC ebook record available at https://lccn.loc.gov/2025019848

British Cataloguing in Publication Data
A Cataloguing in Publication record for this book is available from the British Library.

Table of Contents

Detailed Table of Contents

This chapter explores the evolving role of artificial intelligence (AI) in virtual counseling, student guidance, and career advising. It examines foundational AI technologies such as natural language processing, machine learning, and recommender systems, highlighting their applications in mental health support, personalized academic advising, and career planning. The chapter discusses the benefits of AI-driven tools, including scalability, personalization, and accessibility, while addressing challenges related to data privacy, algorithmic bias, transparency, and the need for human oversight. Future directions emphasize hybrid human-AI models, emotionally intelligent systems, culturally adaptive frameworks, and lifelong advising ecosystems. Ultimately, this chapter underscores the transformative potential of AI to enhance educational support through ethical, inclusive, and human-centered approaches, fostering improved student outcomes and well-being.

In our current world, technology has impacted almost every element of human life, changing how we work, communicate, learn, and even take care of our health. One field that has been affected is psychological counseling. Artificial intelligence (AI) is playing significant role in the field of mental health as technology advances, changing how people seek assistance and how psychologist practitioners conduct therapy. There are many exciting opportunities associated with the development of AI-powered solutions for mental health, but there are also important obstacles that must be carefully considered. The function of psychological counseling in the era of artificial intelligence will be examined in this article, along with how AI is being

In recent years, the integration of Conversational AI in education has revolutionized the way students receive support, interact with educational content, and manage their well-being. Conversational AI—comprising chatbots, virtual assistants, and natural language processing (NLP) models—has emerged as a powerful tool for fostering a more inclusive, personalized, and accessible learning environment. With the increasing reliance on digital education and remote learning, AI-driven solutions play a critical role in addressing the diverse needs of students, offering timely assistance, and improving their overall academic experience. Conversational AI systems serve as virtual tutors, academic advisors, and emotional support agents, ensuring that students have access to reliable assistance at all times. These AI-powered tools provide instant responses to queries related to coursework, assignments, deadlines, and general academic concerns.

This chapter explores how a conversational AI teaching assistant can influence second language (L2) writing by giving advice on creating ideas, organizing thoughts, improving grammar, and expanding vocabulary. Using a qualitative approach rooted in Grounded Theory and supported by sentiment analysis, it looked at answers to six open-ended questions. These questions aimed at exploring students' experiences, including how their writing enhanced, the difficulties they met, and suggestions they would provide. Open, axial, and selective coding revealed that most students found that the AI was useful for reducing writing anxiety, building confidence, and providing immediate constructive feedback. Yet, some concerns were also surfaced. Overwhelming feedback and the potential loss of personal writing style were the major concerns. Consequently, effectiveness of conversational AI in L2 writing hinges on its ability to balance structured guidance with learner autonomy through adaptive, context-sensitive support. Several recommendations were provided based on study findings.

In today's evolving educational landscape, conversational AI is emerging as a powerful ally for both learners and educators. This chapter explores how tools like chatbots, voice assistants, and virtual tutors are making education more personalized, supportive, and accessible. By interacting in natural language, these AI systems offer real-time guidance, answer questions, and adapt to individual learning needs. For educators, they reduce workload by handling repetitive tasks and providing insights into student progress. The chapter also addresses important concerns around privacy, bias, and digital inclusion, and shares real-world examples of how conversational AI is creating more engaging and equitable learning environments.

This chapter explores the critical privacy and security challenges posed by AI-powered education tools. It examines how AI enhances student support and personalized learning while highlighting risks associated with chatbots, data collection, and processing. Ethical concerns, including consent and fairness, are discussed alongside the complexities of global regulations such as GDPR and FERPA. The chapter also addresses cybersecurity threats targeting educational AI systems and presents strategies to mitigate these risks. Emerging privacy-preserving techniques like federated learning and differential privacy are evaluated for their potential to safeguard student data. Drawing on case studies, it identifies best practices for ethical AI implementation and offers actionable recommendations for educators and

Preface

Artificial Intelligence (AI) is quickly revolutionizing education by utilizing advanced algorithms and models, leading to significant changes in traditional teaching practices and student advising (Tedre et al., 2021). Interestingly, within the field of conversational AI, applications such as chatbots, virtual assistants, and intelligent tutoring platforms have made significant progress in supporting classroom instruction, academic advising, administrative coordination, emotional well-being (Al-Sayed et al., 2024), and even in the leadership of educational initiatives.

Artificial intelligence systems, empowered by cutting-edge Natural Language Processing (NLP) and machine learning models, are reshaping the learning process by making it more interactive, personalized, and responsive. In particular, companies such as OpenAI, Google DeepMind, Meta, Microsoft, and Amazon which are pioneering the development of NLP and generative AI technologies based on transformer architectures (Vaswani et al., 2017) and deep neural networks. These models such as GPT, Claude, Gemini, and LLaMA are increasingly being integrated into conversational AI systems that can simulate human-like interactions. This integration significantly enhances the educational experience by enabling more natural between learners and digital platforms, thereby supporting more effective and engaging learning environment. Several researchers have been inspired to study the challenges and effectiveness of using such models in education, particularly by comparing them with other models. For example, Lin (2024) discussed the strengths and challenges of using ChatGPT with adult learners, particularly exploring its role as a virtual tutor to facilitate self-directed learning (SDL). Another study conducted by Assayed et al. (2024a) evaluated the effectiveness of ChatGPT 3.5 in comparison with a Seq2Seq-based chatbot, which was built using an Encoder–Decoder architecture and trained on a dataset using a specific domain of student inquiries.

In general, the conversational AI empowers students to become more independent and confident learners (Alqahtani et al., 2023) while encouraging educators and developers to innovate in creating more inclusive, accessible, and effective educational tools. In fact, educators including school teachers or university professors have increasingly included AI in different aspects of education. For instance, teachers use AI tools to track student progress (Fitria, 2021) and customize learning materials, while professors in higher education apply AI for grading assignments, conducting research, and guiding students through intelligent tutoring systems (Pillai et al., 2024).

As AI continues to transform educational environments, its role has also extended to supporting students' mental health and emotional well-being. Intelligent systems now utilize sentiment analysis and behavioral data to identify signs of stress, anxiety, or disengagement, enabling timely and personalized interventions. Assayed et al. (2023) proposed a chatbot designed to detect students' emotions using machine learning algorithms. The authors utilized a dataset of 41,157 COVID-19-related tweets from the Kaggle platform, enabling the system to identify signs of stress and emotional distress based on users' posts.

Furthermore, conversational agents and AI-powered virtual counselors give students a safe and private space to share their feelings and get help with their mental health (Delello et al., 2025). Students often face a lot of stress from heavy schoolwork, deadlines, and high expectations, which can be hard to handle alone (Corazza, 2021; Assayed et al., 2024b)

AI is ready to listen without criticism, offering guidance and support to help students navigate challenging situations. According to the study conducted by Alshammari (2025), a ChatGPT self-help tool was tested to support university students' emotional well-being. Students found it easy to use, helpful for managing stress and anxiety, and capable of offering empathetic advice. While such technologies can improve learning outcomes and boost student engagement, they also present notable challenges in educational settings. According to Eden et al. (2024), a major challenge is ensuring equal access for all students, as differences in technology availability and internet access risk widening existing inequalities. Other concerns include protecting students' data privacy, addressing limited infrastructure, providing sufficient teacher training, and tackling algorithmic bias that may unfairly affect certain groups. Additionally, there is a risk that over-reliance on AI could diminish the essential human connection and guidance vital to effective learning (Farooqi et al., 2024).

This book, *Enhancing Student Support and Learning Through Conversational AI*, presents a comprehensive collection of research and practical implementations focused on the role of Conversational AI across educational contexts. It explores how these technologies contribute to student advising and support, whether in learning, language assistance, administrative processes, or enhancing overall student services. The book aims to provide researchers, IT developers, practitioners, and policymakers with valuable insights into the development, deployment, and impact of AI-powered systems in both K–12 and higher education environments.

Each chapter in this book examines a specific aspect of how artificial intelligence is being integrated into education. Topics range from students' experiences with AI in teaching, learning, and well-being, to the state of the art in generative AI technologies such as generative AI (GenAI) tools, large language models (LLMs), and emerging innovations using transformers and neural networks, along with the roles of educational leaders, decision-makers, developers, and AI engineers.

This book aims to bring together students, educators, school leaders, and technology developers to create a clear understanding of AI technologies like machine learning, deep learning, natural language processing (NLP), and conversational AI. It explains how these tools are transforming education by enhancing learning skills, supporting student wellbeing, providing career and guidance advising, improving language skills, and helping educational leaders. AI-powered student advisers and virtual assistants offer real-time guidance to students and assist teachers and leaders in making better decisions to create a positive learning environment.

ORGANIZATION OF THE BOOK

The book is organized into 9 chapters, each focusing on a key area of artificial intelligence integration in education. Below is a brief overview of the chapters included in each section:

Chapter 1 explores how artificial intelligence (AI) is changing educational leadership by reshaping school leaders' roles. AI supports data-driven decisions and better management, while leadership remains key to empowering staff and students. The authors in this chapter highlight the real-world examples from different countries, showing AI's benefits and challenges, including ethics, privacy, and equity.

Chapter 2 explores the AI's growing role in virtual counseling, student guidance, and career advising. It examines key AI technologies like natural language processing, machine learning, and recommender systems applied in mental health support and academic advising. The authors emphasized the importance of future human-AI collaboration and ethical approaches to improve educational support and student well-being.

Chapter 3 explores the impact of artificial intelligence on psychological counseling and mental health care. The author discusses the ways AI is transforming how individuals seek support and how therapists deliver treatment. The author also addresses the important challenges and limitations as well as highlights why human therapists remain essential in providing compassionate and effective mental health care.

Chapter 4 explores the integration of conversational AI in addressing student mental health within educational settings. It examines how AI-powered chatbots are being utilized to offer scalable, accessible, and timely psychological support. While highlighting the promise of such technologies in reducing anxiety, promoting resilience, and supplementing overburdened counseling services. The authors in this chapter also examine the key ethical concerns, including privacy, algorithmic bias, and the risk of emotional dehumanization.

Chapter 5 explores the integration of conversational AI in education has revolutionized the ways students receive support, engage with learning materials, and manage their well-being. It highlights how tools like chatbots, virtual assistants, and natural language processing models have become essential for creating more inclusive, personalized, and accessible learning environments.

Chapter 6 investigates the influence of a conversational AI teaching assistant on second language (L2) writing by offering advice on idea creation, organization, grammar, and vocabulary. Through qualitative analysis and sentiment evaluation, the study revealed that most students experienced reduced writing anxiety, increased confidence, and immediate constructive feedback, although some expressed concerns about excessive input and potential loss of personal writing style. The authors emphasize that effective AI support in L2 writing depends on balancing structured guidance with learner autonomy through adaptive, context-aware assistance.

Chapter 7 highlights the role of conversational AI as a valuable partner for both students and educators in today's evolving educational landscape. It examines how chatbots, voice assistants, and virtual tutors personalize learning, offer real-time support, and adapt to individual needs while helping educators manage workloads. The chapter also discusses challenges such as privacy and bias, and showcases examples of how conversational AI fosters more engaging and equitable learning environments.

Chapter 8 explores the critical privacy and security challenges posed by AI-powered education tools. It examines how AI enhances student support and personalized learning while highlighting risks associated with chatbots, data collection, and processing. Moreover, the authors discuss the ethical concerns, including consent and fairness, alongside the complexities of global regulations such as GDPR and FERPA. The chapter also addresses cybersecurity threats targeting educational AI systems and presents strategies to mitigate these risks.

Chapter 9 examines the integration of Generative AI (GenAI) in curriculum development using the Taba model, highlighting its role in needs diagnosis, objective setting, content selection, and evaluation. The analysis shows that GenAI can support various curriculum stages effectively when guided by teacher oversight. Additionally, the chapter discusses how GenAI's impact on students' well-being depends on its usage, emphasizing the importance of responsible integration to enhance education quality while protecting mental health.

Suha Khalil Assayed

The British University in Dubai, UAE

REFERENCES

Al-Sayed, S., Assayed, S. K., Alkhatib, M., & Shaalan, K. (2024). Impact of Artificial Intelligence Chatbots on Student Well-being and Mental Health: A Systematic Review. *People and Behavior Analysis*, *2*(2), 10–31098. DOI: 10.31098/pba.v2i2.2411

Alqahtani, T., Badreldin, H. A., Alrashed, M., Alshaya, A. I., Alghamdi, S. S., Bin Saleh, K., & Albekairy, A. M. (2023). The emergent role of artificial intelligence, natural learning processing, and large language models in higher education and research. *Research in Social & Administrative Pharmacy*, *19*(8), 1236–1242. PMID: 37321925

Alshammari, M. E. (2025). Promoting emotional and psychological well-being in students through a self-help ChatGPT intervention: Artificial intelligence powered support. *International Journal of Instruction*, *18*(3), 511–530.

Assayed, S. (2024). *HSGAdviser-BiLSTM-Chatbot*. GitHub. https://github.com/sassayed/HSGAdviser-BiLSTM-Chatbot

Assayed, S., Shaalan, K., Al-Sayed, S., & Alkhatib, M. (2023). Psychological emotion recognition of students using machine learning based chatbot. [IJAIA]. *International Journal of Artificial Intelligence & Applications*, *14*(2).

Assayed, S. K., Alkhatib, M., & Shaalan, K. (2024a). A Comparative Study of ChatGPT and Seq2Seq Chatbot for Effective Students Advising. *ChatGPT and Global Higher Education: Using Artificial Intelligence in Teaching and Learning*, 148.

Assayed, S. K., Alkhatib, M., & Shaalan, K. (2024b). A Systematic Review of Conversational AI Chatbots in Academic Advising. In Al Marri, K., Mir, F. A., David, S. A., & Al-Emran, M. (Eds.), *BUiD Doctoral Research Conference 2023. Lecture Notes in Civil Engineering* (Vol. 473). Springer., DOI: 10.1007/978-3-031-56121-4_3

Corazza, M. S. (2021). *The Senior Year High School Experience and Transition to College: Managing Stress, Expectations, and Coming of Age in the Modern Era* (Doctoral dissertation, Northeastern University).

Delello, J. A., Sung, W., Mokhtari, K., Hebert, J., Bronson, A., & De Giuseppe, T. (2025). AI in the classroom: Insights from educators on usage, challenges, and mental health. *Education Sciences*, *15*(2), 113.

Eden, C. A., Chisom, O. N., & Adeniyi, I. S. (2024). Integrating AI in education: Opportunities, challenges, and ethical considerations. *Magna Scientia Advanced Research and Reviews, 10*(2), 006-013.

Farooqi, M. T. K., Amanat, I., & Awan, S. M. (2024). Ethical considerations and challenges in the integration of artificial intelligence in education: A systematic review. *Journal of Excellence in Management Sciences*, *3*(4), 35–50.

Fitria, T. N. (2021, December). Artificial intelligence (AI) in education: Using AI tools for teaching and learning process. In *Prosiding Seminar Nasional & Call for Paper STIE AAS* (pp. 134-147).

Lin, X. (2024). Exploring the role of ChatGPT as a facilitator for motivating self-directed learning among adult learners. *Adult Learning*, *35*(3), 156–166.

Pillai, R., Sivathanu, B., Metri, B., & Kaushik, N. (2024). Students' adoption of AI-based teacher-bots (T-bots) for learning in higher education. *Information Technology & People*, *37*(1), 328–355.

Tedre, M., Toivonen, T., Kahila, J., Vartiainen, H., Valtonen, T., Jormanainen, I., & Pears, A. (2021). Teaching machine learning in K–12 classroom: Pedagogical and technological trajectories for artificial intelligence education. *IEEE Access : Practical Innovations, Open Solutions*, *9*, 110558–110572.

Vaswani, A., Shazeer, N., Parmar, N., Uszkoreit, J., Jones, L., Gomez, A. N., Kaiser, Ł., & Polosukhin, I. (2017). *Attention is all you need.* In Advances in Neural Information Processing Systems (NeurIPS), 30.

Acknowledgment

I'm deeply thankful to my family and friends for their constant love and support, especially my parents, my husband, and my children. This book would not have been possible without their constant confidence in me and the kindness they showed to help me succeed. I am truly blessed to have their support every step of the way.

A special thank you goes to all the contributors, including the authors and reviewers who played a vital role in this project, especially those who embraced the important responsibilities of both author and reviewer. Your dedication, hard work, and commitment have been truly invaluable. The quality and depth of this book owe much to your thoughtful insights and efforts. Without your contributions, this book would not have become a reality.

Chapter 1
AI-Driven Educational Leadership:
Empowering Leaders, Staff, and Students in the Digital Age

Areej K. Assayed
https://orcid.org/0009-0000-3315-8718
Westcliff University, USA

Suha Khalill Assayed
https://orcid.org/0000-0002-9924-0324
The British University in Dubai, UAE

ABSTRACT

This chapter studies how Artificial Intelligence (AI) is transforming educational leadership by changing the roles and responsibilities of school leaders. AI tools support data-driven decision-making, improve school management, and personalize student learning. Effective leadership plays a vital role in connecting and empowering both staff and students, enhancing collaboration and a positive learning environment. The study also highlights real-world examples of AI implementation in educational leadership from various countries, demonstrating diverse approaches and benefits. While AI offers opportunities to enhance leadership efficiency and instructional support, it also raises challenges related to ethics, data

DOI: 10.4018/979-8-3373-3316-8.ch001

privacy, and equity. The importance of professional development programs that equip leaders with both technical skills and human-centered competencies is emphasized to help navigate AI-driven changes while maintaining core educational values.

INTRODUCTION

Artificial Intelligence (AI) is changing education faster than ever, opening up innovative new ways for schools to work and for leaders to lead. As AI keeps advancing, it's not just improving how we teach and learn, it's also reshaping what it means to be an educational leader, creating fresh opportunities to inspire, guide, and transform schools for the better. As AI continues to grow, it is not only changing how teaching and learning happen, but also how school leaders manage and lead their institutions (Karakose & Tulubas, 2025).

Today's educational leaders work in rapidly changing environments where artificial intelligence (AI) plays a key role in many areas of school management. AI helps with strategic planning, making decisions, handling everyday administrative tasks, and personalizing learning for students. It also supports student advising and promotes well-being (Al-Sayed et al., 2024) by identifying students' needs and helping leaders offer timely, personalized support (Assayed et al., 2024a). As a result, leaders must develop new skills and gain a deep understanding of AI tools to enhance both education quality and the school management. AI is changing leadership by moving away from traditional ways and encouraging leaders to rely on data and stay flexible (Madanchian et al., 2024). This new approach helps leaders adapt quickly and make smarter decisions based on real information.

Moreover, Albooshi et al. (2023) explained that AI changes how leadership skills affect a school's ability to grow and improve over time. Now, it's more important than ever for leaders to use digital tools carefully while keeping students, teachers, and the whole community at the center of their work. When leaders balance new technology with important educational values, they create a positive place where both teachers and students can succeed (Schmitz et al., 2023).

Educational leadership in the age of AI requires more than just familiarity with technology. Leaders must develop a balanced mix of technical expertise and interpersonal intelligence. As Karakose and Tülübas (2024) suggested, today's educational leaders are responsible not only for bringing AI technologies into schools but also for helping their teams grow and adapt. This means leaders must support teachers in developing both technical skills such as using digital tools and analyzing data and soft skills like communication, collaboration, problem-solving, and emotional intelligence. By strengthening these abilities, leaders ensure that their staff can confidently and effectively work in technology-rich environments and respond to the challenges that come with AI integration. Supporting the professional growth of teachers is now a key aspect of effective school leadership in the AI era. (Awodiji & Naicker, 2023).

Similarly, Milton and Al-Busaidi (2023) argued that successful educational leadership in the age of AI depends on a well-balanced integration of both technical and emotional competencies. Their research highlights that, while technical skills such as understanding AI systems, using data-driven tools, and managing digital platforms are essential, they are not sufficient on their own. Leaders must also possess strong emotional and interpersonal abilities, including empathy, adaptability, emotional intelligence, and the capacity to support and motivate others through change.

In the past, school leaders made decisions based on their experience and talked with people face-to-face. They also did many tasks by hand, which took a lot of time. Now, AI helps by doing simple jobs like making schedules and sending messages. This lets leaders spend more time on important planning, As Milton and Al-Busaidi emphasized that this shift requires leaders to move beyond traditional forms of management. They must become visionary thinkers who can guide their institutions through complex transformations, ensure the ethical use of technology, and inspire innovation among staff. This means encouraging everyone including teachers and students to keep learning and growing with new technology. Today's leaders need to be skilled with technology and caring with people. They must balance being smart and efficient with being kind and understanding to lead well in a world shaped by AI.

Interestingly, Quaquebeke and Gerpott (2023) further emphasized that AI is set to automate a wide range of traditional leadership tasks that have historically relied on human effort and decision-making. Routine functions such as scheduling, data analysis, reporting, and even some aspects of performance evaluation are increasingly being handled by intelligent systems, which can process information faster and more accurately than humans. This technological shift fundamentally changes the landscape of leadership, freeing leaders from many operational duties but also raising important questions about their evolving role. Given this transformation, the authors argued that it becomes crucial for educational leaders to concentrate on the uniquely human qualities that AI cannot replicate. Skills such as ethical judgment, where leaders must navigate complex moral dilemmas and ensure fairness in AI use; empathy, which fosters genuine understanding and support among staff and students; effective human communication, necessary for building trust and collaboration; and long-term strategic vision, essential for guiding institutions through rapid change as all vital areas where human leadership remains necessary. This perspective highlights an urgent need to rethink professional development programs for educational leaders. Rather than focusing solely on technical training, development initiatives must prioritize cultivating these irreplaceable human competencies. By equipping leaders with a balanced combination of digital literacy and advanced interpersonal skills, such programs will prepare them to thrive alongside AI tools, leading with insight, integrity, and foresight in an increasingly automated educational environment.

This chapter emphasizes the urgent need to rethink leadership preparation by developing tailored professional development programs that equip educational leaders with the essential competencies to thrive in the AI era. These programs should cover key areas such as digital literacy, ethical governance, collaboration, emotional intelligence, and adaptive thinking. By focusing on these skills, leaders will be better prepared to guide their institutions through AI-driven transformations while upholding core educational values. The importance of this topic lies in the fact that AI is not merely supporting leadership, it is increasingly shaping and guiding leadership practices. As a result, school leaders are expected to play a vital role in empowering both academic and administrative staff. They must also recognize the importance of financial investment in AI integration to ensure its effective and sustainable use in education and leadership (Sterrett & Richardson, 2020).

This study is especially relevant as it contributes to improving how educational leaders manage schools while incorporating AI into their daily practices. As AI continues to evolve, school leaders must embrace innovation to remain effective and forward-thinking. Fengchao and Mingchi (2023) emphasized the need for school leaders to be creative, innovative, and energetic in responding to both the challenges and opportunities that AI presents.

Furthermore, the study provides valuable insights for the design of professional development programs aimed at building both the hard and soft skills required of modern educational leaders. This perspective is supported by Dai et al. (2024), who advocate for intensive training programs that help school leaders become highly qualified and prepared to meet the demands of future educational leadership roles.

THE EVOLVING ROLE OF LEADERSHIP IN EDUCATION

Leadership is commonly defined as the knowledge and ability to guide, motivate, and support individuals in achieving their goals effectively (Supriatna & Zulganef, 2023). It plays a crucial role in shaping the success and direction of any organization. As Saputra (2021) explained, leadership is considered one of the most important indicators of an organization's capability to inspire people and achieve desired outcomes efficiently.

In the educational context, leadership takes on even greater importance. Theoharis (2024) emphasized that school leaders play a significant role in creating a supportive environment by adopting collaboration, commitment, and a shared sense of responsibility among staff. Effective leaders not only guide decision-making but also bring people together to work toward common goals.

Supporting this view, Pisriwati et al. (2024) conducted qualitative research in high schools that underlined the key responsibilities of school principals. These include strategic planning, managing school operations, encouraging teamwork among teachers and staff, designing appropriate school facilities, and creating a positive and engaging learning environment.

During the COVID-19 pandemic, the role of educational leaders became even more critical. Leaders had to navigate a wide range of challenges, including concerns about student and staff well-being, the quality of instruction, and the shift to digital and online learning (Parveen et al., 2022). In response, some principals took proactive steps to promote digital literacy by training teachers to use online platforms and other educational technologies effectively (AlAjmi, 2022).

These experiences have driven researchers and policymakers to place greater emphasis on strengthening educational technology infrastructure. The goal is to ensure that schools can continue to provide high-quality learning experiences both in times of crisis and beyond by equipping leaders with the tools and support they need to succeed.

THE IMPACT OF ARTIFICIAL INTELLIGENCE ON EDUCATIONAL LEADERSHIP

In recent years, educational leaders around the world have increasingly focused on the influence of Artificial Intelligence (AI) on teaching, learning, and school administration. While AI presents clear advantages, such as improving efficiency and supporting instructional design, it also raises concerns regarding equity, policy, and implementation challenges. As Ellis (2024) noted, AI can bring significant value to pedagogy, particularly in designing academic plans and structuring course content to better meet learners' needs.

Complementing this perspective, a qualitative study conducted by Ghamrawi et al. (2024) explored the impact of AI on educational leadership and whether it can effectively support and enhance the roles of school leaders. The research involved interviews with 13 teachers from five different countries. Findings revealed that while some educators viewed AI as a valuable opportunity to develop their technical competencies, this potential could only be realized through access to professional development programs focused on AI tools. Moreover, teachers expressed a need for clear guidelines on how AI can be used to streamline administrative tasks in schools.

Similarly, Kim and Kwon (2023) conducted a quantitative study involving surveys and interviews with 67 primary school teachers from AI-leading institutions in South Korea. Their research found that teachers exhibited the lowest confidence in content knowledge related to AI, though they expressed slightly more confidence in their digital and educational knowledge. These findings highlight the importance of targeted training and support to help educators build both technical skills and pedagogical understanding of AI.

At the policy level, the adoption and regulation of AI in education remain uneven across countries and regions. While it is widely expected that new laws and frameworks will be developed to govern AI use in educational settings, the specific focus, timing, and scope of these policies are likely to vary significantly based on national priorities, cultural contexts, and governance structures. Schiff (2022), in a comprehensive analysis of 24 international AI policies and strategies, found that education is often overlooked or minimally addressed in global AI political discussions. This absence highlights a gap between the rapid technological advancements of AI and the slower pace of policy development in the education sector. As a result, many countries lack clear guidelines on ethical AI implementation, data privacy, equity, and the professional development of educators to work effectively with AI tools. This suggests that integrating AI into educational systems is not yet a central priority on many national agendas, potentially slowing down the responsible and effective use of AI in schools. Addressing this gap is crucial to ensure that AI technologies are used safely and equitably to enhance learning outcomes and leadership practices worldwide.

ETHICAL RESPONSIBILITIES OF SCHOOL LEADERS IN THE AGE OF AI

As Artificial Intelligence (AI) becomes more integrated into education, school leaders find themselves facing not only exciting new possibilities but also serious ethical responsibilities. Beyond improving teaching and administrative tasks, AI brings challenges that directly impact leadership especially around issues like data privacy, fairness, and the future role of educators.

Ghamrawi et al. (2024) pointed out that many school leaders and teachers are growing concerned about how AI might affect their roles. There is a fear that AI could reduce the influence of human decision-makers, turning leaders into mere overseers of technology rather than active guides of school culture and learning.

To help address this, Dai, Thomas, and Rawolle (2024) proposed a human-AI collaboration model. They emphasize that school leaders must not simply adopt AI tools blindly, but instead work alongside technology thoughtfully, ensuring ethical accountability is always at the center. Leaders must make sure AI supports human values, not replaces them. Likewise, Fusarelli and Fusarelli (2024) highlighted key ethical challenges for school leadership, such as protecting student and staff data and ensuring that AI is used fairly for all learners. These concerns require leaders to be both digitally aware and morally grounded able to lead innovation while protecting the rights and needs of everyone in the school community.

In summary, as AI becomes part of everyday school life, educational leaders must take the lead in making sure it is used wisely. Their role is not just to manage technology, but to guide its use in ways that respect privacy, promote equity, and strengthen the human side of education. By doing so, leaders can ensure that AI becomes a tool for empowerment rather than exclusion.

PREPARING EDUCATIONAL LEADERS FOR THE AI ERA THROUGH PROFESSIONAL DEVELOPMENT

Adapting to the demands of the AI era requires educational leaders to engage in continuous, targeted professional development. As technological advancements rapidly reshape the education sector, school leaders must be equipped with both the technical knowledge and adaptive leadership skills necessary to navigate this evolving landscape. In particular, AI-powered tools like chatbots are becoming increasingly important in supporting school operations by handling routine inquiries, providing timely information to students and staff, and assisting with administrative tasks (Assayed et al., 2024b). Understanding how to effectively implement and manage such AI applications enables leaders to enhance communication, improve student advising, and free up time to focus on strategic priorities.

Awodiji and Naicker (2023) emphasized the need for continuous professional development (CPD) programs to ensure school leaders are fully prepared for the Fourth Industrial Revolution an era marked by rapid changes driven by AI, robotics, and the internet. These programs are essential in providing leaders with the qualifications and competencies required to lead effectively in digitally advanced environments. Similarly, Fusarelli and Fusarelli (2024) highlighted the importance of developing both technical and emotional intelligence in future leaders. They cite a leadership training program at NC State University that prepares school leaders by focusing on the soft and hard skills necessary for success in an AI-integrated world. This includes building emotional resilience, ethical reasoning, and digital fluency.

Dai et al. (2024) further supported this view by advocating for intensive training opportunities that develop the skills school leaders need to thrive in the AI era. They argued that educational leadership should not only focus on administrative tasks but also on understanding and implementing emerging technologies in a way that benefits the school community.

GLOBAL PRACTICES IN AI-DRIVEN EDUCATIONAL LEADERSHIP

The practical implementation of Artificial Intelligence (AI) in educational leadership is increasingly being observed through case studies and real-world applications across various global contexts. For example, in South Korea, AI-driven school management systems have been adopted in several primary schools to support principals in making data-informed decisions on student performance and resource allocation (Kim & Kwon, 2023). These tools assist leaders by analyzing academic trends and predicting student needs, allowing for more strategic planning. Similarly, in the United States, the North Carolina State University leadership program integrates AI simulations into principal training, helping aspiring leaders practice decision-making in complex school scenarios (Fusarelli & Fusarelli, 2024). In the UAE, smart education initiatives have introduced AI platforms that automate scheduling, monitor attendance, and track learning outcomes, enabling school leaders to spend more time on instructional leadership and staff development (Almarzooqi & Abouassar, 2024). Moreover, one of the leading example of AI-enhanced school leadership is Singapore's Student Learning Space (SLS), particularly the Data Assistant Tool (DAT) (Alison et al., 2019; Tambyah, 2022). This AI system helps principals and school leaders analyze student learning data in real-time, enabling smarter decisions on lesson planning, student support, and staff development. As part of a national initiative by the Ministry of Education, the tool exemplifies how AI can empower school leaders to respond effectively to diverse learning needs and improve educational outcomes while maintaining ethical oversight and data protection. Furthermore, in China Zhao et al. (2024) highlighted the importance of transformational leadership in successfully integrating AI within China's K–12 education system. Their study shows that while AI enhances personalized learning and overall educational efficiency, its effective use depends on visionary leadership that promotes innovation, motivates staff, and addresses challenges collaboratively. By applying key principles of transformational leadership such as inspiration, individualized support, and intellectual stimulation, school leaders can better manage issues like data privacy, teacher preparedness, and technical limitations, creating a balanced and ethically responsible AI-supported learning environment. The Table 1 below shows a summarized overview of these real-world practices.

Table 1. Examples of AI-Driven Educational Leadership Initiatives Across Different Countries

Country	Initiative / Tool	Description / Application	Reference
South Korea	AI-Driven School Management Systems	Used in primary schools to support principals with data-informed decisions regarding student performance and resource allocation.	Kim & Kwon (2023)
United States	AI Simulations in Principal Training (NC State Univ.)	Integrates AI simulations into leadership training to help aspiring principals practice decision-making in complex educational scenarios.	Fusarelli & Fusarelli (2024)
UAE	Smart Education Platforms	AI platforms automate administrative tasks (scheduling, attendance, performance tracking), freeing school leaders to focus on instructional and staff leadership.	Almarzooqi & Abouassar (2024)
Singapore	Student Learning Space (SLS) & Data Assistant Tool (DAT)	National AI system for real-time analysis of student learning data, supporting lesson planning, student support, and staff development.	Alison et al. (2019); Tambyah (2022)
China	Integration of Transformational Leadership and AI	Combines transformational leadership principles with AI to improve personalized learning and educational efficiency, addressing ethical, technical, and professional development challenges in K–12 education.	Hou, Ahmad, & Zhao (2023)

These real-world applications demonstrate how AI can improve efficiency, enhance strategic planning, and support data-driven leadership practices. However, they also reveal the importance of training school leaders to understand, interpret, and ethically apply AI insights. These cases underline the need for strong professional development programs and ethical guidelines to ensure the successful integration of AI into leadership roles while maintaining a focus on equity, student well-being, and educational quality.

THE CHALLENGES ROLES OF SCHOOL LEADERS IN THE AI ERA

The rise of Artificial Intelligence (AI) is reshaping educational leadership, pushing school leaders to adapt to new expectations and responsibilities. Research increasingly points to the need for a well-rounded skill set that combines both technical and interpersonal strengths.

According to Karakose & Tülübaş (2024), AI technologies enable leaders to handle large volumes of data, enhance transparency, promote collaborative decision-making, and streamline various operational tasks such as resource allocation, human resource management, and student information processing. Additionally, AI-powered learning analytics allow for early identification of student needs and the delivery of personalized educational interventions. However, school leaders must also navigate ethical concerns, ensure meaningful involvement of teachers, students, and parents, and adapt their leadership approaches to meet the evolving demands brought about by AI integration. Successfully managing these complexities is essential for advancing school effectiveness in the AI era. Milton and Al-Busaidi (2023) argued also, that to lead effectively in today's AI-driven environment, educational leaders must master both technical skills and interpersonal abilities. They emphasized that AI is not just changing what leaders do, but also how leadership itself is perceived and practiced within schools. Similarly, Ghamrawi et al. (2023) acknowledged that AI technologies are powerful tools capable of handling a variety of administrative and instructional tasks. However, they cautioned that AI cannot replace essential human elements of leadership such as emotional intelligence, critical thinking, and the ability to nurture social and interpersonal skills in students. These are deeply human capacities that remain vital in any educational setting. Not to mention the fact that many schools, particularly in low-resource or rural settings, lack the essential hardware, software, and reliable internet connectivity required to support AI systems (Kim & Wargo, 2025).

On the other hand, Quaquebeke and Gerpott (2023) presented a more disruptive view. They suggested that AI will gradually take over many traditional managerial duties and even argued that most employee tasks, including those carried out by school leaders, could eventually be replaced by AI systems. Supporting this idea, Karakose and Tülübas (2024) highlighted how AI technologies are already altering the expectations placed on school leaders, particularly by demanding stronger technical (hard) skills to work effectively in increasingly digitized environments. Furthermore, Dai et al. (2024) proposed that developing educational leaders' skills through intensive professional development training is essential for preparing highly qualified future school leaders. However, Table 2 summarize the most important challenges that school leaders might face.

Table 2. Key Challenges Faced by School Leaders in the Adoption and Management of AI Technologies

Challenges of AI for School Leaders	Description
Technical Barriers	Many leaders and staff lack sufficient training and expertise to effectively use AI tools, making adoption difficult.
Data Privacy and Security	Ensuring student and staff data is protected from breaches and misuse is a major concern.
Ethical Issues	Leaders must navigate fairness, bias in AI algorithms, and maintain human-centered education amidst automation.
Infrastructure Limitations	Some schools lack the necessary hardware, software, or reliable internet connectivity to support AI systems.
Change Management	Resistance from teachers, students, and parents can hinder smooth AI integration.
Balancing Human and AI Roles	Leaders must ensure AI supports, not replaces, essential human judgment and relationships.
Continuous Professional Development	Ongoing training is required to keep leaders and staff updated on AI capabilities and ethical standards.

CONCLUSION

This chapter explores the impact of Artificial Intelligence (AI) on educational leadership, highlighting the ways in which AI is transforming not only school operations but also the very essence of leadership in the 21st century. As AI continues to evolve, it is no longer simply a supportive tool, it is becoming a central force reshaping decision-making, planning, communication, and instructional leadership. These developments require school leaders to rethink their roles and acquire a new blend of competencies to remain effective.

Today's leaders must guide their teams through change, help teachers grow, and make sure technology is used in fair and ethical ways. While AI takes over routine tasks such as monitoring students' performance, grades predictions, marks analysis, leaders will focus on what only humans can do: build trust, manage with emotional intelligence and make thoughtful decision.

The chapter also identifies growing concerns around the ethical use of AI, particularly related to data privacy, equity, and the changing dynamics between humans and machines. Educational leaders are expected to navigate these issues with integrity, ensuring that AI enhances rather than diminishes the human experience in education. To succeed in the AI era, schools need strong professional development programs. These should help leaders improve both their technical and soft skills. Ongoing professional development is more important than ever in the age of AI. To lead schools successfully, today's school leaders need training that builds both technical skills like using data and digital tools as well as soft skills such as communication, problem-solving, and ethical decision-making. Well-designed programs that focus on both areas will help leaders feel confident, adapt to change, and guide their schools effectively in this new era.

On the other hand, several challenges stand in the way, as many school leaders face technical barriers due to a lack of training and experience with AI tools. Data privacy and security are also major concerns, as protecting sensitive student and staff information becomes more complex. Ethical issues, including fairness and bias in AI algorithms, must be addressed to ensure that technology serves all students equitably. Some schools also struggle with infrastructure limitations, such as outdated hardware or poor internet connectivity, making AI integration more difficult.

To conclude, preparing school leaders for the age of AI requires more than technical skills. It calls for a strong commitment to lifelong learning, ethical leadership, and human-centered values. With a constructive mindset and support, educational leaders can turn the challenges of AI into opportunities for growth, innovation, and better outcomes for all learners.

REFERENCES

Al-Sayed, S., Assayed, S. K., Alkhatib, M., & Shaalan, K. (2024). Impact of Artificial Intelligence Chatbots on Student Well-being and Mental Health: A Systematic Review. *People and Behavior Analysis*, *2*(2), 10–31098.

AlAjmi, M. K. (2022). The impact of digital leadership on teachers' technology integration during the COVID-19 pandemic in Kuwait. *International Journal of Educational Research*, *112*, 101928. DOI: 10.1016/j.ijer.2022.101928 PMID: 35153373

Alison, C. S. M., Kyoko, U., & Hironari, N. (2019, July). Student Learning Space: The Integration of Curriculum and Technology in Singapore. In *Proceedings of the 3rd International Conference on Education and Multimedia Technology* (pp. 37-40).

Almarzooqi, F. M. A., & Abouassar, P. (2024). Strategic Leadership and Effective Management in Implementing an AI-Enhanced Online Parent-Teacher Communication System for a Primary School in the UAE. *Journal of Research in Curriculum Instruction and Educational Technology*, *10*(2), 39–64.

Assayed, S. K., Alkhatib, M., & Shaalan, K. (2024a). The key challenges in educational advising chatbot dialogue system. In *Innovation in the University 4.0 System based on Smart Technologies* (pp. 74–82). Chapman and Hall/CRC.

Assayed, S. K., Alkhatib, M., & Shaalan, K. (2024b). A Comparative Study of ChatGPT and Seq2Seq Chatbot for Effective Students Advising. *ChatGPT and Global Higher Education: Using Artificial Intelligence in Teaching and Learning*, 148.

Awodiji, O. A., & Naicker, S. R. (2023). *Preparing school leaders for the fourth industrial revolution: An assessment of their continuous professional development needs*. Social Sciences &amp. *Humanities Open*, *8*(1), 100521. DOI: 10.1016/j.ssaho.2023.100521

Dai, R., Thomas, M. K. E., & Rawolle, S. (2024). The roles of AI and educational leaders in AI-assisted administrative decision-making: A proposed framework for symbiotic collaboration. *Australian Educational Researcher*. Advance online publication. DOI: 10.1007/s13384-024-00771-8

Ellis, R. A. (2024). *The Education Leadership Challenges for Universities in a Postdigital Age*. Postdigital Science and Education., DOI: 10.1007/s42438-024-00461-9

Fengchao, X., & Mingchi, J. (2023). School leadership and management innovation in the Internet+ education era. *International Journal of New Developments in Education, 5*(12), 28–34. DOI: 10.25236/IJNDE.2023.051205

Fusarelli, B. C., & Fusarelli, L. D. (2024). Leadership for the Future: Enhancing Principal Preparation through Standards and Innovation. *Education Sciences, 14*(12), 1403. DOI: 10.3390/educsci14121403

Ghamrawi, N., Shal, T., & Ghamrawi, N. A. R. (2023). Exploring the impact of AI on teacher leadership: Regressing or expanding? *Education and Information Technologies, 29*(7), 8415–8433. DOI: 10.1007/s10639-023-12174-w

Karakose, T., & Tulubas, T. (2024). School Leadership and Management in the Age of Artificial Intelligence (AI): Recent Developments and Future Prospects. *Educational Process International Journal, 13*(1). Advance online publication. DOI: 10.22521/edupij.2024.131.1

Karakose, T., & Tulubas, T. (2025). The Role of Educational Leaders in the Age of Artificial Intelligence (AI).

Kim, J., & Wargo, E. (2025). Empowering educational leaders for AI integration in rural STEM education: Challenges and strategies. *Frontiers in Education, 10.* Advance online publication. DOI: 10.3389/feduc.2025.1567698

Kim, K., & Kwon, K. (2023). Exploring the AI competencies of elementary school teachers in South Korea. *Computers and Education: Artificial Intelligence, 4*, 100137. DOI: 10.1016/j.caeai.2023.100137

Madanchian, M., Taherdoost, H., Vincenti, M., & Mohamed, N. (2024). Transforming Leadership Practices through Artificial Intelligence. *Procedia Computer Science*, *235*, 2101–2111.

Milton, J., & Al-Busaidi, A. (2023). *New Role of Leadership in AI Era: Educational Sector. SHS Web of Conferences,* 156, 09005. https://doi.org/ DOI: 10.1051/shsconf/202315609005

Parveen, K., Tran, P. Q. B., Alghamdi, A. A., Namaziandost, E., Aslam, S., & Xiaowei, T. (2022). Identifying the Leadership Challenges of K-12 Public Schools During COVID-19 Disruption: A Systematic Literature Review. *Frontiers in Psychology*, *13*. Advance online publication. DOI: 10.3389/fpsyg.2022.875646 PMID: 35432078

Pisriwati, S. A., Hardi, Y., & Siswanto, D. H. (2024). Enhancing organizational development through principal leadership to improve teacher and staff work discipline. *Journal of Organizational and Human Resource Development Strategies*, *1*(01), 52–62.

Quaquebeke, N. V., & Gerpott, F. H. (2023). The Now, New, and Next of Digital Leadership: How Artificial Intelligence (AI) Will Take Over and Change Leadership as We Know It. *Journal of Leadership &amp. Organization Studies*, *30*(3), 265–275. DOI: 10.1177/15480518231181731

Saputra, F. (2021). Leadership, Communication, and Work Motivation in Determining the Success of Professional Organizations. *Journal of Law. Politic and Humanities*, *1*(2), 59–70. DOI: 10.38035/jlph.v1i2.54

Schiff, D. (2022). Education for AI, not AI for education: The role of education and ethics in national AI policy strategies. *International Journal of Artificial Intelligence in Education*, *32*(3), 527–563.

Schmitz, M. L., Antonietti, C., Consoli, T., Cattaneo, A., Gonon, P., & Petko, D. (2023). Transformational leadership for technology integration in schools: Empowering teachers to use technology in a more demanding way. *Computers & Education*, *204*, 104880.

Sterrett, W., & Richardson, J. W. (2020). Supporting Professional Development through Digital Principal Leadership. *Journal of Organizational and Educational Leadership*, *5*(2), 1–19. https://www.proquest.com/scholarly-journals/supporting-professional-development-through/docview/2430112403/se-2

Supriatna, N., & Zulganef, Z. (2023). The Influence of Innovation Leadership on Employee Performance. *International Journal of Business, Economics, and Social Development*, *4*(1), 20–24. DOI: 10.46336/ijbesd.v4i1.365

Tambyah, S. K. (Ed.). (2022). *Student Growth and Development in New Higher Education Learning Spaces: Student-centred Learning in Singapore*. Taylor & Francis.

Zhao, Y., Yusof, S. M., Hou, M., & Li, Z. (2024). How Can Generative Artificial Intelligence help Teachers in Early Childhood Education with their Teaching? Analyses from the Perspective of Teaching Methods. *International Journal of Academic Research in Progressive Education and Development*, *13*(1). Advance online publication. DOI: 10.6007/ijarped/v13-i1/20958

Chapter 2

The Role of AI in Virtual Counseling, Student Guidance, and Career Advising

Chandra Rajesh

Vel Tech Multi Tech Dr. Rangarajan Dr. Sankuthala Engineering College, Chennai, India

M. Gokuldhev

Vel Tech Rangarajan Dr. Sagunthala R&D Institute of Science and Technology, Chennai, India

V. Shanmugapriya

Jeppiaar Institute of Technology, Sriperumbudur Taluk, India

D. Senthil Kumar

R.M.K. College of Engineering and Technology, Puduvoyal, India

B. Yamini

https://orcid.org/0000-0003-3531-108X

SRM Institute of Science and Technology, Kattankulathur, India

M. G. Dinesh

https://orcid.org/0009-0009-7643-5338

EASA College of Engineering and Technology, Coimbatore, India

P. Girija

https://orcid.org/0009-0000-1691-8180

Panimalar Engineering College, Chennai, India

DOI: 10.4018/979-8-3373-3316-8.ch002

ABSTRACT

This chapter explores the evolving role of artificial intelligence (AI) in virtual counseling, student guidance, and career advising. It examines foundational AI technologies such as natural language processing, machine learning, and recommender systems, highlighting their applications in mental health support, personalized academic advising, and career planning. The chapter discusses the benefits of AI-driven tools, including scalability, personalization, and accessibility, while addressing challenges related to data privacy, algorithmic bias, transparency, and the need for human oversight. Future directions emphasize hybrid human-AI models, emotionally intelligent systems, culturally adaptive frameworks, and lifelong advising ecosystems. Ultimately, this chapter underscores the transformative potential of AI to enhance educational support through ethical, inclusive, and human-centered approaches, fostering improved student outcomes and well-being.

1. INTRODUCTION

1.1 Background: The Shift to Digital Education and Support Services

In the last ten years, the delivery of teaching, learning and student support services in schools has seen major changes everywhere. Rapidly advancing and widely used digital technologies have most importantly caused this transformation. Though digital education was already becoming popular, the COVID-19 pandemic caused the move to happen much faster than before. Because of the need for schools to be closed and everyone to keep a distance, educators and administrators quickly switched to online and hybrid methods to keep students learning. The move to digital has made changes to teaching as well as to the wider student support system. Over the years, students received academic advising, career counseling and mental health support mostly by seeing advisors in person. Yet, as we use digital tools more, these services are now often available online, taking over or adding to face-to-face meetings. Thanks to tele-counseling, virtual guidance and chatbots, students at any location can receive fast and personalized help from their schools. Because of digital transformation, Learning Management Systems (LMS) are now used by teachers and students everywhere. Course delivery, following assignments, talking to students and grading happen mostly through these platforms. Yet, LMSs are now connected to a variety of online support tools that add new features to what they can do. More and more, institutions are using mobile apps, video conferencing and cloud services to make their support systems faster and better linked (Benta et al., 2014; Ouadoud et al., 2021). Because of this, students in harder-to-reach schools are now able to access better education and help(Dhinakaran, D et al., 2025). Now, students can access academic support, book appointments, join workshops and take part in peer groups using virtual platforms. Because many online services are asynchronous, students can get help whenever it's convenient for them. Besides, moving student services online has allowed for more fact-based methods to help and guide students. Now, institutions can gather information on student behavior, grades and comments and use it to guide their actions for students who may be struggling. More and more, predictive analytics and machine learning models are helping to make decisions better and personalize learning for students. In brief, the move to digital education and support services means institutions now interact with students in a new way. Even though not all students can take advantage of digital learning, the chance to make education more suitable for everyone, easier to expand and more personal points to its lasting potential in schools.

1.2 Importance of Guidance and Counseling in Educational and Career Development

Support and guidance are required in schools to help students succeed in school and later in their jobs. Because students have different and changing needs, the value of organized, available and successful support services has become very clear. Services are available for more than academic planning, supporting students' emotions and careers which are essential for their overall success. At university or college, students use counseling to decide on their educational and career plans. Trying to understand the detailed curriculum, many course selections and credit rules can be very hard for students who are learning for the first time or are from disadvantaged families. Selecting the right courses for yourself is made easier with the help of academic advisors. They also help students find and solve problems with time, study habits or comprehension. When students are helped with planning and skill development, academic counselling leads to higher retention, better grades and a self-assured student group. The importance of guidance services to guide career movements is just the same. Because the global job market is changing and tough, students need to be academically skilled and career ready to succeed. Career counselors help students know about their strengths, interests and values and how they relate to different career opportunities. Thanks to personality assessments, career interest lists and labor market studies, students are able to make good decisions about their future careers. Counselors help students by guiding them through resume creation, building their portfolios, interview preparation and using networking skills. Such services help students adapt their learning to the workplace, improving their confidence and getting them ready for their future jobs. In addition to helping students in school and their careers, guidance and counselling services look after their psychological and emotional health. Students in today's world are under pressure from school, relationships, family and money. More and more students at every educational level are dealing with anxiety, depression and burnout. In schools, mental health counselling allows students to understand their feelings, gain helpful coping skills and become stronger. When people have trained counselors, it becomes easier to notice problems early and take action which can keep serious psychological concerns from developing. Because there are now more and different students, the traditional system of counseling faces fresh difficulties. Institutions today have to address the different languages, cultures, learning needs and financial situations of their students. Because of this diversity, guidance should focus more on each individual's needs. At the same time, more people looking for counseling services than can be handled by available human counselors which means waiting longer and having fewer sessions to choose from. The result is that students who depend on timely or ongoing help can face many challenges. Here, using artificial intelligence (AI) and digital technologies in counseling seems to offer a lot of promise. With the help of AI, student support services can be easily expanded, personalized and more efficient. For example, chatbots and virtual assistants can always answer questions about academic routines, important dates and the resources students need (Engelbrecht et al., 2025). Advanced AI systems can look at a user's academic history, how they behave and their interactions to suggest suitable courses, ways to study or career paths. AI-based services in mental health give students self-help advice, help track their emotions and identify the best resources for them (Chen et al., 2020).

AI is being introduced to aid counselors, not to take their roles. Thanks to AI, human counselors are able to concentrate on the most important and feeling-focused parts of their job. When technology and people join forces, support systems can become faster, more inclusive and improve results. AI tools also make it possible for all students to receive assistance, regardless of their reluctance to speak up in class or access help in other ways. All in all, students need guidance and counseling to succeed academically, prepare for work and build emotional strength. Because the needs of students are becoming more varied and schools more complicated, how these services are offered needs to be reconsidered. By adopting artificial intelligence, schools can provide support systems that serve more students, quickly and in a way that is personalized to each student's needs.

1.3 Rise of AI Technologies in the Education and Mental Wellness Sectors

Artificial Intelligence (AI) has quickly become an important factor in improving education and mental health. As more students are enrolled and there are fewer resources for everyone, AI has become very useful because it supports many students, meets their needs and does so more efficiently than older ways(Ponnuviji, N. P et al., 2024). AI is helping to make teaching, learning and supporting students more effective in schools. Many schools are now using AI to help with advising and learning that fits each student. Such systems help by studying lots of data about grades, habits and what someone enjoys to give personal recommendations for courses, learning tips and future careers. These insights guide students to make choices that match what they can do and what they hope to achieve. Suppose a student is doing well in math; they may be advised to take part in advanced classes. NLP helps in making communication and interactivity between students and digital systems much easier (Ansari et al., 2021). More and more, AI-powered chatbots are being introduced to websites and learning management systems to help with routine tasks, give academic assistance and be available all the time. Because of these bots, students can find out about deadlines, registration and available help, without having to wait for someone to respond. As a result, both students and staff have better access and less work to do. Besides helping with education, AI is improving mental health care. More people of all ages are feeling stress, anxiety and depression, making student mental health a bigger concern. Because of high demand, traditional counseling services often find it hard to keep up in large institutions. Because of this, AI has been added to virtual counseling sites to help more people get help sooner. Mental health apps using AI watch for emotions, analyze sentiments and track behaviors to help users stay on track and get advice in real time. Some platforms offer steps to help on your own such as mood tracking and may even advise users when it's time to speak with a professional. AI is expected to make it easier to identify students who are having difficulty. AI systems can find out if someone is struggling by looking at their attendance, grades, how involved they are and their online presence. Because of this, institutions can respond quickly to prevent problems from getting worse. A student's engagement with the course could suddenly drop and the AI would let a counselor or advisor know to get in touch. While AI can be very beneficial in these fields, it does bring up some major issues. Privacy is the most important of all these. The AI systems use a lot of personal details like school results, habits and feelings. The data has to be kept safe, handled ethically and be accessed only by agreement with the subject. To maintain both trust and accountability, people need to know how AI systems decide things. Another important issues are bias and fairness. Existing inequalities can be mistakenly preserved by AI models or the biases present in the historical data can be shown by the models. A recommendation algorithm can harm students who do not belong to the majority group if it is not designed and reviewed correctly. But there's also a danger of ignoring important human decisions in favour of automated systems. AI can behave in such a way that it seems to empathize and decide, but does not have the same understanding, emotional intelligence and ethical approach that professionals do. That's why ethics should watch closely when AI is used in these areas and people should supervise it. AI should be seen as an aide for educators and counselors to provide better, more appropriate and inclusive support to their students. Implemented wisely, AI can give all students access to key resources and support, so they can succeed.

1.4 Scope and Objectives of the Chapter

The Study explores how AI is being used more in virtual counseling, student guidance and career advising. The goal is to review how AI is used in these industries, what it can and cannot do now and what its prospects for the future might be. The main goal is to use knowledge from education technology, psychology, computer science and ethics to look at the changes AI is bringing to support services in schools. By analyzing several methods and instruments, this chapter hopes to guide researchers, practitioners and policymakers in understanding what AI-powered advising means for them.

1.5 Structure of the Chapter

The next sections of this chapter will be arranged in this manner. In section 2, we describe the main technologies that support AI in counseling and advising such as NLP and recommender systems. AI in virtual mental health counseling is the main topic of Section 3 and Section 4 looks at its impact on academic advising and behavioral nudging. Section 5 explains how AI is used for career advice and labor forecasting. In Section 6, the main ethical, technical and operational problems related to these technologies are discussed. Section 7 looks ahead at what's next in this field and Section 8 provides about the conclusion.

2. FOUNDATIONS OF AI IN COUNSELING AND ADVISING

2.1 Overview of AI Technologies

Artificial Intelligence (AI) is the area of technology that tries to imitate or mimic human abilities such as learning, solving problems, reasoning and talking naturally. With AI, the traditional ways people are counselled and advised are being improved to be more personal, faster and able to serve more people. They can support students and clients individually at all times which leads to more opportunities and better quality of support services. AI in counseling is greatly influenced by the technology of Natural Language Processing (NLP). NLP permits machines to understand, explain and create human language that makes sense. Being able to do this is crucial for building systems that can dialog with students, answer their questions and give support in an emotional way (Kumar, A., & Gupta, D. 2021). Text input, speech and replies that are clear and suitable to the context are all possible with NLP-driven systems. As an illustration, virtual counseling assistants use NLP to understand what a student is saying as well as how they are saying it which helps the system give advice that is both human and supportive. NLP is closely related to Machine Learning (ML) and Deep Learning (DL) which allow AI systems to become better as they learn from experience. ML algorithms study vast amounts of data to look for patterns and to make forecasts (Hilbert et al., 2021). In counseling settings, ML is used to assess a student's academic results, their habits and their interests to advise them in the right way. It can also help by spotting students who might not succeed in school and offer options for careers that match what they are good at and what they want to do. Deep Learning which belongs to machine learning, works by modeling data relationships with the help of neural networks that have many layers. This way of working is most useful for data that is not organized such as sound recordings, text messages or facial gestures. Through counseling, DL models can spot small changes in the tone of speech or look for signs of stress, anxiety or disengagement in essay-style replies. With more data being used, these models can give better and more understanding recommendations. A major use of AI in advising is through

Recommender Systems. They are built to study user habits, what they like and past actions in order to suggest useful resources, steps or ways forward. At school, recommender systems can show students what to study, what electives to take and what career or higher education paths to explore. When students get personalized suggestions, these systems allow them to choose wisely and improve their skills or career prospects. In counseling, more and more people are using Conversational Agents and Chatbots which are new AI technologies. Users can talk to these tools either by text or audio and they provide ongoing help at any time. Students are able to ask anything related to registering, financial aid, planning their studies or personal matters and instantly get answers. Today's chatbots use NLP and ML to keep track of what's been discussed and recognize emotions and they transfer difficult cases to a human counselor when necessary. The fact that they are always accessible is very important in places where people cannot easily get immediate human help. AI counseling has seen great advances with Sentiment Analysis and Emotion AI. They look at communication to detect the feelings or emotions people are expressing rather than just looking at the words they use. Sentiment analysis is used to see if a student's message is negative, confused or excited, but Emotion AI can read emotions from facial movements, voice tones and data from the body. Because of emotional intelligence, AI systems are able to adjust their communication on the spot, so that it remains considerate and understanding. When a student talks about feeling anxious about an exam, the AI counselor may suggest help, give them encouragement or point them towards calming resources. All these AI tools join together to form a strong system for delivering top-quality, personalized and responsive advising and counseling services. With them, institutions can reach larger groups, give ongoing help and improve student achievement with data analysis.

2.2 Role of AI in Human-Centered Services

Even though AI can help counseling and advising by being efficient and personal, it must be used with care, understanding and a sense of ethics. Such services call for trust, respect for privacy and emotional intelligence which should be carefully built into the design and use of AI. Protection of privacy and confidentiality is a main issue when people interact with AI

(Munir et al., 2022). A person may have to open up about very personal matters and feel a bit exposed in counseling. Students might discuss their emotions, relationships, problems in school or future dreams with AI tools for academic or mental health advice. Users should be told by these systems how their data is gathered, stored, used and guarded. User trust is maintained by handling data safely and having policies that users can understand. AI systems for advising should also assist in making good moral decisions, not only protect privacy. It means making AI tools that admit their own limitations and leave the important decisions to human experts. When a virtual counselor notices that a user might be in serious distress or thinking about suicide, it should quickly tell a trained human counselor instead of trying to deal with the situation alone. Human knowledge and understanding should not be replaced by AI, mainly when situations call for sensitivity and detailed understanding. Ethical AI also depends on reducing bias. The quality of the data that AI algorithms learn from determines how good they are and if this data is not impartial, the system could unintentionally discriminate against certain people. As an example, if the training data used by a career recommendation system shows more men than women in STEM, it could end up recommending STEM careers to men more often. Developers should therefore rely on balanced and diverse data and include various people in system reviews and tests. This way of doing things makes sure that AI tools are fair, open to all and help everyone. AI designers need to have empathy to make sure the user experiences are truly helpful and worthwhile. Such AI systems pay attention to users' words and also to their emotions as they speak. It requires choosing how the system talks to people, the words it uses and the timing of its replies to make sure they are appropriate and understanding. If a student is worried about not passing a class, an empathetic AI might offer encouragement and useful suggestions, instead of giving a standard or technological answer. Adding empathy to how AI is designed can help users feel more connected which can lead to better user experience and results. Another important aspect of human-centered AI for counseling is to keep human involvement. AI is very skilled at analyzing a lot of data, but lacks the real understanding and moral thinking that human counselors have. So, AI systems ought to have a way to bring attention to complex or risky cases for review by people. Having AI deal with typical tasks and data while humans handle important choices makes sure students experience both technology and empathy. AI could help human counselors by giving them useful advice from data analysis. It is possible for AI to notice that a student might need help by seeing their grades drop or them missing more classes. It is able to deliver alerts, create reports on how students are doing or offer individual engagement plans. Because AI can handle routine jobs, human counselors have more time for meaningful talks with students. Also, AI allows counseling services to be both accessible and scalable. Where mental health or education services are lacking, AI-powered systems can help a lot. Those in remote or underserved areas can get advice, motivation and needed resources without having to travel or wait for meetings in person. With more people getting online and better digital skills, AI might enable everyone to access high-quality counseling and advice globally. Nonetheless, we should make sure AI systems help people, not take away their ability to act independently. Students ought to always be able to decide if they want to use AI or speak with a human counselor. Presenting AI as the only way or making people use it, is never acceptable when emotions are involved. Systems should be set up so that they support users, value their independence and protect their dignity in all advising and counseling. All in all, although AI could greatly improve counseling and advising, its use should always be focused on ethics, empathy and putting people first. If used correctly, AI can guide students and give them support they need which can help them face academic and personal challenges with confidence. If AI and human counselors are used together, institutions can design support systems that are more helpful, attentive and inclusive for the future (Pedro et al., 2019).

3. AI IN VIRTUAL COUNSELING

3.1 AI for Mental Health and Emotional Support

Because mental health issues among students are on the rise, AI-based tools are being built to help more students. Natural language processing and digital chats on these platforms help users handle stress, anxiety and depression. These tools are different from regular therapy because they immediately offer support, remain private and do not judge, allowing anyone hesitant to see a counselor in person to use them. They can recognize people's emotions and feelings by reviewing what users write for hints. Sentiment analysis programs group people's expressions into sadness, anger or anxiety which helps the AI respond appropriately. If a person's messages seem to be under high stress, the system could respond with comforting language and suggest getting professional help. Emotion AI goes past text data to examine both voice and facial features, adding more details to a person's mood. Besides, predictive analytics is helping to find students who might experience mental health crises. Using previous counseling notes, grades and behavior information, AI systems are able to find the early signals of depression, wishing to commit suicide or burnout. As a result, students get automatic notifications or counselors are informed quickly. Because of this, predictive models help to increase the safety of mental health services. Even though these technologies are not finished, they show how mental health support can move from in-person visits to online, consistent support.

3.2 Benefits and Limitations

AI in virtual counseling offers a big advantage: users can connect at any time and keep their identity private. Because AI is always online, anyone can access it for help at any time, from any place. Students who find themselves in a crisis outside the counseling timetable may greatly benefit from being able to contact their counselor at any time. Because AI bots keep users anonymous, they make it easier for hesitant users to talk openly about sensitive matters. Because AI tools can manage many interactions at once, they help overcome the problem of shortages in mental health resources and long waits for counseling. Because they can help more people, they can reach students who usually have a hard time accessing traditional counseling. Still, there are major limits to what AI can do in virtual counseling at this time. Lacking emotion and understanding of people is a major problem. Although AI can imitate empathy with pre-made lines, it cannot really grasp the full range of human emotions. Because of this, users can feel that the interactions are not deep enough for what they need emotionally. AI is not yet able to read the small things in body language, tone or judgment of a situation. There is also a major concern about depending too much and facing ethical challenges. AI bots may make users feel they don't require professional help, so they may put off important treatments. Whenever data is collected, there are worries about privacy, obtaining consent and the chance that information may be used improperly. Telling users about the boundaries of AI systems and suggesting where to contact human advisors is necessary to address these risks. Moreover, AI can be unfair to people from different cultures or languages because the training data includes biases. Vulnerable students may get wrong advice because of AI errors which means it is important to keep monitoring and making improvements(Priyadharshini, S et al., 2025). Simply put, even though virtual counseling can reach many and respond quickly, it is not meant to replace care from a human. It is most valuable because it can support regular counseling by giving help quickly, individually and on any scale, while still making sure human supervision is well defined. Using empathetic, clear and ethical AI will play a major role in helping students with their mental and emotional needs.

4. AI IN STUDENT GUIDANCE

4.1 Academic Advising and Personalized Learning Paths

AI is making a big difference in academic advising by giving every student a learning plan suited to their particular strengths, weaknesses and goals. Adaptive learning systems are one of the main uses, since they automatically change lessons and pace according to a student's involvement and achievements. They use instant data from quizzes, student activity and problem solving to discover what students don't know and change their lesson plans. When students are taught this way, they understand more and learn efficiently, as they go at their own speed instead of being forced to use a uniform curriculum. AI tutors and intelligent mentoring which mimic the guidance a human tutor would provide complement such adaptive systems as well. Natural language processing allows these tutors to have chats, answer questions and even offer support or tips to students. They can notice the difficulties that students have and recommend which exercises or resources will help to overcome those difficulties. Because they give instant responses, these systems help students avoid frustration and work harder which are important for success in school. AI is also used to create early alert systems for those students who may need extra help. They use information from attendance, grades, involvement and behavior to predict students who could face challenges at school. If students receive support early in their studies, institutions can help them with tutoring, counseling or peer mentoring before the problems get worse. In large educational settings, it is especially important to have this predictive function because one-on-one guidance from human advisors is not practical. In general, such tools allow students to guide their learning by providing personalized guidance as needed. Because of this personalization, students keep more information, do better in school and are happier with their education.

4.2 Nudging and Behavioral Guidance

Besides delivering lessons, AI also guides students by giving nudges or small hints, to help them choose better choices. A lot of student guidance involves using recommender systems to guide students in choosing their classes, what to study and what activities to join. They use a student's past education, what they like and their plans for the future to suggest courses or materials that fit their goals and will benefit them. They lower the burden of choosing, direct students to new areas and help them keep moving toward finishing their program and building a career. Artificial intelligence is used to guide students in forming positive study routines and better time use. For instance, systems may watch student behavior and send individual messages to help them complete work, join study groups and maintain a good studying schedule. These helpful tips keep students motivated and help them avoid putting things off which many students tend to do. You can customize how often, in what style and with what content you receive nudges, so they are both helpful and unobtrusive. In addition, AI tools help students make achievable study goals and monitor their progress. Seeing their milestones encourages students to control their own progress and stick with their learning. Thanks to this behavioral advice and the insights it's based on, students can handle their school work more effectively. Academic advising is joined by nudging and behavioral guidance systems to address motivation and organization which are required for student success. They turn people who were just being advised, into people who act on the data and maintain good habits.

5. AI IN CAREER ADVISING

5.1 Career Pathway Recommendation Systems

Today, career advisors use artificial intelligence to allow students to access information that fits their preferences and that suits their abilities to jobs that are available. Machine learning drives these tools to determine a student's school performance, skills, interests and ambitions (Alenezi, H. S., & Faisal, M. H. 2020). These systems are unlike past career counseling in that they provide personalized paths based on a person's profile. These systems have value in how they link student profiles to recent shifts in the job market. AI is pointing to the kinds of jobs that seem to be appearing and what abilities are needed to do them using ongoing analysis of job postings, wage information and growth estimates in different industries. This makes students get the most recent suggestions which meet the needs of the market and hence they can make the right decision and maintain a step ahead. These insights allow students to see where they are deficient and take actions to add related qualifications which makes it easier for them to get jobs. Also, these systems include personal preferences along with economic information to make careers more sustainable and satisfying.

5.2 Resume Evaluation and Interview Preparation

AI has been used to suggest paths along with making resume screening tools used by companies and schools. Using both natural language processing and pattern recognition, they quickly review resumes and rank candidates by how relevant their skills, experience and qualifications are. AI driven resume evaluators help students find out what needs to be updated in their resume, how to lay out resume and what keywords to include to pass ATS programs. This direction enables students to introduce their skills well which raises their chances of receiving an interview. At the same time, AI is helping people practice for interviews by using mock interview platforms. These tools use speech, facial expressions and verbal answers to give positive suggestions on how to improve communication skills, confidence and clarity. Students are able to answer everyday or job-relevant questions in a stress-free environment and get instant, honest feedback about what they should improve. Because of these systems, students without access to professional training can now improve their interview skills.

5.3 Labor Market Analysis and Forecasting

Analyzing and forecasting the labor market is a main function of using AI in career advising. AI systems review a lot of workforce data to understand what skills are needed which industries are growing and changes in the economy. Using data from job boards, reports by governments and company announcements, AI systems can determine both sectors that are growing and those where skills are becoming outdated. The data is important for helping students decide how to best develop their careers. AI helps connect to local and national job databases which allows it to suggest jobs that match the available work in a person's area and the local economy. This integration allows career advisors to give students advice which is suited to their local and social situation. For instance, if it is a place where technology is given a lot of prominence, students can be encouraged to go into software or data science; and if it is an agricultural area, students can be encouraged to pursue agribusiness or environmental sciences. AI in the labor market also helps with forecasting, in order to help educational institutions plan their workforce and guide their curricula towards what will be needed on the future job market. Students will have skills and certificates to fill the gap between education and a job.

6. CHALLENGES AND ETHICAL CONSIDERATIONS

6.1 Data Privacy and Security

One of the main issues in using AI for virtual counseling, student guidance and career advising is student data security. These AI tools collect and work with a very large amount of information about a person's mental health, school records, habits and future career goals. Student data is very sensitive and so it must be very well protected to prevent anyone from getting access to it without permission or misusing it. All schools, AI services should use powerful encryption, keep data safe and limit access to protect student information. In addition to legal requirements, there's a good reason now to ensure people trust schools with their use of AI on student data and that means being open about it. Students and counselors must be sure that their data will not be used for commercial reasons without their agreement. The easier it is for users to trust and use AI tools ethically when they understand data policies and can remove their data.

6.2 Bias, Fairness, and Transparency

The concern with education and counseling is that, because AI systems learn from their data, any biases in the data will be passed on. The data that AI models are trained on can contain biases and AI models can repeat or even enhance those biases. For example, when trained on skewed data, an AI career recommender may advise students against certain careers, thereby reducing diversity and keeping existing barriers. Also, tools for sentiment analysis could interpret student's expression of emotion from different backgrounds in incorrect or inappropriate ways. Regularly working to reduce bias in AI algorithms, we should continue to review and manage these risks. To do this we need to make sure we have diverse and fair training data, we use fairness rules when building the model and we routinely monitor for signs of discrimination in its output. It is very important to have students, counselors and ethicists involved in designing and testing AI tools so that everyone is treated fairly. Another major issue is that AI decision making has to be understandable. Deep learning AI models are hard for users to understand because they do not explain how the recommendations or predictions are made(Ponnuviji, N. P et al., 2023; Ganesan, I et al., 2024). The information is not always clear as the students may find it harder to trust and accept the advice given in areas like counseling and career advising. Explainable AI allows counselors and students to review, question and check the suggestions provided by AI. Systems that are clear make it possible for users to know what information they need to make good choices about their education and career.

6.3 Trust and Human Oversight

For these systems to be used effectively, people need to trust them. Even though AI can do many things, both students and counselors are still doubtful about using it for decisions that matter a lot to them. The accuracy, empathy and ethics of AI lead us to see why using automation and human input together is important. AI is best seen as something that helps people, not as something that can take their place. Having people involved is necessary for cases that require special attention, detailed judgment, understanding and ethics. For instance, if AI identifies a student as having mental health risks, it is the counselor who must review and handle the intervention. By using AI for data work, this model allows people to keep the valuable human qualities required for trust and support. In addition, the way students and counselors view AI systems plays a role in whether they want to use them. If everyone involved knows what AI can do and what it cannot and if users are given chances to provide feedback, AI can be better understood and used by all. Making user interfaces easy to use and putting user autonomy first will help these services be accepted and used for a long time.

7. FUTURE DIRECTIONS

7.1 Integration of AI with Human-Led Hybrid Models

In the future, it's likely that virtual counseling, student guidance and career advising will make the most progress when AI and human insight work together in a single model. AI can handle huge amounts of data, scale up its services and recommend things to users, but human counselors have empathy, understand the context of each situation and make ethical decisions that machines cannot do at present. It is expected that future systems will allow AI to do the simple data tasks and leave complex, sensitive or important decisions to human advisors. In these hybrid models, AI will be set up to meet students first, evaluate them briefly and arrange cases in order of priority or complexity. When needed, human professionals can step in to provide support that fits each person, helping to make the best use of resources and maintain top-quality care. The partnership will support continuous development, as AI systems are updated using advice from experts. The purpose of these hybrid frameworks is to supply students with responsive, efficient and caring services that suit a variety of needs.

7.2 Emotionally Intelligent AI Systems

AI is expected to improve in the future by sensing and responding to the emotions of students. Currently, AI tools can analyze sentiment and detect basic emotions, yet these methods aren't always very accurate. New AI systems will use voice, facial expressions, body signals and context to better understand people's feelings. If AI is emotionally intelligent, it would be able to respond with empathy and in a way that people respond better to, boosting user engagement and positive results in virtual counseling. These systems could spot signs of disengagement or distress early and switch up how they help which helps build trust and good relationships. With affective computing, AI can help people by suggesting emotional regulation exercises, mindfulness and coping strategies which will improve virtual counseling. For these improvements to work, the algorithms must be developed using a wide range of ethical emotional data and carefully checked to prevent misunderstandings or cultural mistakes. Still, AI with emotional intelligence shows great potential in helping to create digital tools that fit well with the work of counselors and advisors.

7.3 Culturally Adaptive Advising Systems

As AI is introduced in schools worldwide, becoming culturally adaptable will matter more. AI systems designed for the future must take into account cultural, language and socioeconomic diversity to help everyone equally. It means changing the way teachers communicate, recommend and intervene to match the values and cultures of their students. With cultural adaptation, AI is able to reduce biases by understanding and respecting the various customs connected to mental health, learning habits and career goals. As an example, systems designed for people from many cultures and languages can automatically adjust their language and expressions to help everyone communicate more clearly. Much the same, recommendations for a career path can consider both the job market in the area and what is expected by the community. For these systems to succeed, we must involve experts in cultural studies, education and ethics and encourage active participation by diverse user communities in the design. Culturally adaptive AI will help make virtual counseling and advising more accessible and useful around the world.

7.4 Cross-Platform and Lifelong Advising Ecosystems

AI will eventually play a big role in counseling and advising by creating ongoing advising systems that work across various platforms and cover a lifetime of education and career choices. Instead of only being used for specific reasons, blended platforms will link insights from data in academic records, mental health apps, career services and even social media to give students fuller, more personalized advice. These ecosystems will provide each user with a personalized dashboard to view their progress, create goals and receive specially made support for mental health, schooling and work prospects. If wearable devices and mobile apps are connected, it is possible to monitor someone's health in real time, allowing problems to be managed sooner. In addition, such platforms will ease the change from school to work, helping people keep learning and adapt their careers as labor markets change. Using AI to predict and analyze information in one system, lifelong advising ecosystems will guide individuals as they deal with challenging life paths.

8. CONCLUSION

This chapter has looked at the many ways artificial intelligence helps with virtual counseling, student guidance and career advising. Thanks to natural language processing, machine learning and recommender systems, educational institutions now offer personalized help to many students at once. Online counselors and emotional support bots are accessible and adaptive learning and behavioral nudges help students with schoolwork. In addition, AI-based tools support students by helping them get through tough job markets, shape their resumes and get ready for interviews. All of these applications show that AI can help education by making help more personal, automatic and available to all. Even so, applying AI to these sensitive areas has its own set of problems. Data privacy issues, unjust algorithms, openness and the need for human involvement show that ethical and trustworthy AI is essential. Making sure AI works with human feelings is making sure that it doesn't replace what humans do best. It is also very important to continue developing AI that is aware of cultural differences and can appropriately emotionally support people. Furthering ahead, education will be hybrid, emotionally aware technologies, culturally aware systems and integrated advising for lifelong learning. They will likely result in environments where teaching responds to students' growing needs in a better way over time. To fully benefit from AI in virtual counseling and advising, we need teachers, technology experts, ethicists and students to join forces. When we focus on ethical, open and people-centered AI, we make sure that learners everywhere benefit from these technologies.

REFERENCES

Alenezi, H. S., & Faisal, M. H. (2020). Utilizing crowdsourcing and machine learning in education: Literature review. *Education and Information Technologies*, *25*(4), 2971–2986.

Ansari, G., Gupta, S., & Singhal, N. (2021). Natural Language Processing in Online Reviews. In *Natural Language Processing for Global and Local Business* (pp. 40–64). IGI Global Scientific Publishing.

Benta, D., Bologa, G., & Dzitac, I. (2014). E-learning platforms in higher education. Case study. *Procedia Computer Science*, *31*, 1170–1176.

Chen, L., Chen, P., & Lin, Z. (2020). Artificial intelligence in education: A review. *IEEE Access : Practical Innovations, Open Solutions*, *8*, 75264–75278.

Dhinakaran, D., Kumar, N. J., & Ponnuviji, N. P. (2025). Safeguarding confidentiality and privacy in cloud-enabled healthcare systems with spectrasafe encryption and dynamic k-anonymity algorithm. *Expert Systems with Applications*, *279*, 127584.

Engelbrecht, J., Oates, G., & de Carvalho Borba, M. (2025). Artificial intelligence and social media in mathematics education. In *social media in the changing mathematics classroom* (pp. 43-65). Cham: Springer Nature Switzerland.

Ganesan, I., Ponnuviji, N. P., Kumar, A. S., Nithya, M., Jambulingam, U., & Lalitha, S. D. (2024). Real-Time Event Detection and Predictive Analytics Using IoT and Deep Learning. In Industry Applications of Thrust Manufacturing: Convergence with Real-Time Data and AI (pp. 1-41). IGI Global Scientific Publishing.

Hilbert, S., Coors, S., Kraus, E., Bischl, B., Lindl, A., Frei, M., & Stachl, C. (2021). Machine learning for the educational sciences. *Review of Education*, *9*(3), e3310.

Kumar, A., & Gupta, D. (2021). Sentiment analysis as a restricted NLP problem. In *Natural language processing for global and local business* (pp. 65–96). IGI Global.

Munir, H., Vogel, B., & Jacobsson, A. (2022). Artificial intelligence and machine learning approaches in digital education: A systematic revision. *Information (Basel)*, *13*(4), 203.

Ouadoud, M., Rida, N., & Chafiq, T. (2021). Overview of E-learning Platforms for Teaching and Learning. *Int. J. Recent Contributions Eng. Sci. IT*, *9*(1), 50–70.

Pedro, F., Subosa, M., Rivas, A., & Valverde, P. (2019). Artificial intelligence in education: Challenges and opportunities for sustainable development.

Ponnuviji, N. P., Murugan, P., Esakkiammal, S., Kumar, S., Vishal, K. S., & Meenakshi, S. (2024, March). AI-Powered Business Intelligence for Transforming Finance and Education. In *2024 2nd International Conference on Disruptive Technologies (ICDT)* (pp. 1287-1291). IEEE.

Ponnuviji, N. P., Sumaiya Begum, A., Gnanasekaran, T., Rajendiran, M., & Shenbaga Ezhil, S. (2023, April). Leveraging Random Forest for Intelligent IoT Systems in Industrial Environments. In *International Conference on Internet of Things* (pp. 46-57). Cham: Springer Nature Switzerland.

Priyadharshini, S. I., Irene, D. S., Beulah, J. R., & Ponnuviji, N. P. (2025). Enhancing real-time health monitoring with hybrid recurrent long short-term tyrannosaurus search for menstrual cups. *Biomedical Signal Processing and Control*, *100*, 107065.

Chapter 3
The Role of Psychological Counseling in the Age of AI

Sana Alsayed
https://orcid.org/0009-0002-1419-219X
Philadelphia University, Amman, Jordan

ABSTRACT

In our current world, technology has impacted almost every element of human life, changing how we work, communicate, learn, and even take care of our health. One field that has been affected is psychological counseling. Artificial intelligence (AI) is playing significant role in the field of mental health as technology advances, changing how people seek assistance and how psychologist practitioners conduct therapy. There are many exciting opportunities associated with the development of AI-powered solutions for mental health, but there are also important obstacles that must be carefully considered. The function of psychological counseling in the era of artificial intelligence will be examined in this article, along with how AI is being included into mental health treatment, its advantages and disadvantages, as well as the reasons why a traditional psychologist is still important.

DOI: 10.4018/979-8-3373-3316-8.ch003

INTRODUCTION

Technological developments in our present world affect every sector of human life by changing work practices and communication methods as well as education and healthcare management. The field of psychological counseling has experienced an impact from modern technology. Artificial Intelligence (AI) plays an important role in mental health treatment and is changing how therapy is delivered to both patients and therapists (Topol, 2019). The development of AI-powered mental health solutions creates various exciting possibilities yet multiple significant obstacles require careful examination (Ajayi, 2025). This chapter investigates how AI modifies psychological counseling practice through its integration into mental health treatments alongside their benefits and drawbacks and reasons why traditional psychologist practitioners remain essential. The objective of connecting mental health technologies involves two components: Chatbots on virtual therapy websites and diagnostic software that support depression, anxiety and post-traumatic disorder (PTSD) (Fitzpatrick et al., 2017). The development of Wysa and Woebot applications shows how artificial intelligence supports mental health by offering digital therapist services to counselees (Inkster et al., 2018; Fulmer et al., 2018). AI applications offer three major benefits to psychological counseling through their ability to increase accessibility while providing virtual counseling and online chatbots and remote mental health counseling services (Naslund et al., 2017). Another important obstacle to mental therapy is cost. Psychological therapy remains expensive in various countries due to extensive therapy sessions and professional dedication but mental health apps provide more budget-friendly psychological support (Torous et al., 2020). Through the application of machine learning algorithms artificial intelligence systems develop personalized mental healthcare that matches individual needs based on demographic factors such as language, age, sex, ethics, religion, social concerns, economic factors, region of living, level of education, and medical and psychological history (D'Alfonso, 2020). The worldwide phenomenon of stigma or the shame of mental illness persists as a challenge even with modern social and technological advancements because it prevents people from discussing their disorders. AI apps establish secret spaces that let people get treatment without revealing their identities. The accessibility of online mental health resources will make these services more accepted which leads people to seek necessary help for discussing their disorders (Gaffney et al., 2019).

AI technology offers numerous advantages for mental health yet it creates multiple critical drawbacks together with moral challenges that must be addressed. The drawbacks of artificial intelligence applications include human therapist replacement problems and excessive electronic device usage and compromised patient mental health data privacy and security (Vaidyam et al., 2019). The essential elements of therapy include human interaction alongside trust and empathy. Many people visit therapy to receive both listening support and psychological and mental problem guidance. The algorithmic responses of AI attempt to replicate empathy yet fail to deliver the genuine human connection which therapists build through their psychological practice from the beginning (Zhou et al., 2019). AI systems maintain advanced capabilities yet they remain incapable of grasping the complete depth of human emotions and experiences (Assayed et al., 2023). The small behavioral cues which human therapists normally detect remain invisible to AI systems which could force them to modify their therapeutic methods including body language, voice tone and eye movement (Blease et al., 2019). Human therapists provide better emotional support than AI during extreme trauma situations because counselees need complete attention while also requiring additional interventions or professional referrals. Data privacy and security stand as the primary concerns when AI applications are used since people worry about data handling methods and data ownership and storage locations and access rights and unauthorized third-party data access. AI platforms must adhere to strict data protection rules while providing full transparency about their data management procedures to maintain user trust and safeguard user privacy (Robbins et al., 2021). AI requires human supervision because its development needs constant human oversight. AI systems have strong capabilities but they do not possess absolute perfection. Insufficient monitoring of AI systems leads to incorrect suggestions or improper data understanding. An AI application might suggest inappropriate coping strategies for a particular disorder (Torous & Wykes, 2020). AI software exists to supplement human therapy instead of replacing human therapists. Human experts should stay involved in therapy sessions throughout the process to provide necessary guidance and suggestions.

THE EVOLUTION OF PSYCHOLOGICAL COUNSELING

The discipline of Psychological Counselling has experienced significant growth throughout multiple years. Mental health problems received minimal discussion during that time while people considered sadness and anxiety as natural weaknesses. The absence of both understanding and support systems forced numerous people to endure their suffering without speaking out. Mental health problems were historically treated as spiritual possessions or divine punishments during past times. People used confinement and other dangerous punishments to treat these "illnesses" yet these methods proved ineffective (Braslow, 2023). Science and reason entered the scene much later to bring an end to the incorrect psychological interpretations.

During the 1900s Frankus and Jung established foundational principles for contemporary psychology through their systematic exploration of human mental processes. Through his work Freud introduced the world to the therapeutic value of emotional conversation for mental and physical health (Freud, 1910). The introduction of "talk therapy" began at this point which allowed professionals to provide structured conversations that helped people discover themselves.

The passage of time brought forth numerous new theories and therapeutic approaches. The development of cognitive-behavioral therapy (CBT) represented a major breakthrough because it helps patients recognize and transform their unconscious negative thoughts that shape their lives (Beck, 1979).

WHAT IS ARTIFICIAL INTELLIGENCE?

AI aims to create methods which enable computer systems to execute human-level intelligence tasks across different levels (Russell & Norvig, 2021). The functions of AI technologies will comprise natural language understanding and speech recognition and pattern recognition and problem solving and decision making capabilities. Simple rule based programs represent the fundamental category of AI technologies whereas sophisticated learning neural networks demonstrate the most advanced category (Assayed et al., 2024).

The AI technology known as machine learning enables computers to enhance their performance through data analysis without requiring human programming. The way machines process information differs from one machine to another until they respond like humans then we call it AI. Human beings acquire knowledge through three distinct learning methods which include imitation and pattern identification and learning from mistakes. The main objective of NLP or Natural Language Processing involves teaching computers to understand human language so they can provide verbal responses which form the basis of chatbots and virtual assistants (Jurafsky & Martin, 2021; Assayed et al., 2025). Computer vision stands as the fourth AI technology among others. Through its functionality machines gain the ability to process images and understand environmental data (Khan et al., 2021). Hence, AI serves various sectors including healthcare and finance and self-driving vehicles and customer support services (Topol, 2019).

ARTIFICIAL INTELLIGENCE AND ITS INTEGRATION INTO MENTAL HEALTH SERVICES

AI has entered multiple sectors of the economy while transforming mental healthcare to provide better access to services. The definition of Artificial Intelligence (AI) explains how computer technology performs human intelligent tasks for learning and problem-solving (Russell & Norvig, 2021). AI technology supports medical evaluations for mental healthcare while diagnosing conditions which results in both quicker treatments and expanded service accessibility (Topol, 2019). AI-based conversational agents or chatbots such as Woebot and Wysa and Tess represent the most advanced AI application. The digital tool combines CBT and DBT principles to offer therapeutic conversations and symptom management for users experiencing anxiety, depression and emotional distress (Inkster et al., 2018). AI chatbots and virtual therapists create emotional connections with users while requesting their responses. The resources provide emotional management strategies that help users control their distress symptoms. The technology provides valuable assistance to both elderly individuals and people who feel ashamed or discriminated against. AI serves as an assistance tool for remote communities which lack sufficient mental health professionals (Fulmer et al., 2018). The accessibility feature stands as one of the main benefits AI brings to mental healthcare. AI tools deliver instant support to patients through all hours including times when clinical services are unavailable (Al-Sayed et al., 2024).

Mental healthcare benefits from artificial intelligence yet this integration creates major ethical problems. AI systems face a critical data security risk because patients must share sensitive personal information with counselors.

AI systems lack the ability to show compassion because it restricts their capacity to understand complex emotional expressions and situational reactions. AI should function as a support system for human therapists to improve mental health care quality and accessibility according to Vaidyam et al. (2019).

OPPORTUNITIES AND BENEFITS OF ARTIFICIAL INTELLIGENCE IN COUNSELING

Artificial Intelligence (AI) transforms many aspects of our existence especially counseling services. AI technology brings enhanced mental health support access as its main beneficial feature. Most people encounter barriers because of expensive therapy costs combined with insufficient mental health professionals and geographical isolation. AI tools together with chatbots and virtual counselors provide continuous assistance to users. These tools deliver their benefits best during emergency situations and situations where conventional therapy services are unavailable (Fitzpatrick, Darcy, & Vierhile, 2017). .AI technology enhances counselor abilities to detect emotional signs that occur in clients. The system evaluates client speech patterns together with tone and writing content to detect signs of depression or anxiety which traditional sessions would miss (Miner et al., 2020). Blease et al. (2019) state that AI maintains longitudinal tracking of client progress which enables therapists to develop personalized treatment strategies.

The system delivers continuous virtual counselor assistance through its virtual counselors. These platforms function best during emergency situations and when standard therapeutic services become unavailable (Fitzpatrick, Darcy, & Vierhile, 2017). These tools enable users to start empathetic discussions while providing stress relief exercises and tools for anxiety and depression management. AI technology enables counselors to better identify emotional signals from their clients. The system can analyze client speech together with tone and writing to detect signs of depression and anxiety which standard sessions would miss. AI systems maintain continuous client progress tracking which enables therapists to create individualized treatment approaches (Blease et al., 2019).

People who prefer not to speak with humans can find privacy and unbiased support through AI systems. AI serves as a gateway which directs users toward professional mental health assistance (American Psychological Association, 2023). The AI system provides silent help through smartphones or computers without causing any stigma. This makes more people seek help (IBM, 2023). AI systems assist mental health practitioners by performing administrative tasks that include writing reports and scheduling appointments and taking notes. The system provides therapists with extended time to spend with their patients (HealthIT.gov, 2021). AI delivers training to future counselors through virtual simulations that mimic real-world situations in educational settings. Through these simulations trainees develop better skills for handling actual situations (Shore et al., 2018). AI provides significant advantages by offering services to diverse groups of people. The system operates with multiple language capabilities and understands different cultural backgrounds. The system enhances the inclusion of diverse groups through its ability to show empathy toward different communities (World Health Organization [WHO], 2022). AI functions as an information-sharing tool that assists healthcare providers to enhance their delivery of care without replacing human emotional intelligence or deep understanding. The system analyzes extensive data collections to determine which specific treatments work best for different individuals. Blease et al. (2019) explain that this method produces personalized treatments which yield superior results.

CHALLENGES AND ETHICAL CONSIDERATION OF USING ARTIFICIAL INTELLIGENCE IN MENTAL HEALTH

Artificial Intelligence (AI) functions as an essential tool for mental health support. Practitioners use this technology to identify patients and deliver treatment while monitoring their health status. The technology provides numerous benefits yet creates significant obstacles and moral dilemmas which need thorough examination. The main challenge with AI systems stems from their accuracy and dependability. AI systems reach their decisions by processing data for learning purposes. The outputs from models become misleading or worse when they are built from training data that lacks completeness or shows bias or lacks representation. An AI system trained with data mainly from young Western subjects will demonstrate reduced accuracy when working with older people or those from different cultural backgrounds (Obermeyer et al., 2019). This may lead to incorrect diagnoses or ineffective treatment planning, which can even cause damage to clients.

Privacy is also a challenge. Mental health data is very confidential, and use of AI entails collecting, storing, and processing individual information. This information can leak if not properly managed through data breaches or misuse. This will be harmful to patients, who may become embarrassed, ashamed, or discriminated against if their mental condition is disclosed. Maintaining confidentiality of patients is highly important, and mental health professionals must ensure that the security of any AI application they use is strong.

Ethical dilemmas emerge when AI is tasked with decisions that directly affect the lives of individuals, in health care contexts involving diagnosis and treatment choices that have an impact on an individual's welfare. When an AI system recommends a course of treatment or raises an alarm about risks without justification or explanation provided to the individual involved in their care process questions of accountability come into play. Determining who should take responsibility for errors made by an AI system whether it's the company overseeing its operations the healthcare professionals interpreting its recommendations or the developers responsible, for its design becomes an issue to address. In comparison, to professionals like doctors and therapist's artificial intelligence lacks the ability to consider the context show empathy or understand the intricate emotional nuances crucial, in mental healthcare. This can lead AI programs to come across as cold and impersonal towards patients diminishing trust and potentially deterring them from seeking help. Another ethical issue revolves around the risks of relying on technology in this field. While AI can support health professionals in their work it cannot replace the judgment and decision making they provide. In the realm of health care lies a personal touch rooted in human connection. Trust is vital, for nurturing relationships while emotions play a pivotal role, in the healing process; qualities that no computer can replicate the compassion or empathy offered by a proficient therapist who possess these attributes wholeheartedly. Relying excessively on AI might lead professionals to overlook skills or overlook nuances that machines are incapable of detecting (Vayena et al., 2018).

In addition, to that point raised on about AI tools not ensuring fairness in access to resources among all groups of people equally; it's worth noting how certain AI powered mental wellness apps and services require tools like smartphones and internet connectivity along with possible subscription costs, a scenario that may pose financial challenges for marginalized communities such as individuals with low income status and older adults living in remote areas. The uneven availability of AI applications for health across populations can worsen preexisting disparities and widen the gap, between those who can benefit from such technology and those who cannot (Topol, 2019).

HYBRID MODELS: COLLABORATION BETWEEN COUNSELORS AND ARTIFICIAL INTELLIGENCE

Counselors and artificial intelligence (AI) have teamed up to enhance health services jointly now. AI is becoming more advanced. Is no longer a futuristic concept but is presently integrated into therapy sessions. Devices such, as chatbots and data analysis platforms assist therapists, in their work than taking over their roles entirely.

AI can analyze a clients' data to detect signs of health problems early on as an illustration. Chatbots such, as Woebot and Wysa offer users advice and mental health resources in the gaps between therapy appointments

(Fitzpatrick et al. 2017). When it comes to utilizing AI in the field of health ethics plays a role in the discussion, at hand. It is essential for therapists to contemplate the accuracy of AI systems along with their respect for privacy and diverse norms. Any biases or complexities within these systems could potentially result in diagnoses or breaches of confidentiality (as noted by O'Neil in 2016). Moreover, AI lacks the ability to fully grasp emotions. Therefore, cannot serve as a substitute for the profound human connection that is fundamental, in therapy sessions.

Therapists should maintain authority. View AI, as an aid than a substitute in their practice methods according to Reamer (2018). Current counselor education involves understanding technology and ethics to guarantee AI utilization. Furthermore, it is crucial for developers of AI to partner closely with health professionals in order to create inclusive and evidence based tools. Collaboration among experts, from disciplines will enhance the efficiency and reliability of AI systems.

Imagine it as a physician collaborating with an aide; through adhering to ethical standards and prioritizing teamwork and the clients' welfare as key factors, in their approach. AI and counselors have the potential to build a more empathetic and effective mental health system.

WHY COUNSELORS STILL MATTER

Mental wellness application growth through artificial intelligence technology creates questions about whether society still requires counselors to manage all aspects of daily life. The consensus remains affirmative. The increasing number of online therapy resources including self-help literature and digital tracking tools and YouTube influencers do not replace the exclusive value counselors provide with their human connection and specialized expertise and secure emotional recovery space.

A fundamental issue in counseling practice is establishing connection because it remains crucial for developing trust between the therapist and client throughout the therapeutic process. Technology delivers convenience alongside basic therapeutic tools but fails to replace the essential experience of human connection and active listening. According to Psychologist

Carl Rogers (1961) genuine listening from someone who does not criticize nor attempt to control creates a powerful feeling. That's something an app can't replicate.

The work of professional counselors exceeds advice-giving and listening since they possess trained expertise and a strict ethical commitment that exceeds what a supportive friend could provide. Professional counselors use evidence-based approaches including Cognitive Behavioral Therapy (CBT) and Person-Centered Therapy as well as trauma-informed methods to help clients understand their emotional responses and behavioral patterns in life (Corey 2016). Their area of expertise extends beyond symptom recognition because they specialize in discovering the fundamental causes of problems they encounter. Each client receives specific intervention and tailored strategies as part of their professional practice. The focus is on offering qualified assistance combined with empathy instead of attempting to solve problems.

People from all walks of life actively seek counseling services because they need a dependable environment which our current fast-paced world desperately needs. Sessions at this establishment enable customers to work with an expert on emotion management and goal setting as well as obstacle resolution. The continuous bond between counselors and their clients helps clients become responsible and develop personally although online platforms lack the ability to thoughtfully and empathetically engage with your ideas and provide support.

As part of their role counselors perform early intervention and crisis prevention by identifying mental health issues before they reach dangerous stages of escalation. A skilled counselor can identify signs of depression, anxiety disorders and trauma in people while providing assistance to stop severe outcomes including suicidal thoughts. The American Counseling Association (ACA) confirms that seeking help from health professionals leads to reduced permanent damage to our wellness (ACA 2021). Throughout life we encounter transitions which both reshape our identity and transform our relationships and emotional responses. Counselors help people navigate life transitions through their ability to support individuals during times of change and career transformation and marital dissolution and identity exploration. "They not offer resources. They establish a safe space which allows people to handle the challenges that emerge from change.

The utilization of digital technology should be viewed as a supplementary tool rather than an alternative to human interaction and therapy or counseling services. A mindfulness application functions to reduce stress while a virtual conversational agent provides emotional support. A person needs human emotional support from a compassionate person who can validate their suffering while guiding and motivating them during healing when facing difficult situations such as loss or mental health complexities.

CONCLUSION

As we approach the conclusion of this investigation, into the shifting landscape of therapy in the era of intelligence technology reveals a fundamental reality. Advancements may alter our methods and communication mediums while enhancing our understanding of the human psyche; However, they cannot replicate the core essence of empathy and genuine connection, in healing and listening processes.

Artificial Intelligence has made strides in fields of technology and innovation. Its ability to process information rapidly conversations and identify speech and behavioral patterns not easily discernible by humans presents significant opportunities, in the realm of mental healthcare. This technology can play a role in enhancing accessibility and mitigating stigmas. Chatbots have the capacity to provide solace to individuals feeling isolated, at night. Mood tracking tools offer clients insights into their cycles that they may have previously overlooked. Furthermore, sophisticated algorithms can alert professionals to crisis indicators even before a client reaches out for help.

At its peak performance level but still AI serves as a mirror reflecting the information it has absorbed than possessing a soul or a heart, with lived experiences; it lacks the ability to offer companionship by holding your hand or deciphering the sorrow hidden in prolonged silences. Moreover, it cannot shed tears alongside you. Comprehend the profundity of quietness. In that hallowed interaction, between therapist and patient where much restoration originates no mechanical device can supplant the power of human connection.

In the realm of counseling shines an bright light of support and understanding beyond mere techniques or test result analysis, by professionals known as counselors—they serve as observers of sorrow and joys evolution amid adversity and change They are skilled not solely in methods but in the delicate craft of being truly present for others They create a safe haven, for the vulnerable aspects of ones self—those tangled in messiness fear embarrassment or doubt In a world focused heavily to boost performance and streamline processes counseling bravely chooses to pause and inquire gently;"What emotions are you experiencing?"

In the era of AI advancement and technology integration, into our lives does not reduce the importance of this type of nurturing and attention; in fact it accentuates it further. As our interactions increasingly take place through screens and algorithms influence our self-perception and relationships dynamics some individuals might experience a sense of disconnection from their selves. There is an increasing desire for environments where individuals are valued not merely as figures or personality categories but as human beings, with intricate and evolving identities.

Counselors currently face a twofold challenge. To leverage the aspects of AI without succumbing to its restrictions and drawbacks. This involves incorporating technology in a manner that enhances and supports the process of substituting it.It entails staying of the tools clients utilize. Such, as apps, chabots and digital diaries. Additionally, it necessitates advocating for guidelines, data security and human rights, in an era where mental health data is becoming increasingly commodified.

In today's era of avatars and carefully crafted personas counselors have a unique opportunity to assist individuals in navigating the complexities of digital life itself a role that may be considered a calling, in its own right. Exploring the concept of self-awareness amidst the realm poses questions; How do we define our identity when surrounded by avatars and digital representations of ourselves that others perceive online? Furthermore; How do we cope with loss and mourning when memories of our loved ones persist in their imprints? Additionally; In a world where artificial intelligence has the capacity to predict our desires before we even voice them aloud. How does this affect our memory recall abilities as our capacity, for intimacy and creativity? These inquiries extend beyond musings; they delve into the realm of psychology and are increasingly surfacing within the confines of therapy sessions.

Looking ahead to the future requires us to move beyond viewing things in a and white manner of humans, versus machines. Than sticking to this perspective we should consider a new approach where technology and human beings work together as partners with human principles taking precedence. In this scenario AI can assist in reducing tasks offer support in between sessions and flag potential issues. However the essence of healing inevitably lies within interactions and connections.

In each era, throughout history psychological therapy has evolved to address the challenges—be it war, social unrest, pandemics or the ongoing digital transformation. One constant remains unchanged; the counselors' duty as an observer of pain and a supporter in the journey towards recovery. In this era dominated by AI technology the counselors' role is not diminishing; rather it is extending its reach. For long as individuals seek acknowledgment listening ears and empathy the necessity for human engagement, in therapy will endure.

In the light emanating, from our devices stands a reminder to cherish the essence of compassion and connection in all that we do.

REFERENCES

Ajayi, R. (2025). AI-powered innovations for managing complex mental health conditions and addiction treatments. *International Research Journal of Modernization in Engineering Technology and Science*, •••, 1–18.

Al-Sayed, S., Assayed, S. K., Alkhatib, M., & Shaalan, K. (2024). Impact of Artificial Intelligence Chatbots on Student Well-being and Mental Health: A Systematic Review. *People and Behavior Analysis*, *2*(2), 10–31098.

American Counseling Association (ACA). (2021). *Why Counseling is Important.* Retrieved from www.counseling.org

American Psychological Association. (2023). AI in psychology: Promise, pitfalls, and potential. https://www.apa.org/news/press/releases/2023/09/artificial-intelligence-psychology

Assayed, S., Shaalan, K., Al-Sayed, S., & Alkhatib, M. (2023). Psychological emotion recognition of students using machine learning based chatbot. [IJAIA]. *International Journal of Artificial Intelligence & Applications*, *14*(2).

Assayed, S. K., Alkhatib, M., & Shaalan, K. (2024). The key challenges in educational advising chatbot dialogue system. In *Innovation in the University 4.0 System based on Smart Technologies* (pp. 74–82). Chapman and Hall/CRC.

Assayed, S. K., Alkhatib, M., Shaalan, K. F., & Alsayed, S. A. (2025, April). HSGAdviser: AI Speech Assistant for Enabling Sustainable Education Solutions. In *2025 1st International Conference on Computational Intelligence Approaches and Applications (ICCIAA)* (pp. 1-6). IEEE.

Beck, A. T. (1979). *Cognitive therapy of depression.* Guilford Press.

Blease, C., Kaptchuk, T. J., Bernstein, M. H., Mandl, K. D., Halamka, J. D., & DesRoches, C. M. (2019). Artificial Intelligence and the future of psychiatry: Insights from a global physician survey. npj. *Digital Medicine*, *2*(1), 1–6. DOI: 10.1038/s41746-019-0182-7

Blease, C., Kaptchuk, T. J., Bernstein, M. H., Mandl, K. D., Halamka, J. D., & DesRoches, C. M. (2019). Artificial Intelligence and the Future of Psychiatry: Insights From a Global Physician Survey. *NPJ Digital Medicine*, *2*(1), 1–6.

Braslow, J. (2023). *Mental ills and bodily cures: psychiatric treatment in the first half of the twentieth century* (Vol. 8). Univ of California Press.

Corey, G. (2016). *Theory and Practice of Counseling and Psychotherapy* (10th ed.). Cengage Learning.

D'Alfonso, S. (2020). AI in mental health. *Current Opinion in Psychology*, *36*, 112–117. PMID: 32604065

Fitzpatrick, K. K., Darcy, A., & Vierhile, M. (2017). Delivering cognitive behavior therapy to young adults with symptoms of depression and anxiety using a fully automated conversational agent (Woebot): A randomized controlled trial. *JMIR Mental Health*, *4*(2), e19. DOI: 10.2196/mental.7785 PMID: 28588005

Freud, S. (1910). *Five Lectures on Psychoanalysis*. Norton.

Fulmer, R., Joerin, A., Gentile, B., Lakerink, L., & Rauws, M. (2018). Using psychological artificial Intelligence (Tess) to relieve symptoms of depression and anxiety: Randomized controlled trial. *JMIR Mental Health*, *5*(4), e64. DOI: 10.2196/mental.9782 PMID: 30545815

Gaffney, H., Mansell, W., & Tai, S. (2019). Conversational Agents in the Treatment of Mental Health Problems: Mixed-Method Systematic Review. *JMIR Mental Health*, *6*(10), e14166. PMID: 31628789

Health, I. T. gov. (2021). Benefits of health IT for behavioral health. https://www.healthit.gov/topic/health-it-health-care-settings/behavioral-health

IBM. (2023). How AI is transforming mental health care. https://www.ibm.com/blog/how-ai-is-transforming-mental-health-care

Inkster, B., Sarda, S., & Subramanian, V. (2018). An empathy-driven, conversational artificial intelligence agent (Wysa) for digital mental well-being: Real-world data evaluation. *JMIR mHealth and uHealth*, *6*(11), e12106. DOI: 10.2196/12106 PMID: 30470676

Jurafsky, D., & Martin, J. H. (2021). *Speech and language processing* (3rd ed. draft). https://web.stanford.edu/~jurafsky/slp3/

Khan, A. A., Laghari, A. A., & Awan, S. A. (2021). Machine learning in computer vision: A review. *EAI Endorsed Transactions on Scalable Information Systems, 8*(32).

Miner, A. S., Haque, A., Fries, J. A., Fleming, S. L., Wilfley, D. E., Terence Wilson, G., & Shah, N. H. (2020). Assessing the accuracy of automatic speech recognition for psychotherapy. *NPJ Digital Medicine*, *3*(1), 82. PMID: 32550644

Naslund, J. A., Aschbrenner, K. A., Marsch, L. A., & Bartels, S. J. (2017). The future of mental health care: Peer-to-peer support and social media. *Epidemiology and Psychiatric Sciences*, *25*(2), 113–122. PMID: 26744309

O'Neil, C. (2016). *Weapons of math destruction: How big data increases inequality and threatens democracy*. Crown Publishing Group.

Obermeyer, Z., Powers, B., Vogeli, C., & Mullainathan, S. (2019). Dissecting racial bias in an algorithm used to manage the health of populations. *Science*, *366*(6464), 447–453. DOI: 10.1126/science.aax2342 PMID: 31649194

Reamer, F. G. (2018). Artificial Intelligence in social work: Emerging ethical challenges. *Social Work*, *63*(3), 233–242. DOI: 10.1093/sw/swy019

Robbins, R., Krebs, P., Rapoport, D. M., Jean-Louis, G., & Duncan, D. T. (2021). Examining the Effects of COVID-19 on Sleep, Mental Health, and Technology Use Among Adults in the United States: Cross-sectional Survey. *JMIR Mental Health*, *8*(1), e22857.

Rogers, C. R. (1961). *On Becoming a Person: A Therapist's View of Psychotherapy*. Houghton Mifflin.

Russell, S., & Norvig, P. (2021). *Artificial Intelligence: A modern approach* (4th ed.). Pearson.

Shore, J. H., Yellowlees, P., Caudill, R., Johnston, B., Turvey, C., Mishkind, M. C., & Hilty, D. M. (2018). Best practices in videoconferencing-based telemental health. *Telemedicine Journal and e-Health*, *24*(11), 827–832. DOI: 10.1089/tmj.2018.0237 PMID: 30358514

Topol, E. (2019). *Deep medicine: How artificial Intelligence can make healthcare human again*. Basic Books.

Torous, J., Myrick, K. J., Rauseo-Ricupero, N., & Firth, J. (2020). Digital mental health and COVID-19: Using technology today to accelerate the curve on access and quality tomorrow. *JMIR Mental Health*, *7*(3), e18848. PMID: 32213476

Torous, J., & Wykes, T. (2020). Opportunities From the Coronavirus Disease 2019 Pandemic for Transforming Psychiatric Care With Telehealth. *JAMA Psychiatry*, *77*(12), 1205–1206. PMID: 32391857

Vaidyam, A. N., Wisniewski, H., Halamka, J. D., Kashavan, M. S., & Torous, J. B. (2019). Chatbots and conversational agents in mental health: A review of the psychiatric landscape. *Canadian Journal of Psychiatry*, *64*(7), 456–464. DOI: 10.1177/0706743719828977 PMID: 30897957

Vayena, E., Blasimme, A., & Cohen, I. G. (2018). Machine learning in medicine: Addressing ethical challenges. *PLoS Medicine*, *15*(11), e1002689. DOI: 10.1371/journal.pmed.1002689 PMID: 30399149

World Health Organization. (2022). Mental health and COVID-19: Early evidence of the pandemic's impact. https://www.who.int/publications/i/item/9789240055672

Zhou, X., Snoswell, C. L., Harding, L. E., Bambling, M., Edirippulige, S., Bai, X., & Smith, A. C. (2019). The Role of Telehealth in Reducing the Mental Health Burden From COVID-19. *Telemedicine Journal and e-Health*, *26*(4), 377–379. PMID: 32202977

Chapter 4
Conversational AI for Student Well-Being:
Transforming Mental Health Support in Education

Abid Aziz
https://orcid.org/0009-0002-1582-9113
Uttara University, Dhaka, Bangladesh

Nabid Aziz
https://orcid.org/0009-0004-2944-7321
Uttara University, Dhaka, Bangladesh

Md Mehedi Hasan Emon
https://orcid.org/0000-0002-6224-9552
American International University, Dhaka, Bangladesh

Md. Adnan Rahman
https://orcid.org/0000-0003-3378-0958
Uttara University, Dhaka, Bangladesh

Zerin Tasnim
https://orcid.org/0000-0002-5705-1648
North South University, Dhaka, Bangladesh

Abu Bakar Abdul Hamid
https://orcid.org/0009-0007-5177-8145
Infrastructure University Kuala Lumpur, De Centrum, Malaysia

ABSTRACT

This chapter critically explores the integration of conversational AI in addressing student mental health within educational settings. Drawing on recent empirical studies and real-world applications, it examines how AI-powered chatbots are being utilized to offer scalable, accessible, and

DOI: 10.4018/979-8-3373-3316-8.ch004

timely psychological support. While highlighting the promise of such technologies in reducing anxiety, promoting resilience, and supplementing overburdened counseling services, the chapter also scrutinizes key ethical concerns, including privacy, algorithmic bias, and the risk of emotional dehumanization. Through a nuanced discussion of case studies, challenges, and governance imperatives, the chapter underscores the need for human-AI collaboration grounded in empathy, equity, and accountability. It concludes by proposing a forward-looking policy and research agenda to ensure that AI serves as a complement not a substitute to human care in fostering student well-being.

INTRODUCTION

In today's changing education systems, the health of students' minds is a major area that needs attention. Recent years have seen more learners suffering from anxiety, depression, stress, and burnout, which has grabbed the attention of educators, policymakers, and mental health workers. These issues do not stay in just one place or affect a particular population. In fact, they are counted as a worldwide issue that crosses different sections of society and education. Competition in school, expectations from their family, uncertainty at home, the influence of social media, and changes in the workplace have combined to make things more challenging and often result in poorer academic performance and well-being for students. The challenge became more obvious during the COVID-19 pandemic. Switching to remote learning greatly interrupted both the academic and social lives of students (Tulaskar & Turunen, 2022). Being isolated, not being well supported by society, and spending a lot of time in front of digital screens led to an increase in reported cases of psychological disorders. Although a lot of colleges and schools tried to increase their counseling services, they could not meet the rising need for help. Many organizations had problems such as staff shortages, insufficient finance, and arranging services, mainly occurring in areas where there was very little mental health care and a common stigma.

As a result, innovations include interventions that are scalable and rely on technology. Among these, Conversational AI, which comes in the form of mental health chatbots, has attracted more users. These instances stand out from traditional platforms by involving users in quick, real-time chats that feel like having a conversation with people. Using NLP, sentiment analysis, and affective computing, they can notice the emotions in conversations and answer with sympathy or guidance when needed (Kusal et al., 2023). It is important that they can be used at any time, since barriers like time, place, and having someone available are removed. The key to Conversational AI's attractiveness is that it can be used anywhere and tailored to someone's needs. Students nowadays are used to interacting with technology in different aspects of life. Making mental health support a feature on things like smartphones, learning management systems, and chat apps likely encourages students to use them when they feel distressed (Alhasani & Orji, 2025). AI technology is capable of spotting signs of mental health conditions in people's language and actions, making it easier to catch them and help at the right time. A few systems include access to academic records and behavioral reports to give a full picture of the student's performance. At the same time, AI is not always simple to use in the context of student mental health. There are many ethical issues, mainly around data privacy, being certain about client consent, genuine client emotion. Since mental health data is sensitive, it should be secured and used responsibly by strong protections (Parker et al., 2019). Students should be trusted and respected by these tools when they use AI in their learning experience. People might think that it is hard for machines to feel and understand human emotions, especially in societies that highly value relationships and direct talks.

There is also the danger that putting too much attention on technology can lead to less human interaction. There is no reason for AI to take the place of trained psychologists and counselors. Rather, it should help human practitioners by offering basic help or regular check-ins in the gaps between real-life counseling sessions. An ideal approach is making sure technology assists and complements the human side and does not just take its place. This chapter takes a fair and critical view of how Conversational AI influences student mental health. First, it explores student emotional well-being as it is today and how conventional support does not always work. It further examines the building blocks and workings of AI-based conversations, showing how they are being used in different school contexts.

Using a few case studies, the chapter demonstrates both the advantages and the disadvantages of these technologies. Finally, the recommendations discuss the ethical, legal, and practical parts that should guide further use of AI and outline how it might make education more supportive, inclusive, and responsive. This implies that teachers, parents, and administrators are now responsible for mental health in education too. This field requires more and more professionals from different areas to work together. People like technologists, ethicists, educators, and students should be involved in developing AI tools that are both useful and caring towards all users. Since student mental health is a pressing matter, we must find a new way that adopts innovative developments but never forgets about the importance of giving emotional support. This chapter helps shape a new conversation that asks educators to focus on emotional intelligence as well as digital proficiency in school design for the future. Moving ahead in a world that is increasingly digital and connected, we must see student well-being as something that keeps changing, and in this, Conversational AI can be of significant help, within certain limits.

THE GROWING NEED FOR MENTAL HEALTH SUPPORT IN EDUCATION

Over the past decade, people have come to see student mental health as very important for academic achievements and personal growth. Whereas education used to be mainly seen as a tool for thinking and learning, it is now viewed as affecting students' emotional and mental health just as much. It is becoming obvious from research that mental health issues may prevent students from doing well academically, remedial learning, exacerbating health and income inequalities, and may lead to lowered life achievements (Johnson & Lester, 2022). Therefore, universities have increased their counseling services, started awareness activities, and included wellness features. At the same time, despite the efforts, there are still not enough resources for everyone, mainly in underfunded learning institutions. Its seriousness calls for the development of modern, reliable ways to assist students in being strong and successful.

The Mental Health Landscape in Education

Research over the past few years has highlighted how much students are distressed. According to the 2022 National College Health Assessment from the American College Health Association, 62.3% of the students had severe anxiety, while 38.7% indicated depression that limited their day-to-day activities (Pinto et al., 2024). Also, in the Healthy Minds Study, episodes of undergraduates considering suicide have gone up, suggesting a crisis linked to serious mental illness (Baumhauer et al., 2025). K-12 settings are experiencing similar developments to HE. According to the Centers for Disease Control and Prevention, one in five adolescents mentions having regular feelings of sadness or hopelessness, and there has been an almost 100% increase in self-harm behaviors in the past decade (Aggarwal et al., 2023). A variety of stresses are causing these worrying problems. With more pressure on high-stakes testing, getting into college, and the need for skills at work, academic competition has increased in recent times. Similarly, social media adds to the culture of comparing oneself, being bullied online, and the feeling of missing out, always keeping people's emotions on high alert (Bernadas et al., 2025). Dealing with financial issues adds more pressure to the situation. The higher cost of tuition and living expenses are pushing many students to find jobs, which eats into their self-care time and increases the possibility of burnout. Moreover, COVID-19 presented many people with constant uncertainty, a sense of isolation, and grief, leading to increased risks for some and the onset of others (Ansari, 2022). Problems with mental health can result in consequences for society as well. Students who have anxiety and depression that is not managed perform poorly in academics, more often withdraw from school, and participate less in campus activities (Haikalis et al., 2022). Its impact can be seen in families, offices, and throughout the neighborhood, raising healthcare budgets for institutions. Though more people are aware of these challenges, schools and universities still find it difficult to come up with long-term solutions. According to a 2021 study, almost 70% of university counseling directors had mentioned staff fatigue and difficulty keeping up with the number of students seeking help (Quijada, 2021). The situation is made worse by culture and logistic challenges. A lot of people are still not sure about mental health care. Talking about needing counseling may make students and families feel weak or worried about confidentiality being broken, respectively. Difficulties with language and the absence of support tailored to minorities mean that these students often do not access help, therefore leading to greater inequality in their health (Pilav et al., 2022; Woldegiorgis & Chiramba, 2025). Limited office hours, lengthy waitlists, and trouble with transportation stand in the way of using health services. Irrespective of the presence of services, students may find that they don't meet their expectations for an immediate and private response. Talking to people over text or chat seems to be a preferred method for many young individuals. As a result, there is an ever-growing gap between what people need and what they receive. Even though traditional care is important, it is not adequate to handle the rapidly increasing distress students face. Without any action, these gaps can damage both people and the good name of schools and society. Because of this, the field of education now looks to Conversational AI as a valuable way to offer more and better services to a broader community.

Constraints of Traditional Counseling Models

In most typical mental health programs in schools, students meet with counselors in one-on-one meetings where trust, skill, and effective methods play a role. Based on psychology and social work, this model is known to be beneficial in addressing stress and more serious issues such as psychopathology (Colizzi et al., 2020). Still, its benefits are reduced when it must address a big and diverse group of students. Scalability is the biggest issue that must be addressed. For human counselors to work well and avoid being overwhelmed, they must receive thorough training, supervision, and keep their caseload manageable. One counselor is not able to support each student individually when they have many others to take care of. For this reason, many institutions use triage, giving the most attention to serious cases and putting mild to moderate ones on a waiting list. It is reported that students may have to wait two to four weeks for a first meeting, which not only makes their symptoms worse, but also increases the danger (T. Wang et al., 2025). Accessibility further constrains traditional services. Usually, counseling centers in higher education are open during normal school or work hours for students. Sometimes, mental health services for students in K–12 schools are only offered by providers who are not on the school campus. A lack of adequately trained doctors is common in rural areas, resulting in students traveling a long way or handling the complications caused by slow internet connections (Vaiyapuri et al., 2023). Even in schools where tutoring can be accessed, it may not be possible for students to schedule it for times that suit them, which might stop them from participating. Being physically and emotionally exhausted is another issue counselors have to face. Having to encounter students' challenges for a long time may create compassion fatigue, secondary traumatic stress, and lower their job satisfaction (Ormiston et al., 2022). When employees in mental health leave their jobs at high rates, it interrupts the continuity of patients' support and results in greater cost of recruiting and training staff. When requests for services increase, some counselors discover they are unable to give the same level and frequency of support as they once did.

Disagreements in culture and language between the counselor and students may also affect how effectively they can help. It is often challenging for diverse institutions to find mental health professionals who can communicate with students in their native languages and know about their culture. When there is a difference between patient and provider, communication may fail, trust may drop, and patients are likely to follow their treatment less (Lee, 2021). Individuals with immigration or minority experience may believe that counselors do not know what it is like to go through their unique challenges. Feelings of shame and privacy issues act as a barrier to using traditional counseling. Some students are afraid that seeking assistance will result in being discriminated against by others at the school. Even though confidentiality is very important, students are sometimes concerned that their information will be shared outside of the school (Seo et al., 2021). Such fear can mean that students do not use the limited help that is available to them. Also, the fact that in-person counseling is just an occasional session is very different from how mental health is experienced by students. You can have an emotional crisis at any time, not just during workday. The number of calls goes up before tests, late in the evening, or during holidays when the service will not be available. Outside of therapy, students usually turn to self-help guides or friends for support, which may produce bad advice. Since there is a gap, there is a need for unstoppable resources to help fill the time between seeing a health professional.

CONVERSATIONAL AI AS A MENTAL HEALTH SUPPORT TOOL

As mental health problems among students keep expanding, therapeutic chatbots have appeared as an interesting solution. Previously basic scripted chatbots, virtual agents, and AI-based companions have improved over time and now can both talk naturally and respond emotionally to people. They can respond right away, adapting to each user, and offering support, treating users as more than just informed people. In relation to students' mental health, conversational AI allows for mental health services to be given more widely than they can presently be with standard resources (Gao, 2025). Conversational AI does not stop after a campaign by talking to someone one time; it is designed to have ongoing, realistic conversations just like people have. Such tools focus on providing immediate assistance for students and often help them organize thoughts better, sending students to real therapists when the situation calls for it. This section investigates the ways in which conversational AI can work as a useful tool for mental health support in education.

Mechanisms of Emotional Support via AI

They rely on natural language understanding as well as natural language generation to have conversations that are easy for users to understand. They support emotions by using features like computational empathy, prepared psychological structures, and responsiveness. The main feature of mental health-focused chatbots lies in their programming related to different therapies and aims, for example, improved moods, lower stress, and thinking changes. Woebot, Wysa, and Youper use evidence-based psychological approaches as part of their algorithms. Woobot applies principles of CBT and gives users suggestions for having conversations with themselves to adjust their mindset, engage with their thoughts, and learn more about psychology. The use of CBT, DBT, motivational interviewing, and mindfulness are all part of the conversations Wysa uses to support users regulate their emotions and improve their behaviors (Nelson et al., 2025). To suit what students, prefer, AI friends are set up to be non-judgmental, supportive of privacy, and accessible all the time. They provide immediate feedback, monitor people's emotions over a period, and offer exercises that suit the user's current mood. The most crucial aspect is that students do not have to schedule appointments, manage their transportation, or face language problems (Wang et al., 2025). There is scientific evidence supporting how effective these tools are for mental health. Various research has verified that just a few daily chats with artificial intelligence agents about health issues help to ease anxiety and depression, enhance a person's emotional strength, and improve their sense of being in control of their mental health (Denecke et al., 2021). This indicates that AI may be a valuable tool for behavior change, if it uses positive reinforcement, promotes thinking about one's behavior, and suggests positive coping solutions.

NLP and Sentiment Analysis in Mental Health Chatbots

The basic function of any conversational AI system is NLP, which allows machines to comprehend, explain, and create language that humans speak. Within mental health support, NLP is teamed with sentiment analysis to learn the emotional meaning of the user's words, so the system provides a helpful and appropriate response (Mohamed Jasim et al., 2025). In sentiment analysis, large volumes of annotated text are used to teach models to spot language that matches different emotions and moods. As a result, the chatbot can tell if a student is feeling sadness, stress, loneliness, anger, or optimism and change its actions accordingly. In case a student types, "I can't deal with another exam," an AI system might interpret this as stress or losing motivation and respond with positive statements, relaxation advice, or information about available counseling services. As a result of LLMs such as OpenAI's GPT-4, the systems have advanced further. Chat GPT can hold longer and more organized discussions and understand the context, purpose, and feelings behind the conversation. Handling sarcasm, metaphor, and the way people express emotion is a major leap for AI and humans to connect emotionally (Olujimi & Ade-Ibijola, 2023). Systems based on emotion AI or affective computing can read things like changes in tone and overall rhythm in people's writing. Usually, AI mental health apps gather information using voices and facial expressions to know their users' feelings better. Even though they are not fully ready and present some privacy issues, they could lead to a more intuitive and convenient use of AI. However, challenges remain. Such systems should be thoroughly trained so that they do not misunderstand sensitive information, limit wrong judgments, and uphold the right standards of care. In addition, being open about what the system can do and what it cannot do helps prevent people with no tech experience from trusting it too much. Students should be made aware that even though the chatbot helps, it does not replace a mental health evaluation or an emergency form of support.

Integration With Existing Student Support Systems

Conversational AI in education really shines when it is teaming up with other tools and services that help students. To operate correctly and morally, AI should be included in the way institutions work, ensuring that procedures are always followed, answers are given, and results are recorded. Furthermore, interoperability with LMSs such as Moodle, Blackboard, or Canvas, conversational AI tools can be adjusted to respond according to when exams, assignments, or other academic activities take place. During stressful times, the system may check in with students, give advice on managing time, or show them which campus wellness events they could join. Doing so makes it possible for schools to respond quickly to students with targeted help when they are needed. Also, AI technology should be attached to the right referral protocols and procedures for escalation. When a user talks about suicide, is very distressed, or hints at being abused, the chatbot must know how to contact and alert specialists as soon as possible. At Stanford University, MIT, and the University of Edinburgh, AI triage tools are put in place to help immediately and identify people at high risk, who are then followed up by medical staff (Subramanian & Rajendran, 2024). Information gathered by these systems is useful for making decisions in the planning process. Collecting reactions and emotions from large students' groups can help administrators target those programs more accurately, make the best use of their resources, and spot those who might be at risk. In addition, data collection and use should adhere to both data protection laws and respect student's rights and privacy (Sule et al., 2021). It is important to note that success depends on people from different fields collaborating. These tools should be created by IT departments, counseling centers, faculty, and student affairs together to guarantee that they fit the students' backgrounds and needs. Users of the website, namely students, need to be part of the design, giving input to make the website easily accessible and improve the overall experience.

CASE STUDIES AND REAL-WORLD APPLICATIONS

Conversational AI is now being used in large-scale ways in schools and colleges, moving ahead quickly from small trials. In this area, we investigate cases of AI-based chatbots and virtual agents in practicing schools and colleges, study evidence of their effects on student well-being, research how they are introduced across institutions, and use those findings to plan.

AI Chatbots in Action

"Tess" at the University of Southern California (USC)

In 2019, USC became one of the main North American universities to add X2AI's conversational AI, Tess, to its student mental health services. Tess uses text or in-app messaging to engage students, providing modules on mental health, prompting them to track their moods, and giving cognitive restructuring tasks made for them individually. If Tess finds phrases such as "overwhelmed" or "can't cope" in users' inputs, she starts an interactive check-in, shares ideas on diaphragmatic breathing, and occasionally suggests meeting a human counselor if needed. By the end of six months after deployment, USC reported that almost a fifth of students had tried Tess, and most of them liked that it was quick and did not judge them (Bolia et al., 2021).

"Eloise" at the University of Auckland

In 2021, the University of Auckland released Eloise, a chatbot that was created with student feedback to deal with stress in academics and elsewhere. Eloise has mindfulness sessions, practical sleep routine lessons, and tests users using well-known questionnaires such as the PHQ-9 and GAD-7. Eloise also brings together various sources of local support, including counseling centers, peer mentors, and cultural liaison officers, to guarantee that referrals are culturally sensitive. Results from the university's evaluation found that more than two thirds of those who used the service experienced a decrease in self-reported stress for four weeks, and more than three-quarters became more confident managing their schoolwork.

Woebot in Multi-Institutional Trials

Many universities have carried out RCTs on Woebot, one of the first AI mental health chatbots. For a study in 2018 at Stanford, 83 college students were divided into those who used Woebot and those who got just information. The members of the Woebot cohort saw a strong decrease in depressive symptoms during the two-week period (effect size d = 0.44) using the PHQ-8, as well as a decrease in anxiety during the period (d = 0.37), marked by the GAD-7 (Crawford et al., 2024). In another 2023 study, researchers used Woebot with 560 students across three U.S. universities and observed a more significant symptom reduction for the Woebot group compared to those in the control group (Pavunraj et al., 2025).

"Youper" in Corporate-University Partnerships

Youper, which uses ACT, has been trialed as an AI assistant for universities and their EAPs. Graduate students at the University of Michigan were able to use Youper as an addition to the usual counseling services. It was discovered that 42% of those involved with Youper interacted with it during evenings or weekends, since they are the times when counseling is not accessible. User reviews noted that Youper plays a quick role in offering mini-interventions that lower stress levels before they negatively affect students' studies (Theodore et al., 2025).

Reducing Stress and Enhancing Resilience

Apart from helping reduce symptoms, conversational AI has proved efficient in helping people become emotionally stronger and improve how they deal with stress.

Just-in-Time Interventions for Exam Anxiety

Wysa's impact on pre-exam stress reduction was evaluated in a collaboration between the University of Cambridge's Institute of Education and startup Wysa. When a pilot study was conducted before the 2022 test period, Wysa used automated prompts to remind students about evidence-based ways of managing their stress such as progressive muscle relaxation and cognitive reframing. Self-reported anxiety declined by 25% in Wysa users relative to their control counterparts on the STAI, between their first break and peak exam week (Pillai & Tedesco, 2023). It seems that AI-based nudges can help people boost their resilience before such situations even arise.

Data-Driven Early Warning Systems

Many organizations are combining AI that can talk with academic and behavioral analytics to create early alert systems. The University of Sydney obtained students' mood ratings from its chatbot and used activities like logging on or submitting assignments on the LMS to spot those at highest risk of dropping out or failing their courses. Any observations of major drops in academic scores and mood scores led the system to notify the student support office which reached out to the student. This model reduced the percentage of first-year students exiting by 8% in just one year as compared to previous years (Delen et al., 2024).

SCALING ACROSS DIVERSE EDUCATIONAL SETTINGS

Although most studies begin with prestigious research universities, conversational AI has proven useful in all kinds of academic environments, from local community colleges to the country's most rural secondary schools.

Project Listen at MIT

MIT has partnered with the Boys and Girls Clubs to allow high school students to access conversational AI support using Project Listen. The project introduces a copy of the empathic dialogue engine from the MIT AI Lab to mobile apps used by club members which gives real-time assessment of their feelings and access to various helpful resources. An evaluation using both qualitative and quantitative approaches showed that most participating students came by the center every week and valued having someone to talk to after school (Williams et al., 2023).

Rural District Implementations in Australia

A lack of mental health care workers is a longer-lasting problem for rural and remote schools. A program called "Outback Well-Being" distributed tablets to Queensland with the conversational agent "Sparky" loaded on them for areas where the internet is inconsistent. Due to its light design, Sparky could work without Internet, automatically transferring changes when a network became available. During the pilot, the program continued to be used for more than three months and students and teachers both agreed that emotional problems became less of a challenge in class.

Community College Adaptations in the United States

The student body at community colleges is made up of adults from all walks of life and includes many who are the first in their family to go to school. The college brought in "MoodMe," a chatbot, to help students with financial problems, family duties and career-related issues, thanks to student focus groups. The team chose to display MoodMe on the college's portal with academic advising services to make it easily visible and accessible. Based on the initial reports, students took part in more on-campus mental health workshops thanks to AI prompts.

Insights from Student Feedback and Continuous Improvement

In every context, some common topics appear in student feedback and multiple development processes, guiding future approaches.

Importance of Co-Design and Cultural Adaptation

Students regularly request tools from Artificial Intelligence that fit with their daily lives. It is essential that developers engage in co-design workshops with those who will use the app, to make sure its instructions, tone and help are up to their needs. As an example, rural Australian students looked for region-specific expressions, so mental health organization Origins suggested using the phrase "taking a reef break." On the other hand, UK teens said they wanted to see more emoticons and colloquial terms to feel more relaxed. Awareness of different cultures also means using language: with multilingual chatbots, more francophone and international students can access support with greater equity.

Balancing Automation and Human Oversight

Automation helps with large student records, but students feel more trust when they know someone is watching their information. Combining automatic AI checks with reviews by counselors has resulted in a very satisfied clientele. Adhering to Stanford's guidelines, Woebot receives fortnightly clinical oversight, as experts go over anonymized chat sessions to edit and guarantee their accuracy and safety. The presence of the same oversight principles at USC's Tess gives students confidence in the strong focus on their human needs.

Transparent Communication of Capabilities and Limitations

A difference in what partners believe can cause trust to weaken. It's important for students to have a clear idea of what a chatbot can and cannot do during a crisis. It is effective practice to include a welcome discussion that explains how AI is not a crisis intervention service and that it gives people a list of emergency contacts at the start.

CHALLENGES AND ETHICAL CONSIDERATIONS

Since conversational AI is being introduced into educational and mental health fields more quickly, it's crucial to carefully review the many ethical and technical challenges linked to it. Although these tools claim to make things more efficient, broaden access and personalize support, any introduction to sensitive areas such as student mental health should be overseen by secure ethical processes. This area examines important privacy issues, along with excessive trust, biased algorithms and the role of public institutions, using recent studies as evidence.

Privacy and Data Security

There is a big ethical challenge around AI-powered conversational agents, since the conversations in mental health areas are emotionally personal and private. In comparison with other data inputs, conversations with chatbots often expose people's feelings, mental struggles and often sensitive characteristics about them. A security lapse in this part of cybersecurity is more than a technical problem. It breaks users' trust in the service. Any learning organization using conversational AI for mental health needs to guarantee it is following data protection laws such as the GDPR from Europe and HIPAA from the United States. These frameworks stress that people should have joined consent, a right to have their information deleted, minimal handling of their data and clarity about how decisions are made using machines (Almeida & Barr, 2025). Apart from guidelines, ethical data use means individuals are given true choices when they consent. It's possible that students do not fully realize what happens when an AI system records, sorts and may share their communication. It is now stressed by researchers that users must be told how the system is set up, what information it collects, what causes its responses and who uses that data (Emon et al., 2025; Iyamu, 2018). The virtue of opt-in models makes them superior to default enrollment and anonymity of input data should be a regular feature. Additionally, companies need to ensure they encrypt data from start to finish, secure files on the cloud and manage staff access points to stop any unauthorized leaking of information. Babylon Health demonstrates how mistakes in data protection can cause both lawsuits and problems with the company's reputation (Ganesan, 2025). Breaches can be especially frustrating for students under medical care for major medical conditions such as depression, self-harm or substance use.

Risks of Over-Reliance and Dehumanization

Improved conversations with AI might encourage people to view empathy of machines as the same as empathy from humans. Woebot and Tess and similar AI systems, can act compassionately and offer programming based on cognitive therapy, yet they can't match people trained in counseling with unique human experiences and ethical awareness. Therefore, certain scholars point out that many decision-makers think technological improvements prove that a therapy is good for patients (Aravind & Arun, 2024). AI chatbots are considered a better choice for schools with limited resources because administrators may believe they are less costly than hiring more counselors. The appeal of being able to reach many can sometimes lead organizations to give more importance to depth, relationships being damaged in the process. It has been found that while students like having access to AI tools all the time, they still prefer real interactions with other humans (Yadav, 2025). Moreover, people are worried that those with social anxiety or trust problems may overuse AI systems because of their challenges. Alternatively, instead of helping to connect someone to professional help, chatbots could stop people from engaging in deeper therapy. AIs might have trouble recognizing what to do in more complicated cases involving people from, trauma survivors or those who have different brains. That's why an ethical AI model should operate as part of the wider medical care environment. Artificial intelligence helps with triage, spotting signs early, keeping track of my moods and teaching me new information. In addition, if a patient presents high complexities, this should be reported and handled by licensed healthcare professionals right away. An approach using hybrid care which mixes AI responsiveness and ethical care from specialists should be chosen (Barr et al., 2025).

Bias and Fairness in AI Responses

Algorithmic bias which appears in machine learning when data is biased, is a particularly dangerous ethical issue. A lot of the training goes into conversational AI systems using resources that skew towards some ways of talking or cultural norms. So, marginalized students might not feel that the system really supports them. Empirical research revealed that different types of models can reflect biases in feelings and conversation based on race, gender and social status (Yadav et al., 2024). Sometimes, if someone uses a different dialect or cultural expression, that emotional distress can be misjudged as not serious. Also, AI-based emotional words are usually set up with Western-centric psychological thoughts which make them less useful for students in different parts of the world. It is important for developers to put more emphasis on having diverse data when collecting or annotating. Inclusivity can be improved by getting feedback on chatbots development directly from students. Forever forming feedback into their system, institutions should also regularly review AI outcomes. Moreover, fairness is a concern not only for the dialogue of the website, but also for access and usefulness. Some students may not be digitally prepared to use AI systems because they have learning issues, language restrictions or no or limited internet. Therefore, deploying ethically means some interfaces need to accept multiple languages and respond to speech and services must be compatible with assistive technology.

Institutional Accountability and Governance

AI in mental health support creates new sorts of responsibilities for organizations. Universities and colleges take an active role in how technological tools are put into use, looked after and connected with other aspects of healthcare. For this reason, the use of AI demands firms to put strong governance in place. Currently, an emerging trend is to appoint internal Ethics Committees with people having expertise in technology, ethics, psychology, the law and education. The committees can advise on buying, installing and checking how AI systems work. They also could watch over the organization, help with grievances, see that rules are kept and update policies for new issues as needed. In addition, institutions should have open and clear relationships with their vendors. Businesses that provide AI chatbots usually keep how they use customer data and what algorithms they have secret, along with details on their service promises. Universities ought to make sure contracts are transparent, that systems are audited and that there is the authority to adjust or close systems in case of ethical issues (Avasthi et al., 2022). Colleges and schools should also teach students how to act ethically with artificial intelligence. Every mental health initiative in schools should be matched with digital learning programs that make students aware of AI strengths and weaknesses. It will encourage individuals to rethink how much they believe in technology and the influence of automation.

Emotional Authenticity and User Trust

The idea of emotional authenticity is as significant ethically as the other questions above, though it is not always as clear. A lot of the time, students share how they feel with the help of AI systems. At some point, if users learn that their service's answers were set ahead of time, they may end up feeling cynical or disappointed. The real issue for ethics here is not just what is fake, but how emotionally stressful the experience can be and how high the user's expectations (Singh & Kaunert, 2024). Consequently, being transparent should apply to how interaction takes place. All students ought to be frankly explained what happens when interacting with an AI. It is important for chatbots to clarify at the start of the talk that they are not living beings, but assistance tools available for referral. Building trust is not only about technical problems; it is about ethics. Trust grows when a website is transparent, dependable, has accountability and is designed with respect. If an institution looks upon trust as crucial rather than simply paying lip service to it, it will be more likely to make good use of AI that benefits students. The conversation about AI in mental health has a lot of advantages, but it's also intricate. Even though these systems provide flexible, judgment-free communication at any time, using them in class needs close ethical attention. The issues of privacy, dehumanization, algorithmic bias, who is responsible and what people feel all play a main role in making AI acceptable here. Since AI technology is developing rapidly, it's important to regularly review our principles for evaluating AI, since we want the ethical side of AI's growth to keep up with its technological side.

STUDENT PERCEPTIONS AND USER EXPERIENCE WITH CONVERSATIONAL AI

Students' attitudes and actions with conversational AI tools can strongly determine their success in educational mental health. The factors in user experience include usefulness, how easy something is to use, trust in responses from AI, the emotions it triggers and issues related to data privacy. Together, these dimensions decide how widespread AI tools are, how long they are adopted and how much they affect student well-being (Stige et al., 2024). Many new studies have noticed that students appreciate the security and immediate response they get from conversational AI. In case someone feels scared to see a human therapist, thinks it takes too much time or is nervous in social activities, Woebot, Wysa and Tess help them begin seeking support. Students say they feel less judged and more confident interacting with AI, so AI may be offering a different type of therapeutic alliance, one that depends on feeling safe instead of human sympathy. However, though these tools are praised for being so convenient, students have some doubts about how deeply they can make students feel. According to Gkinko & Elbanna, (2022), a lot of users pointed out that chatbots are helpful when they deal with stress, but they are not convinced the chatbots can genuinely empathize. This lack of feeling shows up even more when therapists are required to understand emotions deeply, show cultural understanding or build close bonds with client's areas that people are often better at than chatbots. Most students therefore view conversational AI as helping them, instead of taking the place of human counselors. The way something is designed on screen can strongly boost or reduce user engagement. A majority of students select platforms that are easy to use, have neat designs and feature smooth communication interactions. A person's view of how reliable the tool is can be reduced by slow answers, repeating requests or missing or incorrect commands.

In addition, filmmakers should be clear about how they handle personal details when communicating with people. Students often share personal details if they believe their talks are kept confidential and safe and no one else has access to them. Finally, trust, practicality of conversational AI, emotions involved and openness within an institution determine student views of technology (Rahman et al., 2024).

FUTURE DIRECTIONS AND POLICY IMPLICATIONS

As conversational AI is used more in student mental health support, we need carefully plan its future and how it will be managed. Due to the rapid AI growth and the sensitivity of mental health, there is a strong need for action, collaboration from many areas and technologies that value honesty and care for people. This section discusses the main approaches for regulation, growing AI emotions and ever-changing collaborative education between humans and AI in mental health.

Regulation and Governance

Adopting conversational AI in services for student wellness brings up many questions about who should be held accountable, how information is managed transparently and how to guarantee the safety of at-risk students. It is necessary for policies to work as powerfully as the regulations for medical and psychological actions. At present, the GDPR in Europe and HIPAA in the U.S. stand as main frameworks for data safety and privacy, but they typically miss the details of AI applications in the mental health sector (Gambhir et al., 2024). The main necessity is making certain there are clear, workable rules about informed consent. Students are advised to have a clear awareness of how data is handled by conversational agents, including collection, processing, storage and use and what AI's impact is on their route of treatment. Making AI decision-making transparent or explainable is very important to earn trust, mainly when chatbots give advice on mental health or emergency care. Policymakers need to direct the use of these tools only after their accuracy, safety and fairness are checked by independent parties on an ongoing basis. Moreover, methods for handling problems should be written down, so if students or institutions find misuses of data and errors in algorithms from AI, they can easily report and receive help. The involvement of ethicists, mental health professionals, technologists and students in overseeing bodies helps keep important conversations happening (Rahman, 2025). A clay foundation to governance could lead to a fall in student trust and result in unequal and biased AI-driven mental health help.

Enhancing Emotional Intelligence in AI

The future of AI should concentrate on improving emotional intelligence, as it's needed to move beyond simple chatbot support. Currently, most models focus on processing sentences and measuring sentiment which can capture only a tiny portion of a person's emotions (Reddy et al., 2025). Emotional intelligence for AI means checking, understanding and responding sensitively to many different emotional indications. Today, researchers are combining voice tone analysis with facial emotion recognition and spotting behavioral habits to find out more about a user's psychological state (Almadani, 2024). These vocal stress markers and micro facial gestures which appear even when a person writes or speaks neutrally can let the therapist respond sooner. Ensuring an emotional detection system is right for each culture and setting is necessary, considering the many ways emotion is expressed by people. Moreover, emotionally intelligent AI needs to change the way it converses, responds and offers choices instantly, matching the user's feelings and involvement (Chundru & Whig, 2024). The use of personalization in mental health care grows partners' trust, lowers their stress and motivates them to stay in therapy, all of which supports good mental health outcomes. It is crucial that these systems clearly show that they use AI, so that students are aware of the limits of AI support. Educational benefits will be realized by investing in research that blends affective computing, psychology and education. The design of ethically sound emotionally intelligent AI will rely on end-user's students and mental health practitioners being involved.

Human-AI Collaboration in Mental Health

AI may offer significant results when we find a way to team it up with mental health experts. Instead of treating AI as a straight alternative, the idea is to let AI enhance how humans look after patients. AI chatbots can look after common daily tasks, track a client's mood, achieve psycho-education and complete first-line triage, easing pressure on counseling centers that are often overloaded (Anand et al., 2025). Therefore, human counselors can concentrate on complicated and risky cases that involve diverse skills and emotional intelligence. AI can be used successfully in mental health work when professionals receive training to know what AI can do and what it cannot and when they can effectively add it to their routines (Daisy, 2024). For example, AI can help find out if patterns in student well-being are developing, so counselors can plan early and use-ful group workshops. It is just as necessary to develop clear guidelines that link AI findings to instant human response when dangerous distress is identified. This method helps mental health care stay strong and pro-tected from the risks of depending too much on technology. People and computers also work on ethical issues together. Professionals in mental health need to join technologists in ensuring the design and evaluation of AI tools are fair, open and respectful of student freedom (Yambal & Waykar, 2025). It makes sure that AI is useful and meaningful to every student population. There is huge potential for conversational AI to make a major difference in how student mental health is managed. Still, making this happen means navigating complicated regulations, improving AI 's ability to sense emotions and teaming up to match high technology with caring for people. All these experts should collaborate to draft policies, create learning environments and use AI to aid and help strong, supported learners.

CONCLUSION

Conversational AI is now playing a major role in changing the way mental health support is given in schools and universities. The use of AI-driven chatbots and virtual assistants for student well-being means mental health support can be increased, given to more learners and answered with care for different students. This new development gives hope for dealing with persisting difficulties stemming from resource restrictions, mental health stigma and delay in finding psychological distress. However, despite the many uses for conversational AI, several important ethical, practical and theoretical problems should be managed with everyone in mind. Conversational AI basically makes mental health care in colleges simpler, since it provides continuous support on demand. It is especially significant since many students struggle to use traditional counseling, due to extended waits, a lack of professionals and fears about confidentiality or what others might think. Chatbots like Woebot, Tess and Eloise that provide psychoeducation and mental skills discussions have helped many students relax about using counseling, reducing their anxiety and depression faster and more consistently. The quick and simple way this tool is used makes it a valuable addition to the current mental health system, helping to relieve counseling centers and increase early care. At the same time, we should be aware of what conversational AI is not capable of and what. Privacy is very important because private conversations with AI agents require strong methods to safeguard data. School systems need to keep to GDPR and HIPAA and tell pupils clearly about the ways their information is collected and how they consent to it. Breaches and unapproved access to patient data can harm trust and prevent people from using available technology which makes the original efforts useless. In addition, conversational AI tries to be empathetic, but it cannot replicate the cheer and understanding that real human beings bring to mental health services. It might happen that students believe relying on AI counselling is better than seeing a professional which means they might skip the real advantages of professional help. This highlights that computer models should assist health workers by taking care of common cases while specialists look after the more serious or involved ones. This way of working values the unique judgment and moral sense of every mental health caregiver.

It's also a big concern that AI can contain bias. The emotions of underrepresented or marginalized students can be unintentionally overlooked or confused when datasets are not balanced which can make existing problems worse instead of better. Including these biases can be addressed by gathering inclusive data, following design processes with community input and always keeping an eye on fairness and cultural understanding. AI tools can become fair and effective only when schools give meaningful roles to a wide range of student opinions. Going forward, it is very important to strengthen AI's emotional intelligence, too. By using voice, facial gestures and actions as indicators, schools may better determine how students are feeling. Adjusting responses in response to the user's emotions may create a stronger bond and more trust. At the same time, more technology should come along with appropriate openness and checks to help stop deception. Meanwhile, laws and rules should change along with these new technologies. Such aspects as agreeing to (consent), sharing important details and being highly accountable should all be standard in polices and written laws for AI mental health usage. The success and security of AI tools must be assessed independently, since it guarantees responsible and proper usage of them. In addition to other stakeholders, leaders in educational technology should include teachers, mental health professionals, technologists, policymakers and students when considering this approach.

Educational mental health using conversational AI depends on the relationship were human skills and AI work together. By automating repetitive duties, counselors can put more effort into cases that require the highest level of human feeling and right thinking. If mental health experts are taught about AI, they will be able to get the most from its advantages while managing risks. Also, when AI forms part of an institution's mental health policies, users can expect better coordination, accountability and support for teaching activities. Conversational AI opens a new door for educational organizations to think about and offer mental health support. Its ability to give scalable, personal and accessible help with emotions far exceeds any other system, making it essential for boosting student well-being in today's busy and complicated academic life. The positive promise of AI should not hide the many ethical, technical and social issues that appear with its use. As experts at the interplay among pedagogy, psychology and technology, we direct the growth of conversational AI based on sound evidence and a continuous concern for human respect. Supporting designs that are linking and simple can enable these technologies to assist, rather than replace, efforts to care for and cultivate minds, building up more robust students and better school communities.

REFERENCES

Aggarwal, S., Wright, J., Morgan, A., Patton, G., & Reavley, N. (2023). Religiosity and spirituality in the prevention and management of depression and anxiety in young people: A systematic review and meta-analysis. *BMC Psychiatry*, *23*(1), 729. DOI: 10.1186/s12888-023-05091-2 PMID: 37817143

Alhasani, M., & Orji, R. (2025). Promoting Stress Management among Students in Higher Education: Evaluating the Effectiveness of a Persuasive Time Management Mobile App. *International Journal of Human-Computer Interaction*, *41*(1), 219–241. DOI: 10.1080/10447318.2023.2297330

Almadani, N. (2024). *Emotional Intelligence.*, DOI: 10.4018/979-8-3693-7372-9.ch004

Almeida, D., & Barr, N. (2025). Innovations in Health Data Protection Ethical, Legal, and Technological Perspectives in a Global Context. In *Navigating Privacy, Innovation, and Patient Empowerment Through Ethical Healthcare Technology* (pp. 171–196). IGI Global. https://doi.org/DOI: 10.4018/979-8-3693-7630-0.ch007

Anand, S., Miglani, S., & Anand, R. (2025). *Multimodal AI for Enhanced Emotional Intelligence in the Cloud Computing Era.*, DOI: 10.4018/979-8-3693-9694-0.ch008

Ansari, D. (2022). An accumulation of distress: Grief, loss, and isolation among healthcare providers during the COVID-19 pandemic. *SSM. Mental Health*, *2*, 100146. DOI: 10.1016/j.ssmmh.2022.100146 PMID: 36104985

Aravind, K., & Arun, S. (2024). *S., I. R., & Pazhamalai, V.* Transforming Healthcare., DOI: 10.4018/979-8-3693-1243-8.ch002

Avasthi, S., Sanwal, T., Sareen, P., & Tripathi, S. L. (2022). *Augmenting Mental Healthcare With Artificial Intelligence.* Machine Learning, and Challenges in Telemedicine., DOI: 10.4018/978-1-7998-8786-7.ch005

Barr, N., Lopes, D. G., Schwendinger, M., & Gafaro, S. (2025). Ethical Implications and Patient-Centered Innovations in Digital Healthcare. In *Navigating Privacy, Innovation, and Patient Empowerment Through Ethical Healthcare Technology* (pp. 107–138). IGI Global. https://doi.org/ DOI: 10.4018/979-8-3693-7630-0.ch005

Baumhauer, J., Mortenson, L. Y., Rion, E., & Hong, V. (2025). Management of College Student Mental Health Emergencies. *Current Psychiatry Reports*, *27*(5), 337–346. DOI: 10.1007/s11920-025-01603-x PMID: 40097778

Bernadas, J. M. A. C., Soriano, C. R., Cabañes, J. V. A., & Tarroja, M. C. H. (2025). Ambivalent visibilities : Social media bullying and disconnective practice of the youth. *Convergence (London)*. Advance online publication. DOI: 10.1177/13548565251328774

Bolia, I. K., Savvidou, O. D., Kang, H. P., Chatzichristodoulou, N., Megaloikonomos, P. D., Mitsiokapa, E., Mavrogenis, A. F., & Papagelopoulos, P. J. (2021). Cross-cultural adaptation and validation of the Musculoskeletal Tumor Society (MSTS) scoring system and Toronto Extremity Salvage Score (TESS) for musculoskeletal sarcoma patients in Greece. *European Journal of Orthopaedic Surgery & Traumatology*, *31*(8), 1631–1638. DOI: 10.1007/s00590-021-02921-5 PMID: 33721082

Chundru, S., & Whig, P. (2024). *Future of Emotional Intelligence in Technology.*, DOI: 10.4018/979-8-3693-7011-7.ch024

Colizzi, M., Lasalvia, A., & Ruggeri, M. (2020). Prevention and early intervention in youth mental health: Is it time for a multidisciplinary and trans-diagnostic model for care? *International Journal of Mental Health Systems*, *14*(1), 23. DOI: 10.1186/s13033-020-00356-9 PMID: 32226481

Crawford, J., Allen, K.-A., Pani, B., & Cowling, M. (2024). When artificial intelligence substitutes humans in higher education: The cost of loneliness, student success, and retention. *Studies in Higher Education*, *49*(5), 883–897. DOI: 10.1080/03075079.2024.2326956

Daisy, A. (2024). Digital Mental. *Health Education*, •••, 143–180. DOI: 10.4018/979-8-3693-8242-4.ch006

Delen, D., Davazdahemami, B., & Rasouli Dezfouli, E. (2024). Predicting and Mitigating Freshmen Student Attrition: A Local-Explainable Machine Learning Framework. *Information Systems Frontiers*, *26*(2), 641–662. DOI: 10.1007/s10796-023-10397-3 PMID: 37361887

Denecke, K., Abd-Alrazaq, A., & Househ, M. (2021). *Artificial Intelligence for Chatbots in Mental Health: Opportunities and Challenges* (pp. 115–128). https://doi.org/DOI: 10.1007/978-3-030-67303-1_10

Emon, M. M. H., Khan, T., Rahman, M. A., Hamid, A. B. A., & Yaakub, N. I. (2025). GreenTech Revolution: Navigating Challenges and Seizing Opportunities. In *AI and Green Technology Applications in Society* (pp. 63–90). IGI Global Scientific Publishing. https://doi.org/DOI: 10.4018/979-8-3693-9879-1.ch003

Gambhir, A., Jain, N., & Pandey, M., & Simran. (2024). Beyond the Code: Bridging Ethical and Practical Gaps in Data Privacy for AI-Enhanced. *Health Care Systems*, •••, 37–65. DOI: 10.1007/978-981-97-6790-8_2

Ganesan, A. (2025). *Transforming Wellness.*, DOI: 10.4018/979-8-3693-9521-9.ch018

Gao, Y. (2025). The impact and application of artificial intelligence technology on mental health counseling services for college students. *Journal of Computational Methods in Sciences and Engineering*, *25*(2), 1686–1701. DOI: 10.1177/14727978241302641

Gkinko, L., & Elbanna, A. (2022). Hope, tolerance and empathy: Employees' emotions when using an AI-enabled chatbot in a digitalised workplace. *Information Technology & People*, *35*(6), 1714–1743. DOI: 10.1108/ITP-04-2021-0328

Haikalis, M., Doucette, H., Meisel, M. K., Birch, K., & Barnett, N. P. (2022). Changes in College Student Anxiety and Depression From Pre- to During-COVID-19: Perceived Stress, Academic Challenges, Loneliness, and Positive Perceptions. *Emerging Adulthood*, *10*(2), 534–545. DOI: 10.1177/21676968211058516 PMID: 35382515

Iyamu, T. (2018). Collecting qualitative data for information systems studies: The reality in practice. *Education and Information Technologies*, *23*(5), 2249–2264. DOI: 10.1007/s10639-018-9718-2

Johnson, A. P., & Lester, R. J. (2022). Mental health in academia: Hacks for cultivating and sustaining wellbeing. *American Journal of Human Biology*, *34*(S1). Advance online publication. DOI: 10.1002/ajhb.23664 PMID: 34357661

Kusal, S., Patil, S., Choudrie, J., Kotecha, K., Vora, D., & Pappas, I. (2023). A systematic review of applications of natural language processing and future challenges with special emphasis in text-based emotion detection. *Artificial Intelligence Review*, *56*(12), 15129–15215. DOI: 10.1007/s10462-023-10509-0

Lee, C. (2021). Patient loyalty to health services: The role of communication skills and cognitive trust. *International Journal of Healthcare Management*, *14*(4), 1254–1264. DOI: 10.1080/20479700.2020.1756111

Mohamed Jasim, K., Malathi, A., Bhardwaj, S., & Aw, E. C.-X. (2025). A systematic review of AI-based chatbot usages in healthcare services. *Journal of Health Organization and Management*. Advance online publication. DOI: 10.1108/JHOM-12-2023-0376 PMID: 39865955

Nelson, J., Kaplan, J., Simerly, G., Nutter, N., Edson-Heussi, A., Woodham, B., & Broman-Fulks, J. (2025). The balance and integration of artificial intelligence within cognitive behavioral therapy interventions. *Current Psychology (New Brunswick, N.J.)*, *44*(9), 7847–7857. DOI: 10.1007/s12144-025-07320-1

Olujimi, P. A., & Ade-Ibijola, A. (2023). NLP techniques for automating responses to customer queries: A systematic review. *Discover Artificial Intelligence*, *3*(1), 20. DOI: 10.1007/s44163-023-00065-5

Ormiston, H. E., Nygaard, M. A., & Apgar, S. (2022). A Systematic Review of Secondary Traumatic Stress and Compassion Fatigue in Teachers. *School Mental Health*, *14*(4), 802–817. DOI: 10.1007/s12310-022-09525-2 PMID: 35694002

Parker, L., Halter, V., Karliychuk, T., & Grundy, Q. (2019). How private is your mental health app data? An empirical study of mental health app privacy policies and practices. *International Journal of Law and Psychiatry*, *64*, 198–204. DOI: 10.1016/j.ijlp.2019.04.002 PMID: 31122630

Pavunraj, D., Mathan Kumar, A., & Anbumaheshwari, K. (2025). *AI in Personalized Treatment Planning*., DOI: 10.4018/979-8-3373-1275-0.ch006

Pilav, S., De Backer, K., Easter, A., Silverio, S. A., Sundaresh, S., Roberts, S., & Howard, L. M. (2022). A qualitative study of minority ethnic women's experiences of access to and engagement with perinatal mental health care. *BMC Pregnancy and Childbirth*, *22*(1), 421. DOI: 10.1186/s12884-022-04698-9 PMID: 35585579

Pillai, A. S., & Tedesco, R. (2023). *Machine Learning and Deep Learning in Natural Language Processing*. CRC Press., DOI: 10.1201/9781003296126

Pinto, A. M., Bazzoli, A., & Mercedes, J. (2024). Mental health and lifestyle health behaviors among commuter college students. *Cogent Mental Health*, *3*(1), 1–25. DOI: 10.1080/28324765.2024.2436432 PMID: 38550624

Quijada, M. A. (2021). My Mental Health Struggle in Academia: What I Wish All Business School Faculty, Students, and Administration Knew. *Journal of Management Education*, *45*(1), 19–42. DOI: 10.1177/1052562920958433

Rahman, H. (2025). The Ethical Dimensions of Digital Interactions. In *Digital Citizenship and Building a Responsible Online Presence* (pp. 123–164). IGI Global., DOI: 10.4018/979-8-3693-6675-2.ch005

Rahman, M. A., Emon, M. M. H., Khan, T., & Siam, S. A. J. (2024). Measuring the Influence of Brand Image on Consumer Behavioral Intentions by using AI: Exploring the Mediating Role of Trust. *2024 IEEE International Conference on Computing, Applications and Systems (COMPAS)*, 1–7. https://doi.org/DOI: 10.1109/COMPAS60761.2024.10796396

Reddy, B. A., Nayak, U. A., Srinivasan, S., Angela Jean Mary, E., Chauhan, A., & Rajagopal, R. (2025). Sentiment and Emotion Analysis Using Machine Learning Techniques. In *Exploring Psychology, Social Innovation and Advanced Applications of Machine Learning* (pp. 173–190). IGI Global. https://doi.org/DOI: 10.4018/979-8-3693-6910-4.ch009

Seo, K., Tang, J., Roll, I., Fels, S., & Yoon, D. (2021). The impact of artificial intelligence on learner–instructor interaction in online learning. *International Journal of Educational Technology in Higher Education*, *18*(1), 54. DOI: 10.1186/s41239-021-00292-9 PMID: 34778540

Singh, B., & Kaunert, C. (2024). *Augmented Reality and Virtual Reality Modules for Mindfulness*., DOI: 10.4018/979-8-3693-1123-3.ch007

Stige, Å., Zamani, E. D., Mikalef, P., & Zhu, Y. (2024). Artificial intelligence (AI) for user experience (UX) design: A systematic literature review and future research agenda. *Information Technology & People*, *37*(6), 2324–2352. DOI: 10.1108/ITP-07-2022-0519

Subramanian, Y. R., & Rajendran, R. (2024). *Transforming Healthcare: The Convergence of IoT and AI* (pp. 357–394). https://doi.org/DOI: 10.1007/978-3-031-65022-2_20

Sule, M.-J., Zennaro, M., & Thomas, G. (2021). Cybersecurity through the lens of Digital Identity and Data Protection: Issues and Trends. *Technology in Society*, *67*, 101734. DOI: 10.1016/j.techsoc.2021.101734

Theodore, S. J., Jr., Lodhi, A. R., Upadhyay, P., & Yadav, S. P. (2025). Augmenting Mental Healthcare Using Artificial Intelligence Advancements. In *Demystifying the Role of Natural Language Processing (NLP) in Mental Health* (pp. 127–144). IGI Global. https://doi.org/DOI: 10.4018/979-8-3693-4203-9.ch008

Tulaskar, R., & Turunen, M. (2022). What students want? Experiences, challenges, and engagement during Emergency Remote Learning amidst COVID-19 crisis. *Education and Information Technologies*, *27*(1), 551–587. DOI: 10.1007/s10639-021-10747-1 PMID: 34690527

Vaiyapuri, S., Kadam, P., Chandrasekharuni, G., Oliveira, I. S., Senthilkumaran, S., Salim, A., Patel, K., de Almeida Gonçalves Sachett, J., & Pucca, M. B. (2023). Multifaceted community health education programs as powerful tools to mitigate snakebite-induced deaths, disabilities, and socioeconomic burden. *Toxicon: X, 17*, 100147. DOI: 10.1016/j.toxcx.2022.100147 PMID: 36632238

Wang, T., Bruckman, A. S., & Yang, D. (2025). The Practice of Online Peer Counseling and the Potential for AI-Powered Support Tools. *Proceedings of the ACM on Human-Computer Interaction*, *9*(2), 1–33. DOI: 10.1145/3711089

Wang, Y., Wang, Y., Crace, K., & Zhang, Y. (2025). Understanding Attitudes and Trust of Generative AI Chatbots for Social Anxiety Support. *Proceedings of the 2025 CHI Conference on Human Factors in Computing Systems*, 1–21. https://doi.org/DOI: 10.1145/3706598.3714286

Williams, R., Ali, S., Devasia, N., DiPaola, D., Hong, J., Kaputsos, S. P., Jordan, B., & Breazeal, C. (2023). AI + Ethics Curricula for Middle School Youth: Lessons Learned from Three Project-Based Curricula. *International Journal of Artificial Intelligence in Education*, *33*(2), 325–383. DOI: 10.1007/s40593-022-00298-y PMID: 35935456

Woldegiorgis, E. T., & Chiramba, O. (2025). Access and success in higher education: Fostering resilience in historically disadvantaged students in South Africa. *Journal of Applied Research in Higher Education*, *17*(2), 759–771. DOI: 10.1108/JARHE-05-2023-0217

Yadav, M., Kanwal, P., & Luu, T. M. N. (2024). *Overcoming Imposter Syndrome*., DOI: 10.4018/979-8-3693-3144-6.ch004

Yadav, S. (2025). Leveraging AI to Enhance Teaching and Learning in Education. In *Optimizing Research Techniques and Learning Strategies With Digital Technologies* (pp. 211–238). IGI Global., DOI: 10.4018/979-8-3693-7863-2.ch008

Yambal, S., & Waykar, Y. A. (2025). *Future of Education Using Adaptive AI*. Intelligent Systems, and Ethical Challenges., DOI: 10.4018/979-8-3693-6527-4.ch006

KEY TERMS AND DEFINITIONS

Conversational AI: AI technology is created to involve users in talking with the system using normal language processing.

Chatbot: An application designed to help users through conversations and is commonly added to websites to give quick support or facts.

Emotional Support AI: Software that can detect and respond to users' feelings is created to help with psychological support.

Natural Language Processing (NLP): A branch dealing with giving machines the skills to process and make use of human speech.

Sentiment Analysis: A procedure for identifying and figuring out which emotions are mentioned in written text.

Digital Well-being: A complete method to look after mental, emotional and social health in online settings.

Algorithmic Bias: Errors in AI results that are caused by biased data, wrong data usage or programming can result in unfair treatments.

Human-AI Collaboration: A model where AI helps, instead of taking over from, humans in giving services.

Chapter 5
The Impact of Conversational AI on Student Well-Being and Mental Health

P. Selvakumar
https://orcid.org/0000-0002-3650-4548
Department of Science and Humanities, Nehru Institute of Technology, Coimbatore, India

R. Devi
https://orcid.org/0009-0000-1968-2222
R.M.K. Engineering College, Chennai, India

Prashant Kalshetti
https://orcid.org/0000-0003-3553-2093
Global Business School and Research Centre, Dr. D.Y. Patil Vidyapeeth, Pune, India

Shilpa Gaidhani
Sri Balaji University, Pune, India

Shaista Md. Mumtaz Khan
https://orcid.org/0009-0004-5202-7608
Datta Meghe Institute of Management Studies, Nagpur, India

Mohit Sharma
https://orcid.org/0009-0007-2280-8077
Maharshi Dayanand University, Rohtak, India

T. C. Manjunath
https://orcid.org/0000-0003-2545-9160
Rajarajeswari College of Engineering, Bangalore, India

DOI: 10.4018/979-8-3373-3316-8.ch005

ABSTRACT

In recent years, the integration of Conversational AI in education has revolutionized the way students receive support, interact with educational content, and manage their well-being. Conversational AI—comprising chatbots, virtual assistants, and natural language processing (NLP) models—has emerged as a powerful tool for fostering a more inclusive, personalized, and accessible learning environment. With the increasing reliance on digital education and remote learning, AI-driven solutions play a critical role in addressing the diverse needs of students, offering timely assistance, and improving their overall academic experience. Conversational AI systems serve as virtual tutors, academic advisors, and emotional support agents, ensuring that students have access to reliable assistance at all times. These AI-powered tools provide instant responses to queries related to coursework, assignments, deadlines, and general academic concerns.

INTRODUCTION TO CONVERSATIONAL AI IN EDUCATION

In recent years, the integration of Conversational AI in education has revolutionized the way students receive support, interact with educational content, and manage their well-being. offering timely assistance, and improving their overall academic experience. Conversational AI systems serve as virtual tutors, academic advisors, and emotional support agents, ensuring that students have access to reliable assistance at all times. These AI-powered tools provide instant responses to queries related to coursework, assignments, deadlines, and general academic concerns. Unlike traditional support systems, which may be limited by staff availability, conversational AI enables 24/7 student engagement, reducing delays in obtaining help. This adaptability ensures that every student receives customized support, addressing their unique challenges and knowledge gaps. Additionally, conversational AI plays a key role in automating administrative support. Universities and schools increasingly deploy AI chatbots to assist students with registration, scheduling, financial aid inquiries, and general campus-related concerns. By handling routine administrative tasks, these systems alleviate the burden on human staff, allowing them to focus on more complex issues that require personal attention (Ahmed & Hassan, 2024). Beyond academic assistance, conversational AI is becoming an essential tool for promoting student mental health and emotional well-being. The pressures of academic life, social expectations, and personal challenges can impact students' mental health, leading to stress, anxiety, and burnout. AI-driven mental health chatbots serve as first-line support systems, offering a safe and confidential space for students to express their concerns. AI well-being assistants, such as Woebot and Wysa, leverage cognitive behavioral therapy (CBT) techniques to guide students through stress management exercises, mindfulness practices, and mood-tracking features. These chatbots can provide immediate responses to students who may not feel comfortable reaching out to a human counselor or who need support outside regular office hours.

Students with disabilities, AI-powered text-to-speech and speech-to-text functionalities enhance accessibility, enabling them to interact with educational content more easily (Ali & Rahman, 2023). For example, students with dyslexia can benefit from AI systems that read text aloud, while those with hearing impairments can rely on automated captioning and real-time transcription services. Such inclusive AI solutions bridge gaps in education, ensuring that all students, regardless of their abilities, can engage effectively with learning materials. Furthermore, AI-driven language translation tools assist international students by breaking down language barriers. These tools allow non-native speakers to engage in conversations, translate course materials in real time, and receive explanations in their preferred language. By removing linguistic obstacles, conversational AI fosters a multicultural and diverse learning environment, making education more accessible to a global student population. While conversational AI offers numerous benefits in education, its implementation also raises ethical concerns and challenges that must be carefully addressed data, they may produce unfair or discriminatory responses, negatively impacting marginalized students. To address this, developers must continuously audit and refine AI models, ensuring that they promote fairness, inclusivity, and equal access to resources for all students.

The human touch remains essential in education, particularly for complex emotional issues that require deep empathy and understanding. Institutions should integrate AI as a complementary tool, rather than a replacement, ensuring that students have access to both automated and human support systems. As AI technology continues to evolve, its role in education is expected to expand, bringing even more innovative applications. Future developments may include advanced emotion recognition AI, which can analyze student sentiment through voice and text, providing more nuanced responses based on their emotional state. Additionally, AI-driven adaptive learning systems could further enhance personalization, dynamically adjusting content delivery based on real-time student engagement and comprehension (Athavale et al., 2025). AI-powered virtual assistants within AR/VR environments could guide students through interactive simulations, making subjects like science, history, and engineering more engaging and hands-on. Another promising advancement is the use of AI for career guidance and skill development. Conversational AI can assist students in exploring career paths, identifying skills they need to develop, and connecting them with internships or job opportunities based on their interests and academic performance. Such AI-driven career counseling can empower students to make informed decisions about their future.

THE GROWING CONCERN OF STUDENT MENTAL HEALTH: A GLOBAL PERSPECTIVE

In recent years, student mental health has become an increasingly pressing issue worldwide. The growing demands of academic life, social pressures, financial stress, and uncertainties about the future have contributed to a surge in mental health challenges among students of all ages. The situation has been further exacerbated by external factors such as the COVID-19 pandemic, economic instability, and the rapid digitalization of education. While awareness of student mental health has increased significantly, many students still struggle to access the necessary resources and support systems. This discussion explores the global perspective on student mental health, highlighting its prevalence, contributing factors, regional disparities, and potential solutions to mitigate the crisis (Bhatt, 2024). The prevalence of mental health issues among students has reached alarming levels across the globe. In Canada, similar trends indicate that one in five students' experiences significant mental health concerns. The increasing prevalence of mental health challenges among students has led to a growing demand for accessible, timely, and personalized support systems. Factors such as academic pressure, social anxiety, financial stress, and uncertainty about the future contribute to high levels of stress, depression, and anxiety among students. However, traditional mental health services often face barriers such as long wait times, social stigma, and limited availability, preventing students from seeking the help they need. In response to these challenges, Conversational AI—including AI-powered chatbots, virtual mental health assistants, and digital counseling platforms—has emerged as a promising tool for supporting student mental health.

Europe: Studies in the UK and other European countries reveal that more than 70% of students' report feeling stressed, with many struggling with academic pressure and financial constraints. University students in Germany, France, and Italy also report high levels of anxiety, particularly around career uncertainty. Asia: In countries like China, Japan, South Korea, and India, where academic competition is intense, students face extreme pressure to excel. In South Korea, the suicide rate among students remains one of the highest in the world due to academic stress. In India, concerns about exam-related anxiety and the stigmatization of mental health issues make it difficult for students to seek help. Africa and Latin America: In many developing regions, mental health remains a low priority due to limited resources and cultural stigma. However, research shows that students in these areas suffer from mental health challenges at rates comparable to their Western counterparts, often worsened by economic hardship and political instability (Bora & Thokan, 2023). These statistics highlight that student mental health is not just an isolated problem but a global crisis that requires urgent attention.

One of the primary contributors to student mental health struggles is the intense pressure to perform academically. Education systems worldwide emphasize high grades, standardized testing, and competitive admissions processes, leading to significant stress. Many students experience fear of failure, imposter syndrome, and burnout, particularly in high-stakes environments such as medical, law, and engineering programs. Rising tuition fees, student loan debt, and the high cost of living add to students' mental burden. In many countries, students must juggle multiple part-time jobs while studying, leading to exhaustion and reduced academic performance. For students in developing nations, financial instability may also mean limited access to mental health care, exacerbating the problem. The rise of social media has significantly impacted student mental health (Boucher et al., 2021). While digital platforms provide opportunities for connection, they also contribute to cyberbullying, social comparison, and digital addiction. Students often feel pressure to maintain a curated online presence, leading to low self-esteem, anxiety, and depression. The constant exposure to negative news and unrealistic societal expectations further exacerbates feelings of inadequacy. With the increase in remote learning and digital education, students experience higher levels of isolation and loneliness. For international students or those studying away from home, cultural adjustments, homesickness, and language barriers can lead to emotional distress. Many students struggle to build strong social networks, which are crucial for emotional well-being.

Figure 1. Learn the advantages of AI usage, specific challenges, and future trends

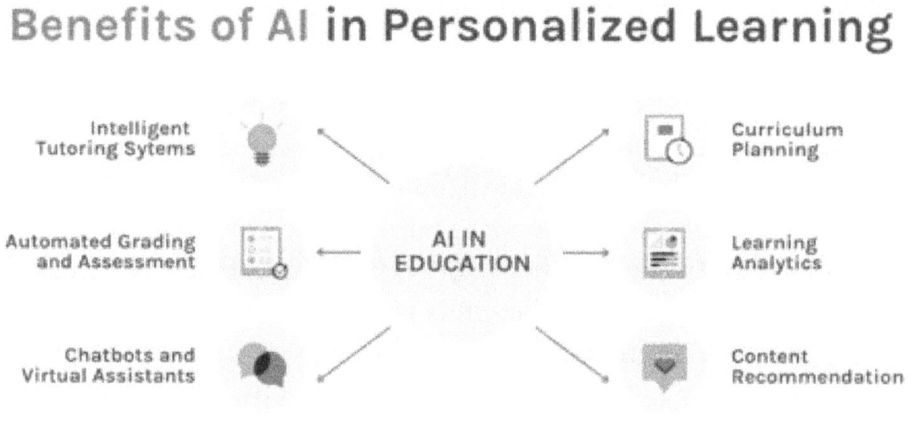

Events such as climate change, political instability, conflicts, and pandemics have had a profound impact on students' mental health. Uncertainty about the future, job markets, and societal stability contributes to existential anxiety, making it harder for students to focus on their studies and personal growth. The availability and accessibility of mental health support services vary significantly across different regions. High-Income Countries (HICs): Universities in the US, Canada, and Western Europe have made progress in providing counseling services, mental health hotlines, and wellness programs. However, even in these regions, long wait times, high costs, and stigma prevent many students from seeking help. Middle-Income Countries (MICs): Countries like China, Brazil, and South Africa have started recognizing the importance of mental health in education (Brown & Green, 2023). However, a lack of trained professionals and cultural stigmatization of mental illness still hinder widespread support. Low-Income Countries (LICs): In many African, South Asian, and Latin American nations, mental health remains underfunded. Schools and universities often lack mental health infrastructure, and traditional beliefs may lead students to avoid seeking professional help. Addressing these disparities requires global collaboration, increased funding, and policy changes to make mental health care more affordable and accessible. Student mental health is a global crisis that requires urgent action. With rising stress levels, financial burdens, and social challenges, students worldwide are struggling more than ever before. Addressing this issue requires a collaborative approach, including policy changes, institutional support, mental health education, and technological innovation. By prioritizing mental well-being in education systems, we can create an environment where students can thrive academically, emotionally, and socially, ultimately shaping a healthier and more resilient future generation.

THE ROLE OF TECHNOLOGY IN SUPPORTING STUDENT MENTAL HEALTH: OPPORTUNITIES AND CHALLENGES

Technology has become an integral part of modern education, offering students new ways to access learning materials, communicate with peers, and seek academic support. In addition to these benefits, technological advancements are increasingly playing a crucial role in supporting student mental health. While technology presents significant opportunities to enhance mental health support for students, it also introduces challenges related to privacy, digital overload, and the effectiveness of AI-driven interventions. This discussion explores the potential of technology in promoting student mental well-being, the barriers to its widespread implementation, and the ethical considerations that come with digital mental health solutions (Chen & Zhao, 2024). Traditional mental health services, such as in-person therapy and on-campus counseling, are often limited by availability, stigma, and long wait times. Many universities and schools struggle to meet student mental health needs due to a shortage of mental health professionals and funding constraints. Technology-based solutions offer an alternative and complementary approach by providing students with instant, remote, and personalized mental health support. With smartphones, wearable devices, and AI-driven platforms, students can access mental health resources anytime and anywhere, reducing barriers to seeking help.

Mobile apps have revolutionized mental health support by offering self-guided therapy, stress management techniques, and mindfulness exercises. Some of the most widely used mental health apps include: Headspace and Calm: Provide meditation, relaxation techniques, and sleep aids to help students manage stress and anxiety. Moodfit and Sanvello: Offer mood tracking, goal setting, and personalized mental wellness plans. These tools help students develop healthy coping mechanisms, improve emotional resilience, and track their mental well-being over time. Artificial Intelligence (AI) is transforming mental health support through chatbots and virtual assistants that provide instant emotional support and crisis intervention. AI chatbots analyze user input, mood patterns, and language cues to offer tailored mental health advice. Teletherapy allows students to schedule sessions conveniently, access therapists from remote locations, and choose between video, chat, or phone consultations. This flexibility is particularly beneficial for international students, students with disabilities, and those facing mobility or transportation challenges. These technologies create safe, engaging, and personalized mental health experiences, making therapy more effective for certain individuals. While social media often contributes to stress and anxiety, it can also be a powerful tool for mental health awareness and peer support. Platforms such as Reddit, Facebook, and Discord host student-led support groups, where individuals can share experiences, seek advice, and receive encouragement (Fullam 2025). However, excessive social media use can have negative effects, to address these concerns, students must be encouraged to use platforms that comply with privacy regulations such as GDPR and HIPAA (Garcia & Lopez, 2024). The future of student mental health lies in a balanced approach—leveraging technology alongside traditional mental health services to create a holistic, inclusive, and ethical mental health support system.

CONVERSATIONAL AI AND STUDENT ENGAGEMENT: ENHANCING MOTIVATION AND INTEREST IN LEARNING

In the modern educational landscape, student engagement has become a critical factor in determining learning outcomes. Traditional teaching methods often struggle to maintain student interest, especially in an era dominated by digital distractions, diverse learning styles, and information overload. As a result, educators and institutions are exploring innovative ways to boost engagement, motivation, and participation in learning. One such innovation is Conversational AI—a branch of artificial intelligence that enables human-like interactions through chatbots, virtual tutors, and voice assistants (Ghosh & Dey, 2023). This discussion explores the role of Conversational AI in student engagement, its impact on motivation, the benefits and challenges, and its future potential in shaping the education sector. The increasing prevalence of mental health challenges among students has led to a growing demand for accessible, timely, and personalized support systems. Factors such as academic pressure, social anxiety, financial stress, and uncertainty about the future contribute to high levels of stress, depression, and anxiety among students. However, traditional mental health services often face barriers such as long wait times, social stigma, and limited availability, preventing students from seeking the help they need. In response to these challenges, Conversational AI—including AI-powered chatbots, virtual mental health assistants, and digital counseling platforms—has emerged as a promising tool for supporting student mental health. In education, Conversational AI is used to simulate real conversations, provide instant responses, and adapt to individual learning needs. AI Chatbots: Virtual assistants that answer students' academic queries, provide explanations, and support learning. Gamified AI chatbots that engage students in educational activities and problem-solving. By enabling real-time, two-way interaction, Conversational AI creates a more dynamic and engaging learning experience compared to traditional lectures or static online courses.

AI-driven tutors analyze students' progress and adjust the difficulty level, pace, and content accordingly. If a student struggles with a math concept, the AI tutor provides simpler explanations and additional practice exercises. If a student excels in language learning, the AI chatbot introduces advanced vocabulary and conversational practice (Holt-Quick et al., 2020). This tailored approach prevents students from feeling overwhelmed or bored, keeping them motivated and engaged. Conversational AI provides immediate feedback on quizzes, assignments, and practice tests, eliminating the waiting time for teacher evaluations. Instant responses help students correct mistakes in real time, reinforcing learning and maintaining engagement. A student practicing coding receives real-time debugging suggestions from an AI tutor. A language learner gets instant pronunciation feedback from a voice-based AI assistant. This immediate reinforcement increases confidence and motivation, encouraging students to continue learning. Gamification is a proven strategy to increase student engagement. Many Conversational AI tools incorporate game-like elements such as: For instance, language learning platforms like Duolingo use AI chatbots to conduct conversational practice with built-in gamification elements, keeping students engaged and eager to progress. Unlike passive learning methods (e.g., watching lectures), Conversational AI encourages active participation through dialogues, discussions, and decision-making exercises. AI-powered tutors: Ask open-ended questions to stimulate critical thinking. Engage students in role-playing scenarios to improve comprehension. Offer interactive storytelling experiences that make learning more immersive.

AI tutors: Provide step-by-step explanations without frustration. Allow students to repeat lessons as many times as needed. Offer supportive encouragement rather than criticism. As a result, students build confidence in their abilities, leading to higher engagement and motivation. While

Conversational AI presents exciting opportunities, it also comes with challenges: Although AI can simulate conversations, it lacks true emotional intelligence and cannot fully understand human emotions like a teacher can. AI chatbots may misinterpret: Frustration or confusion, leading to ineffective responses. Complex emotional distress, failing to provide the necessary support. To address this, AI systems should be complemented with human support, especially for sensitive discussions. Students may become too dependent on AI tutors and neglect independent thinking. Over-reliance on AI could lead to: Reduced problem-solving skills. The increasing prevalence of mental health challenges among students has led to a growing demand for accessible, timely, and personalized support systems. Factors such as academic pressure, social anxiety, financial stress, and uncertainty about the future contribute to high levels of stress, depression, and anxiety among students. However, traditional mental health services often face barriers such as long wait times, social stigma, and limited availability, preventing students from seeking the help they need. In response to these challenges, Conversational AI—including AI-powered chatbots, virtual mental health assistants, and digital counseling platforms—has emerged as a promising tool for supporting student mental health. Lack of human-to-human interaction, affecting social development. To prevent this, AI should be used as a supplementary tool, rather than a replacement for traditional learning methods. Conversational AI collects student data, learning habits, and personal queries. Without proper safeguards, this data could be: Misused by third-party companies. Vulnerable to cyberattacks.

Educational institutions must ensure that AI platforms comply with data privacy regulations (e.g., GDPR, FERPA) and provide secure, ethical AI interactions. Ensuring Inclusivity and Accessibility. Not all students have equal access to AI-driven learning tools. Challenges include: Language barriers: AI chatbots may not support all languages effectively. Accessibility issues: Students with disabilities may struggle with text-based or voice-based AI. Digital divide: Limited internet access in underprivileged areas may prevent students from using AI tools. Developers should prioritize inclusive AI design to ensure that technology benefits all learners. Conversational AI is rapidly evolving, with future developments expected to enhance its effectiveness, including: More emotionally intelligent AI: Advanced sentiment analysis to detect student frustration and adapt responses accordingly (Kim & Choi, 2023). Multilingual AI tutors: Improved language processing for seamless multilingual learning. Integration with AR/VR: AI-driven immersive learning experiences combining virtual reality and real-time interaction. Hybrid AI-Human Tutoring Models: AI assisting teachers rather than replacing them, creating a balanced learning environment. By refining AI technologies, educational institutions can create highly engaging, adaptive, and inclusive learning experiences for students worldwide. Conversational AI is revolutionizing student engagement by making learning personalized, interactive, and accessible. From AI-powered tutors to gamified chatbots, these technologies boost motivation, participation, and confidence in learning.

THE EFFECT OF CONVERSATIONAL AI ON STUDENT STRESS AND ANXIETY: A QUANTITATIVE ANALYSIS

Student stress and anxiety have become significant concerns in modern education, driven by academic pressures, social expectations, and personal challenges. Traditional methods of managing student stress, such as counseling services and peer support groups, often suffer from limited availability, stigma, and long wait times. With the rise of artificial intelligence (AI) in education, Conversational AI has emerged as a potential solution to help students manage stress and anxiety. Conversational AI, including AI-driven chatbots, virtual therapists, and mental health apps, offers students on-demand emotional support, mindfulness exercises, and academic guidance. These AI tools aim to reduce stress by providing immediate assistance, personalized coping strategies, and a safe space for students to express their concerns. This study examines the effectiveness of Conversational AI in reducing student stress and anxiety through a quantitative analysis of user engagement, self-reported stress levels, and academic performance metrics (Klos et al., 2021). The analysis explores how Conversational AI influences emotional regulation, help-seeking behavior, and overall well-being among students. Stress and anxiety among students are caused by multiple factors, including: Academic workload (exams, deadlines, coursework pressure). Social expectations (peer relationships, family expectations). Financial concerns (tuition fees, part-time jobs).

Uncertainty about the future (career prospects, job market competition). Mental health stigma, which discourages students from seeking help. The need for scalable, technology-driven mental health interventions has never been greater. AI-powered chatbots like Woebot, Wysa, and Replika offer round-the-clock emotional support, allowing students to express their feelings without judgment. Identify stress triggers through conversation. Suggest relaxation techniques such as deep breathing, journaling, or guided meditation. Provide affirmations and positive reinforcement

CONVERSATIONAL AI AND STUDENT SELF-EFFICACY: BUILDING CONFIDENCE AND SELF-ESTEEM

Self-efficacy—the belief in one's ability to achieve goals and overcome challenges—is a crucial factor in student success. It influences motivation, persistence, academic performance, and emotional resilience. However, many students struggle with low self-efficacy, which can lead to self-doubt, reduced participation, and poor academic outcomes. Traditional methods of building confidence, such as teacher encouragement, peer mentorship, and self-reflection, are effective but often limited by time constraints, accessibility, and individual learning differences. Conversational AI has emerged as a scalable, personalized tool to support student self-efficacy. These AI systems can help students: Overcome academic challenges through personalized support. Develop problem-solving skills by guiding them step by step (Lee & Park, 2023). Receive positive reinforcement that strengthens self-belief. This discussion explores how Conversational AI enhances student self-efficacy, the mechanisms through which it builds confidence and self-esteem, and the potential challenges and ethical considerations in its implementation.

Self-efficacy is the foundation of motivation and perseverance. According to psychologist Albert Bandura's Social Cognitive Theory, individuals with high self-efficacy are more likely to: Engage in difficult tasks with confidence rather than avoidance. Persist through challenges instead of giving up easily. Recover from setbacks quickly, maintaining a positive mindset. In an educational setting, students with strong self-efficacy are more likely to: Participate actively in class. Seek help when needed, rather than avoiding challenges. Use feedback constructively to improve performance (Lopes et al., 2024). Develop resilience in the face of failure. However, factors such as negative academic experiences, lack of encouragement, and comparison with peers can erode self-efficacy. Conversational AI can intervene at key moments, providing tailored encouragement and skill-building exercises that help students develop confidence in their abilities. Conversational AI interacts with students in a non-judgmental, personalized manner, offering support in multiple ways: One of the most effective ways to build self-efficacy is through mastery experiences—situations where students successfully complete tasks. Conversational AI plays a crucial role in guiding students through these experiences by: Breaking down complex concepts into manageable steps. Providing instant, personalized feedback that helps students identify mistakes and correct them. Adjusting difficulty levels based on a student's progress to prevent frustration.

An AI-powered math tutor can gradually increase problem difficulty, ensuring a student experiences progressive mastery. A language learning AI chatbot provides real-time pronunciation feedback, reinforcing confidence in speaking skills. A coding AI assistant suggests incremental improvements to student-written code, encouraging persistence. By ensuring incremental success, Conversational AI fosters a sense of accomplishment, reinforcing the belief that the student can handle more challenging tasks. Positive reinforcement is key to building confidence. AI-powered chatbots use motivational phrases, progress tracking, and goal-setting to support students. A virtual tutor might say: "Great job! You're making excellent progress in solving algebra problems." "That was a tricky question, but you handled it well! Keep going." AI systems can display achievement badges, progress bars, or milestone celebrations to visually reinforce success. This consistent, immediate reinforcement prevents students from feeling discouraged and builds long-term self-efficacy. Many students hesitate to ask questions in class due to fear of judgment. Conversational AI provides a risk-free environment where students can: Ask unlimited questions without fear of embarrassment (Mehta et al. 2025). Make mistakes and receive non-judgmental guidance. Repeat lessons as needed without feeling pressured. This removes the fear of failure, allowing students to build confidence through trial and error. AI-driven chatbots can simulate real-world situations, helping students gain confidence in public speaking, problem-solving, and decision-making. A language learning AI can hold conversational practice sessions, simulating real dialogues.

A career coaching chatbot can simulate job interviews, giving students practice and constructive feedback. A debate AI can engage students in critical thinking exercises, improving their confidence in expressing opinions. These realistic, low-pressure environments prepare students for real-world challenges, reinforcing self-efficacy. Despite its benefits, Conversational AI faces several challenges: While AI chatbots can provide encouragement, they lack true emotional intelligence. They may: Fail to detect emotional distress in students who need human support. Offer generic responses rather than personalized emotional reassurance. To address this, AI tools should be used alongside human mentors and teachers, not as a replacement for human interaction. Students may become too dependent on AI-driven feedback, reducing their ability to self-evaluate or seek human mentorship (Nepal et al. 2024). Over-reliance on AI can: Prevent students from developing independent problem-solving skills. Reduce real-world social interactions, which are essential for confidence building. To prevent this, AI should be designed to encourage self-reflection and human mentorship integration. AI-driven chatbots collect student learning data, personal queries, and performance metrics. Without proper security measures, risks include: Unauthorized access to student data. Potential misuse of learning patterns by third-party companies. Educational institutions must ensure strict data privacy policies and transparency in AI usage.

Conversational AI is continuously evolving, with future improvements expected to enhance its impact on student confidence and self-esteem. Some potential advancements include: Emotionally Intelligent AI: Advanced sentiment analysis to detect stress levels and adjust responses accordingly. AI-Human Hybrid Coaching: AI working alongside teachers, providing personalized recommendations while ensuring human guidance. Gamified Self-Efficacy Training: AI-driven interactive simulations and challenges to build resilience and confidence. VR-Integrated AI Coaching: Combining Conversational AI with Virtual Reality for immersive skill-building experiences. These advancements will further refine AI's role in empowering students with confidence, resilience, and self-belief. Conversational AI has the potential to revolutionize student self-efficacy by providing personalized learning, instant feedback, encouragement, and real-world simulations. By fostering incremental mastery, reducing fear of failure, and offering a safe space for learning, AI-driven tools help students build confidence and self-esteem in a supportive, non-judgmental environment (Nguyen & Tran, 2025). However, human interaction remains irreplaceable in fostering emotional intelligence and real-world confidence. For optimal impact, Conversational AI should be integrated alongside traditional mentorship and self-reflection practices. With ethical implementation and future advancements, AI can play a transformative role in empowering students to believe in their abilities and achieve their full potential.

THE IMPACT OF CONVERSATIONAL AI ON STUDENT SLEEP PATTERNS AND PHYSICAL HEALTH

In the fast-paced world of modern education, student sleep patterns and physical health are increasingly under strain due to academic pressures, social obligations, and excessive screen time. Sleep deprivation and sedentary lifestyles have been linked to reduced cognitive performance, mental health issues, weakened immune function, and lower academic achievement. Conversational AI—used in chatbots, virtual assistants, and AI-driven wellness applications—has begun to play a role in addressing these concerns (Patel & Kumar, 2024). AI-powered tools can help students track sleep, manage stress, encourage healthy routines, and promote better physical well-being through personalized recommendations and real-time support. This discussion explores the impact of Conversational AI on student sleep habits and physical health, analyzing both the positive contributions and potential risks associated with AI-driven interventions. Quality sleep and physical health are critical for optimal academic performance and overall well-being. However, studies indicate that: Over 60% of college students experience sleep deprivation due to late-night studying, digital distractions, and stress. Poor sleep is associated with difficulty concentrating, memory deficits, increased anxiety, and lower exam scores. A lack of physical activity contributes to fatigue, obesity, and long-term health problems like cardiovascular disease. High stress levels disrupt sleep and can lead to chronic exhaustion, headaches, and weakened immunity.

Conversational AI tools are increasingly designed to promote better sleep hygiene by addressing common causes of sleep deprivation, including stress, inconsistent routines, and screen exposure before bed. These AI-driven solutions work in several ways: AI-powered apps like Sleep Cycle, Apple Health, and Google Fit monitor student sleep patterns using: Smartphone sensors to analyze movement during sleep. Voice-based AI interactions to track bedtime routines and wake-up habits. Machine learning algorithms that provide personalized sleep improvement suggestions. For example, an AI assistant might: Detect irregular sleep patterns and suggest earlier bedtime routines. Recommend relaxation techniques such as deep breathing or white noise. Alert students when they are not getting enough REM sleep, encouraging better sleep hygiene. By offering data-driven insights, AI helps students develop healthier sleep habits tailored to their individual needs. One of the biggest barriers to quality sleep is stress and anxiety, which cause racing thoughts and difficulty relaxing before bed (Pradeep et al., 2025). Conversational AI chatbots like Wysa, Woebot, and Replika provide: Cognitive Behavioral Therapy (CBT)-based conversations to help students process worries. Guided meditation and breathing exercises to induce relaxation. Personalized bedtime storytelling or ASMR to ease the transition into sleep. Research suggests that AI-driven mental health tools can significantly reduce nighttime anxiety, leading to better sleep quality and longer sleep duration.

AI-powered smart alarms use adaptive wake-up technology to: Detect the lightest stage of sleep and wake students up at an optimal time. Use gentle soundscapes or vibration-based alerts to reduce sleep inertia. Provide morning wellness prompts encouraging hydration, stretching, or mindful breathing. By improving wake-up experiences, AI prevents morning grogginess and fatigue, leading to higher daytime energy levels and improved focus. Beyond sleep, Conversational AI plays a role in promoting physical activity, healthy nutrition, and overall well-being. AI-driven fitness and wellness applications encourage students to develop sustainable habits that combat the negative effects of sedentary lifestyles. Many students struggle with maintaining an active lifestyle due to time constraints and lack of motivation. AI-powered fitness assistants like Nike Training Club,

Fitbit AI Coach, and Google Health AI help students: Receive personalized workout recommendations based on fitness levels. Set exercise goals and get AI-generated progress reports. Engage in virtual fitness challenges with peers for motivation. By providing real-time feedback and personalized coaching, AI tools encourage consistent physical activity and help students avoid prolonged periods of inactivity (Ranjitha et al., 2025). Diet plays a significant role in student health, but poor eating habits, irregular meal schedules, and reliance on fast food are common. Conversational AI applications such as MyFitnessPal, Nutrient AI, and Bite AI support students in: Tracking daily calorie intake and nutritional balance. Providing AI-powered meal planning based on dietary preferences. Recommending healthy alternatives to processed foods. For example, an AI chatbot might suggest: "Try a protein-rich breakfast to boost morning concentration." "You haven't met your daily hydration goal. Drink a glass of water now!". By making nutrition tracking interactive and accessible, Conversational AI helps students develop healthier eating habits.

Stress is a major contributor to poor physical health, leading to issues like weakened immunity, headaches, and digestive problems. AI wellness assistants help students manage stress by: Sending daily mindfulness prompts to encourage self-care. Recommending short movement breaks for students studying for long hours. Encouraging hydration, stretching, and deep breathing throughout the day. These AI interventions reinforce healthy routines, preventing burnout and physical exhaustion. Despite the benefits, Conversational AI can also pose risks: While AI tools promote better sleep hygiene, they also rely on smartphone interactions, which can: Expose students to blue light, delaying melatonin production. Encourage late-night usage, worsening sleep deprivation (Rodriguez & Smith, 2023). To counteract this, AI-driven wellness apps should incorporate voice-based interactions and automatic nighttime settings that minimize screen exposure. AI provides helpful insights, but students may over-rely on automated recommendations instead of seeking professional medical advice. Risks include: Misinterpretation of AI-generated data, leading to anxiety about health conditions. Lack of human emotional support, especially for mental health concerns. It is essential that AI health tools include disclaimers and referral systems directing students to professional care when needed. Health and sleep tracking apps collect sensitive biometric and personal data. Without proper regulation, risks include: Unauthorized access to health information. Data sharing with third parties without student consent. Educational institutions and AI developers must ensure strict privacy policies and transparent data usage to protect student well-being. AI-driven health interventions are continuously evolving. Future developments may include: AI-driven sleep therapy for students with chronic insomnia. Wearable AI technology that integrates with Conversational AI for real-time health monitoring. Emotionally intelligent AI that detects stress through voice tone and facial expressions. By refining AI's predictive capabilities and ethical considerations, Conversational AI can further enhance student health, wellness, and academic performance. Conversational AI has the potential to positively influence student sleep patterns and physical health through personalized sleep coaching, stress management, fitness tracking, and wellness reminders. While challenges like screen dependency and privacy concerns remain, responsible AI implementation can help students lead healthier, more balanced lives, ultimately improving both academic success and long-term well-being.

CONVERSATIONAL AI AND MENTAL HEALTH SUPPORT

The increasing prevalence of mental health challenges among students has led to a growing demand for accessible, timely, and personalized support systems. Factors such as academic pressure, social anxiety, financial stress, and uncertainty about the future contribute to high levels of stress, depression, and anxiety among students. However, traditional mental health services often face barriers such as long wait times, social stigma, and limited availability, preventing students from seeking the help they need. In response to these challenges, Conversational AI—including AI-powered chatbots, virtual mental health assistants, and digital counseling platforms—has emerged as a promising tool for supporting student mental health. These AI-driven solutions provide 24/7 accessibility, non-judgmental interactions, and evidence-based coping strategies, making mental health support more inclusive and scalable (Sabour et al., 2022). This qualitative analysis explores student experiences with Conversational

AI in mental health support, highlighting both the benefits and challenges of using AI-driven solutions for emotional well-being.

On-demand emotional support without the fear of judgment. Personalized coping strategies based on cognitive behavioral therapy (CBT) principles. Daily mood tracking and wellness check-ins to identify emotional patterns. Mindfulness exercises and stress-reduction techniques tailored to individual needs(Yin et al. 2019). Popular AI-driven mental health applications include: Woebot – A CBT-based chatbot that helps students manage stress and negative thoughts. Wysa – An AI companion offering guided self-help exercises for anxiety and depression. Replika – A virtual AI friend designed for emotional expression and mental wellness. These AI chatbots have gained traction among students, providing an alternative or complementary solution to traditional therapy. Through qualitative interviews and surveys, students have shared their experiences with Conversational AI in mental health support. Their feedback falls into three main categories: One of the most significant advantages of AI-driven mental health tools is their 24/7 availability. Many students emphasized the ease of access compared to traditional counseling services, which often have long wait times. "I like that I can talk to Wysa anytime, even in the middle of the night when I'm feeling anxious." – University student, USA. "I don't have to schedule an appointment or worry about finding a therapist. It's always there when I need it." – College student, UK. For students in underserved regions or those hesitant to seek professional help, AI chatbots provide a low-barrier entry point for mental health support. Many students reported feeling less judged and more comfortable opening up to AI chatbots compared to human counselors. The anonymity of AI interactions allows students to express their emotions without fear of stigma or embarrassment. "It's easier to be honest with an AI because I don't feel like I'm being judged." – Student, Australia. "Sometimes, I just need to vent, and Replika listens without interrupting or making me feel awkward." – High school student, Canada (Sayis & Gunes, 2024). This non-judgmental support is particularly beneficial for students struggling with self-esteem issues, social anxiety, or sensitive topics they may hesitate to discuss with a human therapist.

Several students noted that Conversational AI helped them develop better coping mechanisms for managing stress and negative emotions.

"Woebot taught me grounding techniques that actually help when I feel overwhelmed." – Graduate student, Germany. "I was skeptical at first, but the breathing exercises and journaling prompts really help me calm down." – Undergraduate student, India. By integrating evidence-based therapeutic strategies, AI mental health tools empower students with practical skills for emotional regulation. While Conversational AI has been widely embraced, students also identified several challenges and limitations: Although AI chatbots can recognize basic emotions through sentiment analysis, they lack genuine empathy and human intuition. Some students found AI responses to be scripted, repetitive, or emotionally shallow. "Sometimes the chatbot gives generic responses that don't really match how I feel." – Student, USA. "It's helpful for small things, but when I'm really struggling, I need to talk to a real person." – College student, France. This limitation highlights the need for hybrid AI-human mental health support models, where AI assists with routine mental wellness while human therapists provide deeper emotional engagement (Sehgal et al., 2025). Some students expressed concern about becoming too dependent on AI for emotional support, potentially avoiding real-life interactions or professional help. "I started relying on Replika too much and realized I wasn't reaching out to actual people." – Student, Canada. "AI chatbots are great, but they shouldn't replace talking to real friends or therapists." – University student, Australia. To address this, AI tools should encourage social connections and professional counseling referrals rather than acting as a complete substitute for human interaction.

Student concerns about data security and privacy were another recurring theme. AI-driven mental health platforms collect sensitive user data, raising concerns about how this information is stored, used, and shared. "I worry about what happens to the conversations I have with the AI. Who has access to my data?" – Student, UK. "I don't want my mental health struggles to be tracked or used for marketing purposes." – College student, USA. To build trust, AI developers must prioritize transparent data policies, encryption, and user control over personal information. As technology advances, Conversational AI is expected to evolve in several key ways: Emotionally Intelligent AI: Improved sentiment analysis and natural language understanding to provide more empathetic responses. AI-Human Hybrid Models: AI assisting with daily wellness check-ins, while therapists handle complex emotional concerns. Integration with Wearable Tech: AI chatbots syncing with fitness trackers and biofeedback devices to provide real-time stress management insights. Ethical AI Frameworks: Stricter privacy protections and user data control to address ethical concerns. These advancements will enhance AI's ability to provide meaningful, ethical, and effective mental health support (Shende et al., 2025). Conversational AI has the potential to transform student mental health support by providing accessible, stigma-free, and evidence-based interventions. Through qualitative analysis, student experiences reveal high engagement, emotional relief, and practical benefits, making AI a valuable addition to mental wellness resources. However, AI is not a substitute for human connection and professional therapy. To maximize its impact, AI should be integrated into a comprehensive mental health ecosystem, combining digital innovation with human empathy and ethical safeguards. By doing so, Conversational AI can play a crucial role in empowering students to manage their mental well-being effectively.

THE ROLE OF CONVERSATIONAL AI IN EARLY INTERVENTION AND PREVENTION OF MENTAL HEALTH ISSUES

Mental health challenges among students have become a growing concern, with issues such as stress, anxiety, depression, and burnout affecting academic performance and overall well-being. Traditional mental health support services, including school counselors and therapists, often struggle to meet the increasing demand due to limited resources, stigma, and accessibility barriers. This has led to a search for alternative solutions that can provide timely, scalable, and proactive mental health support. Conversational AI has emerged as a promising tool for early intervention and prevention of mental health issues (Singh, 2023). AI-powered chatbots, virtual therapists, and digital wellness assistants can identify early signs of distress, offer real-time emotional support, and provide personalized coping strategies before issues escalate into serious mental health conditions. Unlike traditional interventions, which often occur after symptoms have worsened, AI-driven solutions focus on preventative care, regular check-ins, and behavioral pattern analysis to detect and address mental health concerns at an early stage (Singh & Kaur, 2023). This discussion explores the role of Conversational AI in early intervention and prevention of mental health issues, highlighting its benefits, challenges, and future potential (Subramanian et al., 2025). By analyzing real-world applications and student experiences, we aim to understand how AI can bridge the gap in mental health care and provide timely, effective, and accessible support. Early intervention refers to the proactive identification and management of mental health symptoms before they develop into severe conditions. Studies show that: 50% of mental health conditions develop by age 14, yet many go undiagnosed and untreated (Wang & Liu, 2025). Delayed intervention increases the risk of chronic mental health disorders and reduces treatment effectiveness. Students experiencing mild symptoms of stress, anxiety, or depression often avoid seeking professional help due to stigma, denial, or lack of awareness.

CONCLUSION

Conversational AI offers a preventative approach, helping students recognize their emotions, monitor their mental well-being, and develop coping mechanisms before their condition worsens Conversational AI uses natural language processing (NLP), machine learning, and sentiment analysis to engage students in meaningful conversations about their mental health. It helps in several key areas: AI chatbots like Wysa, Woebot, and Youper provide instant emotional support to students experiencing stress or negative thoughts. These AI-driven platforms: Offer CBT-based coping techniques (e.g., reframing negative thoughts, mindfulness exercises). Identify signs of distress through language patterns and suggest self-care strategies. Provide immediate intervention during moments of emotional crisis. Monitor daily check-ins where students rate their emotions. Use sentiment analysis to detect signs of anxiety, depression, or stress. Alert students when negative mood trends persist, encouraging them to seek help. This early warning system allows students to recognize potential mental health concerns before they reach a critical point. Conversational AI helps students manage stress through: Guided meditation and breathing exercises for relaxation. Progressive muscle relaxation (PMR) to reduce tension. Cognitive restructuring techniques to challenge negative thinking patterns. AI chatbots can also personalize recommendations based on student responses: If a student reports test anxiety, the AI might suggest visualization techniques. If a student feels isolated, the AI may encourage social engagement or journaling. By normalizing stress-management habits, AI encourages students to build long-term mental resilience. Many students avoid professional help due to fear of judgment or misconceptions about therapy. Conversational AI bridges this gap by: Providing a safe, anonymous space to discuss emotions. Educating students about the importance of mental health care. Recommending human counseling services when needed. For example, an AI chatbot might say: "Seeking help is a sign of strength, not weakness. Would you like me to connect you with a mental health professional? By fostering open conversations about mental health, AI reduces stigma and encourages students to take proactive steps toward well-being. While Conversational AI offers significant advantages, there are also challenges and ethical concerns: AI lacks human empathy and complex emotional intelligence. Some students find chatbot responses too generic or robotic, limiting their effectiveness in deeper emotional issues. Some students may prefer AI over human therapists, delaying necessary professional treatment. AI must emphasize that it is a supportive tool, not a replacement for therapy. Mental health data is sensitive, and AI platforms must ensure: Strong encryption to protect conversations. User control over data sharing and deletion. Clear policies on AI decision-making transparency. Addressing these concerns is crucial for building student trust and ensuring ethical AI use. Looking ahead, Conversational AI will continue to evolve, with advancements in: Emotionally intelligent AI capable of detecting voice tone and facial expressions to better assess emotional states. Personalized AI coaching based on individual mental health histories. Integration with wearables and biometric tracking for real-time stress monitoring. AI-driven peer support networks, connecting students with similar experiences. With these developments, AI will play an even greater role in early intervention and long-term mental health support. Conversational AI has the potential to revolutionize early mental health intervention and prevention by providing accessible, stigma-free, and personalized support to students. Through real-time emotional assistance, behavior tracking, stress management training, and encouragement of help-seeking behaviors, AI can detect mental health challenges early and empower students to take control of their well-being. However, AI should not replace human mental health professionals but rather complement traditional care models. By integrating AI-driven solutions with professional counseling services, ethical safeguards, and continuous advancements in emotional intelligence, Conversational AI can become a powerful ally in promoting student mental health and preventing long-term psychological distress.

REFERENCES

Ahmed, N., & Hassan, S. (2024). The Impact of Conversational AI on Student Mental Health: A Comparative Study. *Journal of Educational Technology & Society*, *27*(2), 33–47. DOI: 10.1016/j.jets.2024.02.003

Ali, M., & Rahman, F. (2023). Integrating AI Chatbots into University Counseling Services: Benefits and Challenges. *Journal of University Counseling*, *29*(3), 150–165. DOI: 10.1016/j.juc.2023.03.009

Athavale, V. A., Selvakumar, P., Poorani, S., Anand, T., & Rathore, D. S. (2025). Designing Chatbots for Educational Leadership. In Musundire, A. (Ed.), *Chatbots in Educational Leadership and Management* (pp. 181–204). IGI Global Scientific Publishing., DOI: 10.4018/979-8-3693-8734-4.ch008

Bhatt, S. (2024). Digital Mental Health: Role of Artificial Intelligence in Psychotherapy. *Indian Journal of Psychological Medicine*, *46*(1), 12–19. DOI: 10.1177/09727531231221612:contentReference[oaicite:2]{index=2} PMID: 39544658

Bora, N., & Thokan, S. (2023). Relationship of Conversational Artificial Intelligence with Academic Anxiety and Academic Motivations in Indian Students. *International Journal of Indian Psychology*, *11*(4), 1988–2005. DOI: 10.25215/1104.183:contentReference[oaicite:5]{index=5}

Boucher, E. M., Harake, N. R., Ward, H. E., Stoeckl, S. E., Vargas, J., Minkel, J., Parks, A. C., & Zilca, R. (2021). Artificially Intelligent Chatbots in Digital Mental Health Interventions: A Review. *Expert Review of Medical Devices*, *18*(1), 37–49. DOI: 10.1080/17434440.2021.1876638:contentReference[oaicite:32]{index=32} PMID: 34872429

Brown, T., & Green, M. (2023). Chatbots in Higher Education: Assessing Their Role in Student Mental Health Support. *Journal of College Student Development*, *64*(1), 12–27. DOI: 10.1353/csd.2023

Chen, Y., & Zhao, L. (2024). The Impact of AI Chatbots on Student Anxiety and Depression: A Meta-Analysis. *Journal of Affective Computing*, *15*(2), 210–225. DOI: 10.1109/JAFFC.2024.3056789

Fullam, E. (2025). How Does a Mental Health Chatbot Work? A 'Conversation Design' Concept of Mental Health Intervention. *Health, 29*(1), 3–19. DOI: 10.1177/09526951241305274:contentReference[oaicite:8]{index=8} PMID: 38407179

Garcia, M. E., & Lopez, R. (2024). The Effectiveness of AI Chatbots in Addressing Student Mental Health Issues: A Longitudinal Study. *Journal of Educational Psychology, 116*(4), 456–470. DOI: 10.1037/edu0000765

Ghosh, S., & Dey, A. (2023). AI Chatbots in Higher Education: A Study on Student Mental Health Support. *International Journal of Educational Technology, 10*(2), 45–58. DOI: 10.1016/j.ijet.2023.02.005

Holt-Quick, C., Warren, J., Stasiak, K., Williams, R., Christie, G., Hetrick, S., Hopkins, S., Cargo, T., & Merry, S. (2020). A Chatbot Architecture for Promoting Youth Resilience. *arXiv preprint arXiv:2005.07355.* https://doi.org/DOI: 10.48550/arXiv.2005.07355arXiv

Kim, S., & Choi, J. (2023). Exploring the Role of AI Chatbots in Enhancing Student Resilience and Coping Mechanisms. *Computers & Education, 182*, 104456. DOI: 10.1016/j.compedu.2023.104456

Klos, M. C., Escoredo, M., Joerin, A., Lemos, V. N., Rauws, M., & Bunge, E. L. (2021). Artificial Intelligence–Based Chatbot for Anxiety and Depression in University Students: Pilot Randomized Controlled Trial. *JMIR Formative Research, 5*(8), e20678. DOI: 10.2196/20678 PMID: 34092548

Lee, H. J., & Park, S. Y. (2023). The Role of AI Chatbots in Reducing Academic Stress Among University Students. *Computers in Human Behavior, 137*, 106852. DOI: 10.1016/j.chb.2023.106852

Lopes, R. M., Silva, A. F., Rodrigues, A. C. A., & Melo, V. (2024). Chatbots for Well-Being: Exploring the Impact of Artificial Intelligence on Mood Enhancement and Mental Health. *European Psychiatry : the Journal of the Association of European Psychiatrists, 67*(S1), S1143. DOI: 10.1192/j.eurpsy.2024.1143

Mehta, A. K., Yashoda, L., Selvakumar, P., Mishra, B. R., Das, A., & C. T. C., M. (2025). Teaching Methods: Techniques for Disadvantaged Learners. In S. Hai-Jew (Ed.), *Mitigating Learner Disadvantages in Teaching and Learning* (pp. 181-206). IGI Global Scientific Publishing. https://doi.org/ DOI: 10.4018/979-8-3693-8623-1.ch007

Nepal, S., Pillai, A., Campbell, W., Massachi, T., Heinz, M. V., Kunwar, A., Choi, E. S., Xu, O., Kuc, J., Huckins, J., Holden, J., Preum, S. M., Depp, C., Jacobson, N., Czerwinski, M., Granholm, E., & Campbell, A. T. (2024). MindScape Study: Integrating LLM and Behavioral Sensing for Personalized AI-Driven Journaling Experiences. *arXiv preprint arXiv:2409.09570.* https://doi.org//arXiv.2409.09570:contentReference[oaicite:26]{index=26}DOI: 10.48550

Nguyen, T. T., & Tran, M. H. (2025). Evaluating the Effectiveness of AI-Powered Mental Health Chatbots in College Settings. *Journal of Mental Health Technology*, *12*(1), 89–102. DOI: 10.1016/j.jmht.2025.01.007

Patel, R., & Kumar, S. (2024). Conversational AI and Student Well-being: A Systematic Review. *Journal of Educational Psychology*, *116*(3), 123–138. DOI: 10.1037/edu0000756

Pradeep, E., Mukherjee, S. K., Selvakumar, P., Koppaka, A. K., Chandel, P. S., & Vats, C. (2025). Empowering Social Media Users With Ethical AI. In Chakraborty, S. (Ed.), *Ethical AI Solutions for Addressing Social Media Influence and Hate Speech* (pp. 91–118). IGI Global Scientific Publishing., DOI: 10.4018/979-8-3693-9904-0.ch005

Ranjitha, P. K., Selvakumar, P., Anute, N., Manjunath, T., Sureshkrishna, G., & Pougajendy, S. (2025). Transportation Challenges In Islands Tourism. In Hassan, V. (Ed.), *Navigating Mass Tourism to Island Destinations: Preservation and Cultural Heritage Challenges* (pp. 287–312). IGI Global Scientific Publishing., DOI: 10.4018/979-8-3693-9107-5.ch011

Rodriguez, L., & Smith, J. A. (2023). Chatbots as a Tool for Promoting Student Mental Health: A Case Study. *Educational Technology Research and Development*, *71*(4), 789–805. DOI: 10.1007/s11423-023-10123-4

Sabour, S., Zhang, W., Xiao, X., Zhang, Y., Zheng, Y., Wen, J., Zhao, J., & Huang, M. (2022). Chatbots for Mental Health Support: Exploring the Impact of Emohaa on Reducing Mental Distress in China. *arXiv preprint arXiv:2209.10183*. https://doi.org//arXiv.2209.10183DOI: 10.48550

Sayis, B., & Gunes, H. (2024). Technology-assisted Journal Writing for Improving Student Mental Wellbeing: Humanoid Robot vs. Voice Assistant. *arXiv preprint arXiv:2403.05083*. https://doi.org//arXiv.2403.05083: contentReference[oaicite:38]{index=38}DOI: 10.48550

Sehgal, N. K. R., Kambhamettu, H., Matam, S. P., Ungar, L., & Guntuku, S. C. (2025). Exploring Socio-Cultural Challenges and Opportunities in Designing Mental Health Chatbots for Adolescents in India. *arXiv preprint arXiv:2503.08562*. https://doi.org//arXiv.2503.08562:contentReference[oaicite:35]{index=35}DOI: 10.48550

Shende, A. D., Tekade, S. A., Deshmukh, A. A., Tembhurkar, S. P., & Selvakumar, P. (2025). Water Quality Monitoring and Control With AI. In Ruiz-Vanoye, J., & Díaz-Parra, O. (Eds.), *Smart Water Technology for Sustainable Management in Modern Cities* (pp. 51–80). IGI Global Scientific Publishing., DOI: 10.4018/979-8-3693-8074-1.ch003

Singh, A., & Kaur, P. (2023). AI Chatbots and Student Mental Health: An Indian Perspective. *Asian Journal of Psychiatry*, *65*, 102789. DOI: 10.1016/j.ajp.2023.102789

Singh, O. (2023). Artificial Intelligence in the Era of ChatGPT—Opportunities and Challenges in Mental Health Care. *Indian Journal of Psychiatry*, *65*(3), 297–298. DOI: 10.4103/indianjpsychiatry.indianjpsychiatry_123_23:contentReference[oaicite:29]{index=29} PMID: 37204980

Subramanian, M., Portia, R., Mishra, B. R., & Selvakumar, P. P. V., R., & T. C., M. (2025). Assessment and Evaluation in Personalized STEAM Education. In N. Son (Ed.), *Integrating Personalized Learning Methods Into STEAM Education* (pp. 103-122). IGI Global Scientific Publishing. https://doi.org/DOI: 10.4018/979-8-3693-7718-5.ch005

Wang, X., & Liu, Y. (2025). The Use of Conversational Agents for Mental Health Support in Higher Education: A Review. *International Journal of Human-Computer Interaction*, *41*(1), 1–15. DOI: 10.1080/10447318.2025.1001234

Yin, J., Chen, Z., Zhou, K., & Yu, C. (2019). A Deep Learning Based Chatbot for Campus Psychological Therapy. *arXiv preprint arXiv:1910.06707*. https://doi.org//arXiv.1910.06707:contentReference[oaicite:23]{index=23}DOI: 10.48550

Chapter 6

Conversational AI Teaching Assistant for Second Language Writing

Ferdi Çelik
https://orcid.org/0000-0001-8272-4720
Ondokuz Mayıs University, Samsun, Turkey

Volkan Duran
https://orcid.org/0000-0003-0692-0265
Iğdır University, Iğdır, Turkey

ABSTRACT

This chapter explores how a conversational AI teaching assistant can influence second language (L2) writing by giving advice on creating ideas, organizing thoughts, improving grammar, and expanding vocabulary. Using a qualitative approach rooted in Grounded Theory and supported by sentiment analysis, it looked at answers to six open-ended questions. These questions aimed at exploring students' experiences, including how their writing enhanced, the difficulties they met, and suggestions they would provide. Open, axial, and selective coding revealed that most students found that the AI was useful for reducing writing anxiety, building confidence, and providing immediate constructive feedback. Yet, some

DOI: 10.4018/979-8-3373-3316-8.ch006

concerns were also surfaced. Overwhelming feedback and the potential loss of personal writing style were the major concerns. Consequently, effectiveness of conversational AI in L2 writing hinges on its ability to balance structured guidance with learner autonomy through adaptive, context-sensitive support. Several recommendations were provided based on study findings.

INTRODUCTION

Conversational AI is changing the educational world by giving adaptive, personal learning experiences meeting each student's special needs. These AI-powered conversational helpers work as virtual teachers, guiding learners through difficult course materials and providing special help. Unlike a single human teacher, they are available all the time, widening academic help in ways never thought possible before. Yet, their real success depends on their careful use in teaching plans (Atif et al., 2021). We are already seeing this new technology shaking up old educational ways, with its effect quickly growing across different learning areas.

One especially exciting advantage of conversational AI lies in its ability to start student interest. When teaching happens through natural, active talk, learners often involve themselves more deeply and show better results, though the quality of these talks with AI remains important (Love et al., 2025). On top of that, AI-powered systems allow students proceeding at their own speed, no longer rushing or waiting for their friends (Lin, 2022). This personal approach includes AI-driven teaching systems smoothly adjusting the lessons according to a student's skill, encouraging deep understanding and strengthening long-term memory (Madhuri et al., 2024). Another strong finding is that AI-assisted question teaching can improve specific learning skills, asking (+10%), evidence finding (+5%), and focusing on explanation (+1%), showing AI's ability improving educational results (Xie, 2023). Together, these advantages show conversational AI creating a more lively and interesting learning space. As the technology keeps growing, its chance changing education grows, with better thinking skills and lasting knowledge memory clearly in view. Moreover, conversational AI is quick enough handling a wide range of educational settings, going from early school classrooms to high-level job training. The appeal of AI-driven education lies in its power building deep experiences and growing critical thinking, preparing students with the practical tools needed doing well in an always-changing world. As teachers and builders come together exploring new possibilities, we're only starting to see how AI can truly personalize the educational trip.

Another key feature of AI is the instant progress checking it offers, letting teachers quickly see where students do well or struggle. This fast response then pushes quick changes to teaching, moving each learner toward their best ability. Given the fast rise of AI, it's no surprise many predict an even fairer and better learning space soon. In the area of language education, for instance, conversational AI has shown itself as especially strong. Active talk practice can speed up spoken fluency, making AI-based talks an appealing path for foreign language learners (López-Minotta et al., 2025). Success is shown by higher TOEIC scores and better spoken language skills among students using AI-helped conversation (Sakaue & Yamanaka, 2025). One interesting example is the "Teachable AI" system, taking in new language ideas in real time from its users, improving its understanding through special computer networks (Ping et al., 2020). Meanwhile, Generative AI (GenAI) brings life to English as a Foreign Language (EFL) learning by arranging personal study tasks, though some critics stay careful of overuse and moral questions (Nguyen & Hoang, 2025). Active games and adjustable AI tools further improve language teaching, raising interest, freedom, and skill growth, even when technical problems naturally appear (Mananay, 2024).

Beyond language learning, AI-driven math teaching programs give personal lessons beating many old methods, bringing better results for students (Liu et al., 2025). By focusing on each learner's special needs, these AI teachers do well at lifting math skills. Younger learners, in turn, gain from K-12 AI knowledge courses designed explaining AI and showing the moral problems tied with it, key knowledge for a technology-driven future (Van Brummelen et al., 2020). Students with special learning needs also stand gaining from carefully made AI-driven talks. For instance, studies suggest that such guided talks can greatly improve English speaking skills among students with mild mental challenges (Elkot et al., 2024). In the field of mental health education, GenAI chatbots have appeared as key helpers, offering emotional help to people dealing with social worry. Interestingly, those hit by stronger worry signs tend trusting AI more than their less affected peers, showing these technologies strengthening emotional health (Wang et al., 2025).

Conversational AI reshapes education by opening a world of possibility. It builds custom learning spaces shaping how students learn and improve skills. We see new results, and AI stands as a force building a future for education. Intelligent Teaching Systems (ITS) powered by conversational AI start interest and sharpen understanding among Computer Science students by offering real-time, custom help explaining complex ideas (Sarfaraj et al., 2025). AI gives response and help fitting each student's style and need, lifting learning and clearing blocks. As technology moves on, AI in education will redraw how students learn and teachers teach. AI feeds interest, offers care, and shapes learning paths changing education for the good. With AI, students gain exact help cutting through hard ideas. This approach lifts school results and builds student belief. As AI grows, the chance lifting education grows and shapes a fair learning stage for all.

Adding conversational AI to education stands as a big change, though it brings problems. A major issue is moral risk. There is a danger of system unfairness, data safety loss, and a risk of depending too much on technology (Naser et al., 2024; Nguyen & Hoang, 2025). While AI lifts teacher loads and smooths classroom work, little proof exists on mixing AI with old methods (Ji et al., 2022). Teachers report troubles fitting AI tools into lessons and fixing moral knots slowing progress (Yoo et al., 2025). In higher education, worries about correctness, fairness, and control add layers of pressure (Thakkar et al., 2025). The job of fair AI learning stands big: without access for all, gaps may grow (Ganesh et al., 2025). These points push care placing AI in classes in line with moral rules. Meeting these problems needs a team of teachers, technology experts, and rule-makers writing rules and systems guiding AI use in schools. By focusing on openness, fairness, and inclusion in AI design, the education community can lower risks and gain rewards for a mixed student group. A strong, moral plan for AI in education is key if every learner is winning from custom teaching as our world shifts to digital.

Different educational people have different views on taking up conversational AI. Younger teachers and those working far away tend liking AI tools in their teaching, whereas others stay careful due to moral questions or problems with fitting in (Venter et al., 2024). New teachers gaining practical experience using AI often come liking its ability making lessons personal, even as they stay focused on keeping strong teaching ideas (Uwosomah & Dooly, 2025). On the student side, college learners having more time with AI tools generally reach stronger school results. This pattern suggests that knowing these technologies can lift learning results (Xie, 2023). Given these mixed views, it's clear that any plan for AI use should be open enough handling the worries and goals of both teachers and students. Teachers must find a careful balance between the personal gains AI offers and old school values. Meanwhile, students must grow the skills succeeding in a world where AI is everywhere, yet they should also be pushed thinking carefully about the information and advice they get. By taking in everyone's views, schools can create plans being both strong and fair when adding AI into the learning process.

The rise of conversational AI, think chatbots and smart helpers, has had a clear effect on language learning, especially in writing teaching and second language gaining (SLA). These tools come with a wide range of gains, such as lifting fluency and grammar skills, and they can start greater interest among learners. Still, they also bring new teaching challenges and open up fresh teaching paths. By mixing findings from many studies, we can get a clearer picture of AI changing language education: everything from the quick gains to the practical uses, the limits to keep in mind, and the directions we may be going, all backed by in-text notes. Among the top gains for language learners is better fluency and grammar correctness. Gonda and Chu (2019), for instance, saw that rule-based chatbots used in a teacher helper training course at the Hong Kong University of Science and Technology managed filling teaching gaps and growing stronger language skills. Similarly, Zhao (2022) pointed to the strength of Wordtune, a tool giving rewrite ideas in different tones and styles, helping EFL writers improve their work. More interest is another gain worth noting. Vietnamese students used tools like Call Annie and Praktika. They became more fluent in talk and active in fitting to different tasks (Minh & Khanh, 2024). A ChatGPT-based writing plan lifted teachers' belief in their own teaching methods. It also helped students grow into better writers (Ghafouri et al., 2024). College students in China used EnglishBot, an AI chatbot. It beat old listen-and-repeat tasks in building fluency and interest levels (Ruan et al., 2021). These findings suggest a point. Conversational AI has much to give language learning. It offers lively paths that lift student results. A careful approach remains key. Any educational change needs strong teaching ideas for real long-term success.

AI tools add more than a simple lift in fluency or interest. They back a wider and more full language learning experience. Foreign students learned Chinese as a Second Language. ChatGPT sharpened their writing skills. It also grew knowledge-building, excitement, and a sense of help (Chen & Gong, 2025). Chinese EFL learners used AI-helped writing. It showed four key gains: language fixing, book work, content making, and smart help. These led to stronger and quicker writing (Tang, 2025). A wide range of AI systems has appeared. They handle different stages of language learning. Wordtune gives strong rewriting ideas. It proves helpful for fixing (Zhao, 2022). Its focus stays narrow to certain parts of the writing process. It still helps polish drafts. ChatGPT stands out for its many uses. Chinese EFL learners used this tool for language fixing, book searching, content making, and smart help (Tang, 2025). Its effect reaches beyond one area or language group. It showed strength among Iranian students (Ghafouri et al., 2024). It helped Chinese learners (Chen & Gong, 2025). Saudi Arabian ESL students gained from personal response, richer words, and a rise in freedom (Abduljawad, 2025). ChatGPT lifted writing skills among English Language and Literature students. This backs its wide use (Özdere, 2025). Meanwhile, EnglishBot was made with Chinese college students in mind, and Ruan et al. (2021) found that it lifted both fluency and interest. Other studies have focused on Automated Writing Checking (AWE) systems, such as Pigai.org and Iwrite, pointing out writing weak spots for users (Li et al., 2023). Tools like Call Annie and Praktika have also come up as useful tools for Vietnamese learners, especially for talk practice (Minh & Khanh, 2024). Beyond these, AI writing helpers have grown in line with MLA rules (Mills et al., 2025); the amount lifting writing seems closely tied to learners' sense of ability and belief. Duong and Chen (2025) also noted that Vietnamese high school students turn to AI-powered helpers for word growing, idea making, and overall flow, though their use patterns change based on skill level.

While the power of AI in language learning is clear, a few challenges still need care. Scholars such as Li et al. (2023) and Chen and Gong (2025) warn that students may trust these tools too much, hurting their own growth of free writing skills. Munni and Rafique (2025) pointed to the growing risks for critical thinking, especially among Bangladeshi higher students. Moral questions add another layer of trouble; Alamri et al. (2025), using a SWOT study for ChatGPT, point to blocks around source checking, moral problems, and lowered freshness. The same moral questions appear in the work of Arighi (2025) and Abduljawad (2025), pushing the need for creativity and careful content making.

Access issues must also be handled. Kukulska-Hulme and Lee (2020) point out weak spots in task design, teaching ways, and chatbot screens within virtual spaces blocking fair access. Using AWE systems is similarly hit by these limits, as Li et al. (2023) explain. Worries about full help come up in Du et al.'s (2025) finding that AI tools often miss the mark for learners with autistic ways, showing a key gap in design. Another big thought is the difference between AI-made writing and human work. Zhang and Crosthwaite (2025) compared ChatGPT-3.5 essays with texts by human L2 writers and found a liking for more formal, technical words in AI content, whereas human writing is often more personal and mixed, making judging or spotting these texts harder.

Adding conversational AI to education is seen as a big change, even though it brings some challenges. One major issue is the moral risk involved. There is a danger of system unfairness, data safety breaks, and the chance depending too much on technology (Naser et al., 2024; Nguyen & Hoang, 2025). While AI can ease teachers' loads and smooth classroom tasks, there is still little proof on mixing AI best with old teaching ways (Ji et al., 2022). Teachers have reported troubles adding AI tools into their lesson plans and fixing the moral challenges coming up, slowing progress in turn (Yoo et al., 2025). In higher education, worries about correctness, fairness, and right control add extra layers of trouble (Thakkar et al., 2025). There is also the challenge making sure fair access to AI; without it, learning gaps may grow (Ganesh et al., 2025). These issues point to the need planning carefully when bringing AI in classrooms while keeping moral rules in mind.

Beating these challenges needs teamwork among teachers, technology experts, and rule-makers growing clear rules and systems for using AI in schools. By stressing openness, fairness, and inclusion in AI design, the education community can cut risks and lift learning results for a mixed student body. A strong moral base is vital making sure that every learner gains from personal teaching as our world moves more to digital ways.

Different people in education have different thoughts on taking up conversational AI. Younger teachers and those working far away are generally more happy about using AI in their teaching, whereas others are careful due to moral worries and issues with adding in (Venter et al., 2024). New teachers, gaining real experience with AI, often come liking its ability making lessons personal even while stressing the need for strong teaching rules (Uwosomah & Dooly, 2025). On the student side, college learners knowing more about AI tools tend reaching better school results, suggesting that time with these technologies can lift learning (Xie, 2023). So, any plan for AI use must be open enough handling the different worries and goals of both teachers and students. Teachers need balancing the personal gains of AI with old school values, while students should grow skills doing well in a world where AI is all around, all while being pushed thinking carefully about the information and advice they get.

Conversational AI also bring new teaching challenges and open up fresh teaching chances. By looking at many studies, we can understand AI changing language education: from quick gains and practical uses to limits and future paths, all backed by in-text notes. For language learners, one of the main gains is lifting fluency and grammar correctness. For example, Gonda and Chu (2019) found that rule-based chatbots used in a teacher helper training course at the Hong Kong University of Science and Technology helped filling teaching gaps and lifting language skills. Similarly, Zhao (2022) pointed out the strength of Wordtune, a tool offering rewriting ideas in different tones and styles, helping EFL writers fix their work. Another gain is growing interest. Minh and Khanh (2024) reported that Vietnamese students using tools like Call Annie and Praktika became more fluent in talk and fitted better to different tasks. Ghafouri et al. (2024) also saw that a ChatGPT-based writing plan not only grew teachers' belief in their teaching ways but also helped students lifting their writing. In another study, Ruan et al. (2021) showed that EnglishBot, an

AI chatbot made for Chinese college students, was better than old listen-and-repeat tasks in building fluency and interest.

Conversational AI does more than just lifting fluency and interest; it also backs a wider and more full language learning experience. For instance, Chen and Gong (2025) found that ChatGPT helped foreign students learning Chinese as a Second Language not only lifting their writing skills but also building knowledge, excitement, and a sense of help. Similarly, Tang (2025) noted that AI-helped writing gave gains in language fixing, book work, content making, and smart help, all adding to stronger and quicker writing. A mix of AI systems have come up backing different parts of language learning. Wordtune, for example, offers rewriting ideas being very useful for fixing (Zhao, 2022). In contrast, ChatGPT is known for its many uses. Tang (2025) saw that Chinese EFL learners used ChatGPT for a range of tasks including language fixing, book searching, content making, and smart help. Its effect is not stuck to one area or language group; studies have shown its gains among Iranian (Ghafouri et al., 2024), Chinese (Chen & Gong, 2025), and Saudi Arabian ESL students (Abduljawad, 2025). Similarly, Özdere (2025) reported that ChatGPT lifted the writing skills of English Language and Literature students.

Meanwhile, EnglishBot, built for Chinese college students, was shown by Ruan et al. (2021) lifting both fluency and interest. Other work has looked at Automated Writing Checking (AWE) systems like Pigai.org and Iwrite, helping users spot weak spots in their writing (Li et al., 2023). Also, tools such as Call Annie and Praktika have proven helpful for Vietnamese learners, especially for talk practice (Minh & Khanh, 2024). Plus, AI writing helpers built following MLA rules have been tied to lifts in writing matching learners' sense of ability and belief (Mills et al., 2025). Duong and Chen (2025) also noted that Vietnamese high school students use AI-powered helpers for word growing, idea making, and overall flow, though use changes with skill. Despite these gains, several challenges stay. Li et al. (2023) and Chen and Gong (2025) warn that students may lean too much on AI tools, hurting their growth of free writing skills. Munni and Rafique (2025) pointed out the risk lowering critical thinking, especially among Bangladeshi higher students. Moral worries also keep going; Alamri et al. (2025) found issues like source checking, moral problems, and less freshness in their SWOT study of ChatGPT. Similar worries are raised by

Arighi (2025) and Abduljawad (2025), stressing the need for creativity and careful content making. Access is another big issue. Kukulska-Hulme and Lee (2020) point out weak spots in task design, teaching ways, and chatbot screens in virtual spaces that can block fair access to AI tools. Li et al. (2023) explain that similar limits hit using AWE systems. Du et al. (2025) found that AI tools sometimes fall short for learners with autistic ways, showing a key need for more open design. Another thought is telling apart AI-made writing and human work. Zhang and Crosthwaite (2025) saw that ChatGPT-3.5 essays tend using more formal and technical words, whereas human writing often shows a more personal and mixed style, making judging harder.

METHODOLOGY

Participants

This study involved twenty-two students who were second language learners enrolled in a writing-focused course. They represented a diverse range of proficiency levels and academic backgrounds, with ages spanning from the late teens to early twenties. Gender distribution was balanced. All students volunteered to integrate a conversational AI tool into their regular writing assignments over several weeks, providing a window into real-world usage rather than a purely experimental setting.

Research Design

A qualitative research design guided by Grounded Theory principles was employed to explore the influence of a conversational AI teaching assistant on second language writing. To complement the qualitative insights, a sentiment analysis was also conducted, allowing for a two-pronged examination of participant responses:

> ***Qualitative Coding:*** Researchers performed open, axial, and selective coding to uncover themes and patterns in the data.

Sentiment Analysis: A computational model evaluated the emotional tone of the students' written feedback, offering measurable data about positive, negative, or neutral sentiments.

This used this double approach to explore both thematic insights and provide a clearer sense of how students felt about using AI in their writing process.

Data Collection

Students used the AI tool to seek feedback on key writing elements, such as idea generation, grammar, vocabulary, text organization, and overall structure throughout the course. Afterward, each participant answered six open-ended questions designed to probe their experiences. These questions addressed:

1. Development and organization of ideas
2. Influence of AI-provided feedback on writing revisions
3. Specific instances of improvement
4. Challenges or limitations in using the AI
5. Effects on confidence and motivation in L2 writing
6. Suggestions for enhancements or new features

Responses were collected via an online survey platform, ensuring consistent formatting. All identifying information was removed for confidentiality, aligning with best practices for ethical research.

Data Analysis

The data analysis took place with two steps. The steps included sentiment analysis and the grounded theory coding.

Phase 1: Sentiment Analysis

In the first phase, a sentiment analysis tool was applied to all responses (132 individual answers from 22 participants, across six questions). This generated sentiment scores ranging from strongly negative to strongly positive, painting an overall picture of the emotional tenor in students' feedback.

Phase 2: Grounded Theory Coding

Building on the sentiment results, researchers engaged in open coding, carefully examining responses line-by-line to identify emerging concepts, such as "idea generation," "feedback overload," and "confidence gain." These initial codes were grouped into broader categories (axial coding). For instance, comments around grammar corrections, sentence structure, and vocabulary expansion were unified under "technical writing improvement." This stage also highlighted key tensions, including balancing the AI's guidance without overwhelming users and maintaining personal style within standardized language norms.

Finally, selective coding identified a central theme: balancing supportive guidance with personal autonomy. To enhance reliability, two additional researchers independently reviewed a subset of the data, and any discrepancies were resolved through discussion until a consensus was reached.

Trustworthiness and Ethical Considerations

Triangulation was achieved by pairing sentiment analysis with qualitative coding, ensuring that thematic observations could be cross-validated with quantified emotional data. A brief follow-up survey allowed participants to confirm whether the emergent categories resonated with their lived experiences. Detailed audit trails documenting coding steps and thematic revisions also supported the credibility of the findings.

All procedures were cleared by the Institutional Review Board (IRB). Participants provided informed consent electronically and were assured of the voluntary nature of their involvement. Personal identifiers were removed prior to data analysis to maintain confidentiality.

Limitations

Although the sample of twenty-two students yielded rich qualitative insights, its size may limit generalizability. Moreover, while sentiment analysis contributed a valuable layer of quantitative insight, it may not fully detect subtler aspects of participant sentiment, such as irony or mixed feelings. Future studies can address these limitations by expanding participant numbers and refining sentiment analysis models for more precise interpretation

FINDINGS

Sentiment and Qualitative Analysis for the Question as "Did the Conversational AI Assist You in Developing and Organizing Your Ideas During the Writing Process? If So, How?"

Most statements, 21 out of 22, carry positive sentiment scores, generally ranging from 0.7 to 0.8, indicating that the vast majority of users found the AI helpful for brainstorming, providing structure, and offering ideas or questions that guided them through the writing process, with many highlighting its ability to help them start when stuck and organize their thoughts more coherently. Several users specifically noted that they often struggle with beginning their writing, but the AI provided first-sentence examples and questions to kickstart the process, while others appreciated how it offered a clear outline or plan to follow, aiding in organizing ideas before diving into writing, and some praised its probing questions that uncovered new angles or ideas they hadn't considered on their own. Only one statement reflects a slightly negative sentiment, scoring –0.3, from a user who found the AI's suggestions repetitive and preferred relying on their own brainstorming, suggesting that while it's a minority perspective, the AI's assistance may not suit everyone, particularly those who favor developing ideas independently.

Figure 1. Sentiment distributions for the question 1

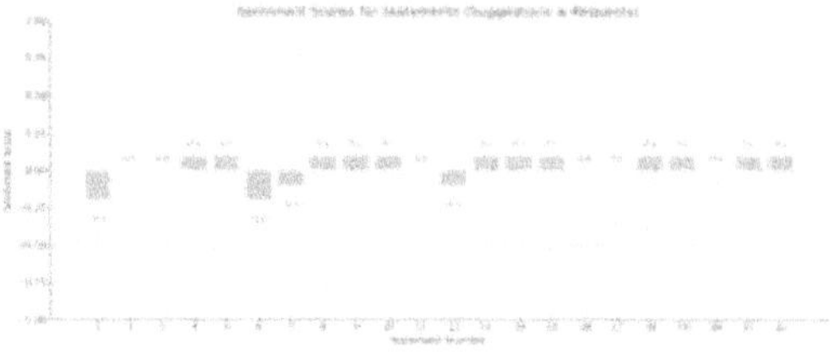

From the sentiment scores, it's evident that the AI was overwhelmingly perceived as beneficial for developing and organizing ideas. Most users appreciated the AI's ability to prompt them with questions, suggest starting points, and help create structured outlines, thus making the writing process smoother and more organized. The single negative response highlights that the experience can vary depending on personal preferences for creative autonomy.

Figure 2. Five categories for the question 1

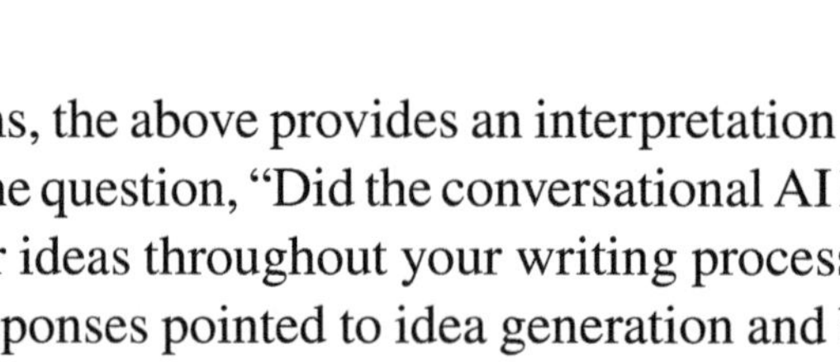

In general terms, the above provides an interpretation of the categories in the context of the question, "Did the conversational AI help you develop and organize your ideas throughout your writing process? If yes, in what way?" Several responses pointed to idea generation and brainstorming as a key benefit, noting that the AI sparked new ideas for users feeling stuck, acting as a creative stimulant by suggesting topics or perspectives they might not have explored independently, making it particularly effective as an initial brainstorming partner when starting feels daunting. Many responses also highlighted organization and structuring, indicating that the

AI helped transform scattered thoughts into a coherent framework, offering structured plans and mapping out the writing process, thus taming the chaotic early stages of an assignment and showing its role extends beyond inspiration to practical guidance in planning and text structuring. Starting guidance, particularly for introductions, was another frequent mention, with users appreciating how the AI provided examples or starting points to overcome the "blank page" problem, serving as a launchpad to ease initial writing anxiety. The aspect of question provocation stood out as well, with the interactive AI posing thought-provoking questions that not only sparked ideas but also encouraged self-reflection about the writing, fostering a dynamic creative process. However, while most feedback leaned positive, some negative criticism or feedback emerged, with a few users noting that the AI's suggestions could feel repetitively prescriptive, and a small group expressed a preference for generating ideas independently, suggesting the imposed structure didn't suit every writer's creative style or process. Overall, these categories reflect a spectrum of experiences where the conversational AI sparks creativity, provides structure, and addresses specific writing challenges for many, though it also reveals that while most find it helpful, some prefer less guided approaches.

Sentiment and Qualitative Analysis for the Question as "Did the AI's Feedback on Grammar, Vocabulary, and Text Organization Influence Your Writing Revisions? If Yes, in What Ways?"

The chart reveals that 21 out of 22 statements express a positive sentiment, with most scoring between 0.75 and 0.9, strongly suggesting that nearly all respondents found the AI's grammar, vocabulary, and structural feedback valuable for revising their work, with many statements pinpointing specific areas of improvement. Several users emphasized enhancements in grammar and syntax, noting that the AI identified unnoticed errors—such as verb tense mistakes, sentence structure problems, or lengthy, confusing sentences—and offered clear guidance to address them. Users frequently highlighted improvements in word choice and vocabulary, appreciating how the AI provided synonyms or alternative words to reduce repetition, resulting in more varied and engaging writing. Some respondents pointed to gains in clarity and organization, explaining that the AI flagged unclear or overly complex sentences, encouraging them to simplify or rearrange their ideas for greater effectiveness. However, there is a single statement, #13, with a negative sentiment score of –0.3, where the user simply "didn't find the feedback very helpful," marking it as an outlier that indicates AI feedback may not align with every writer's needs or preferences.

Figure 3. Sentiment results for the question 2

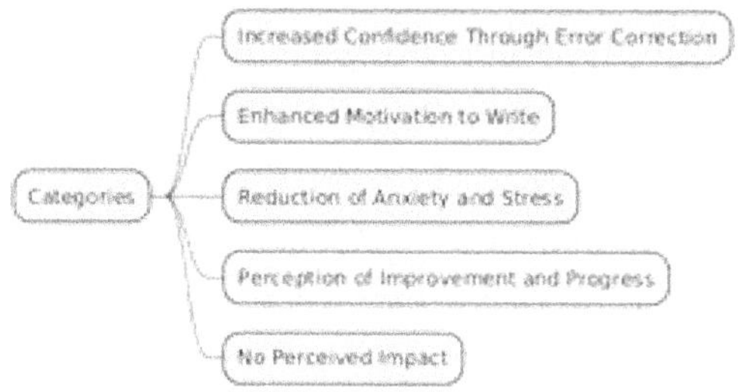

Based on the high proportion of positive sentiment, the vast majority of participants indicate that the AI's feedback directly influenced their writing revisions by enhancing grammar accuracy, expanding vocabulary, and improving text clarity and structure. The lone negative response underscores that such tools may not be equally beneficial to everyone, but for most respondents, the AI appears to have been an effective resource for refining their writing.

Figure 4. Core categories for the question 2

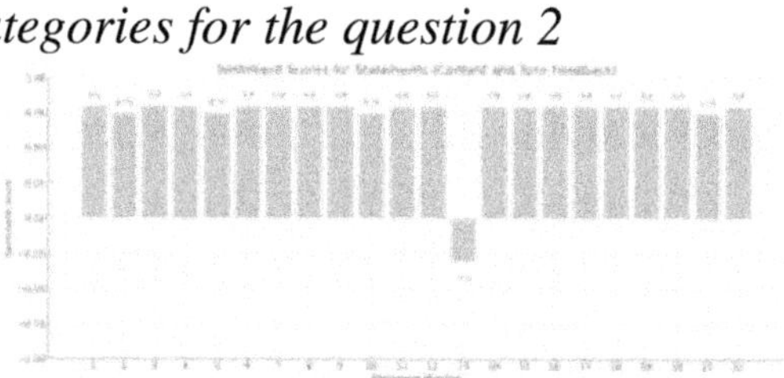

We provided a portrayal of the respective categories as they relate to the question, "Did the revision on writing take into consideration the artificial intelligence suggestions based on grammar, vocabulary, or the organization of text?" A strong consensus among respondents underscores grammar correction and detection of errors as a key benefit, with the vast majority affirming that the AI effectively identifies issues like verb tense errors, sentence structure problems, and overly long or unclear sentences, not only correcting specific mistakes but also helping users recognize recurring errors to enhance self-editing in future revisions. Users also valued vocabulary enrichment and suggestions for synonyms, appreciating how the AI went beyond mere error fixes to recommend better word choices and synonyms, fostering vocabulary growth, reducing repetition, and making writing more engaging—some even found this aspect crucial to their revision process. Another recurring theme was sentence organizing and text clarity, where participants noted that AI feedback improved their writing by simplifying sentences, offering natural phrasing, and advising on restructuring lengthy sentences or combining short ones, ultimately contributing to a more polished and coherent final draft. Beyond immediate fixes, self-correction and learning emerged as a benefit, with several respondents explaining that repeated AI suggestions heightened their awareness of writing weaknesses, encouraging habits of self-correction over time and fostering broader learning by prompting conscious efforts to avoid previously flagged errors. However, not all feedback was universally positive, as mixed or negative perceptions surfaced in a few responses, with some users finding the AI's unsolicited corrections generic or repetitive, suggesting a mismatch with certain writers' needs and indicating variability in how well the tool caters to its audience. In conclusion, the responses reveal that AI feedback influenced multiple facets of writing revisions—technical error correction, vocabulary enhancement, text clarity, and organization—while also serving as a learning tool for many by sharpening self-editing skills, though its effectiveness varied across users.

Sentiment and Qualitative Analysis for the Question as "Can You Describe a Specific Instance, If Any, Where the AI's Support Helped You Improve Your Writing?"

Nearly all statements, 21 out of 22, reflect positive sentiment scores, suggesting that the vast majority of users could identify a specific instance where the AI enhanced their writing. For instance, many statements under clarity and detail highlight how the AI pointed out sentences that were too long, too short, or lacking detail, and after users added or adjusted content based on this feedback, they achieved clearer and more engaging results. Several users noted tone adjustments as a key benefit, explaining that the AI identified inappropriate tones—either too casual or too formal—and offered targeted suggestions, enabling them to revise their writing to better suit the context, such as professional emails. Others focused on grammar and word choice, recalling instances where they overlooked a tense or overused certain words, and the AI's direct feedback allowed them to spot and fix these issues, resulting in immediate improvements. However, one statement, #13, carries a negative sentiment score of –0.3, with the user simply stating that they did not find the feedback very helpful, suggesting they did not experience a significant, positive instance of improvement.

Figure 5. Sentiment results for the question 3

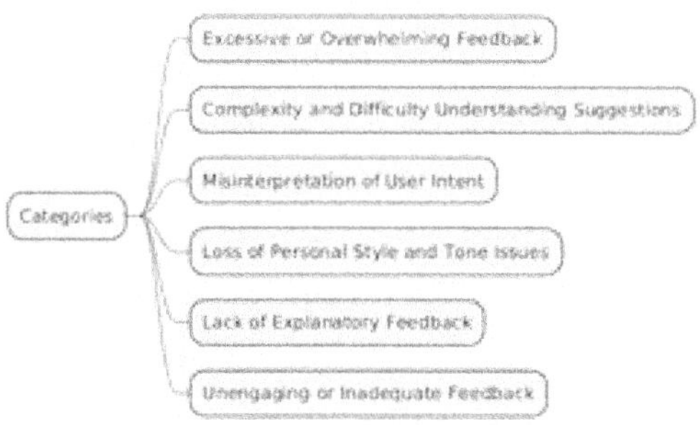

From the high proportion of positive responses, it's clear that most users could cite a specific situation—be it addressing unclear arguments, improving word choice, or refining tone—where the AI's support led to better writing outcomes. The single negative response suggests that experiences may vary, but the general sentiment is that the AI's targeted, instance-specific feedback often proved beneficial.

Figure 6. Core categories for the question 3

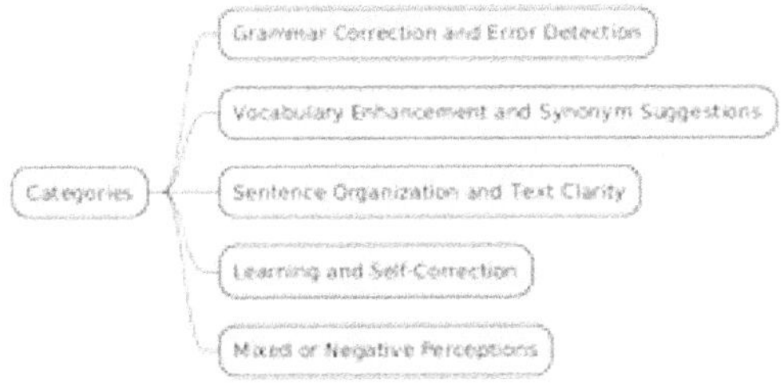

Below is a portrayal of the respective categories as they relate to question 3. In terms of clarity and flow, the AI offers valuable suggestions, such as breaking down overly long, complicated sentences or combining short ones to improve readability, while also recommending transition words to link ideas smoothly and fluidly. For grammar, it effectively identifies issues like incorrect tense and assists users in correcting them. Regarding content, the AI encourages users to expand their ideas, add annotations, and incorporate examples or dialogue to bring more liveliness to their writing. When it comes to arguments, it strengthens them by suggesting additional examples or evidence to bolster the user's points. For tone, the AI can adjust writing, such as making an email more formal, to suit the intended audience. However, there are disadvantages, as some users have reported that the AI fails to provide enough suggestions or doesn't align well with their personal writing style.

Sentiment and Qualitative Analysis for the Question as "4. Did You Encounter Any Challenges or Limitations While Using the AI as a Writing Assistant? If So, What Were They?"

All 22 statements reflect varying degrees of dissatisfaction or difficulty, with sentiment scores clustering between –0.2 and –0.7. This indicates that users frequently encountered challenges or limitations when using the AI. Even the mildest negative statement (#10 at –0.2) still notes that the AI is "too formal," though it also mentions it is "still good." Meanwhile, the strongest negative statement (#3 at –0.7) highlights overwhelming feedback and a lack of understanding from the AI.

Common Complaints

Many users expressed that the AI's feedback was overwhelming or confusing, often delivering too many corrections or suggestions simultaneously, which made it difficult for them to decide what to address first. Several users highlighted formality and tone issues, pointing out that the AI's suggestions frequently came across as too academic or formal, conflicting with the style or tone they aimed to achieve. Some statements indicated a vocabulary mismatch, with the AI recommending words that were too advanced or unfamiliar, requiring users to either look up meanings or ignore the suggestions entirely. Others felt a lack of personalization, noting that the AI failed to grasp their intended message or personal style, resulting in revisions that felt alien and no longer reflected their voice. Finally, some respondents remarked on insufficient explanations, observing that while the AI identified issues, it didn't consistently clarify why a change was necessary, leaving them uncertain about how to enhance their skills moving forward.

Figure 7. Sentiment scores for the question 4

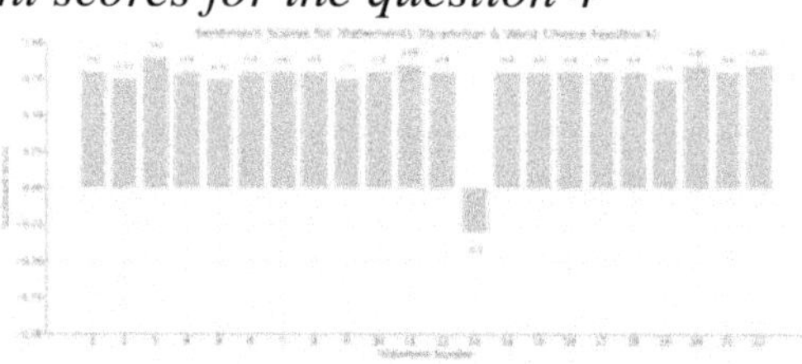

The predominantly negative scores confirm that these users frequently ran into challenges—most notably around overwhelming feedback, mismatched tone, unfamiliar vocabulary, and insufficient explanations. While some found the AI "still good" in parts, the overall sentiment indicates that many felt the AI's suggestions did not align well with their personal writing style or immediate learning needs.

Figure 8. Core categories for the question 4

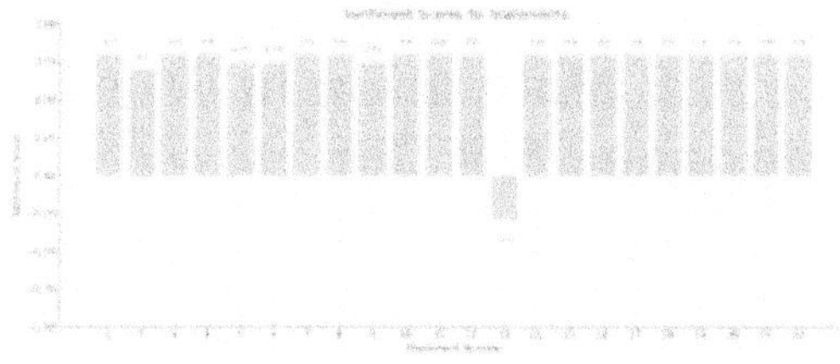

In interpreting categories related to question 4, several key themes emerge from user feedback about their experiences with AI assistance in writing. Most respondents highlighted excessive feedback as a significant issue, noting that the AI often provided overwhelming corrections and suggestions, leaving them confused about what to prioritize; this flood of information made it challenging to narrow down revisions effectively. Several participants pointed to complicated and difficult-to-understand suggestions, describing the AI's use of advanced English as too sophisticated, with tips featuring complex words and phrasing that required extensive effort to decipher, summing up the struggle with overly technical or elaborate feedback. A common observation was the misunderstanding of user intent, where users reported that the AI sometimes misinterpreted their sentences or offered suggestions misaligned with their intended meaning, leading to irrelevant or unhelpful corrections. A few respondents expressed concerns about the loss of personal style and problems with tone, noting that the AI's corrections often made their writing sound overly formal or generic, stripping away their unique voice and highlighting the tension between grammatical accuracy and individuality. Some users were disappointed by the lack of explanatory feedback, mentioning that while the AI flagged errors, it frequently failed to clarify why something was wrong or how to improve, thus limiting the learning potential of its input. Finally, a few responses described inadequate or uninspiring feedback, pointing out that the AI focused on minor mistakes without meaningfully contributing to their learning process, leaving them unconvinced of any significant improvement or new insights in their writing.

Sentiment and Qualitative Analysis for the Question as "5. Did Interacting With the AI Affect Your Confidence and Motivation in Writing in a Second Language? If It Did, How?"

All but one statement, which scored a neutral 0.0, reflect positive sentiments, with most falling in the 0.75–0.85 range, indicating that nearly every respondent experienced a noticeable boost in confidence and motivation when writing in a second language with AI support. Users frequently mention feeling "less nervous," "more comfortable," and "more motivated" to write once they realized the AI could catch and correct their mistakes. Specifically, many statements highlight immediate feedback as a key factor, noting that seeing and correcting errors in real time reduced anxiety and encouraged them to experiment with new words or structures. Respondents also emphasize learning from mistakes, explaining that the AI's corrections and explanations helped them recognize patterns in their second-language writing, gradually building their skills. Several statements point to a reduced fear of error, with users revealing that the previous dread of "writing wrong" had limited their practice, but the AI's role as a safety net gave them confidence to tackle longer or more complex texts. However, one person stated, "No, it didn't change," scoring a neutral 0.0, suggesting they felt no shift in confidence or motivation—though this was the sole non-positive response in the set.

Figure 9. Sentiment scores for the question 5

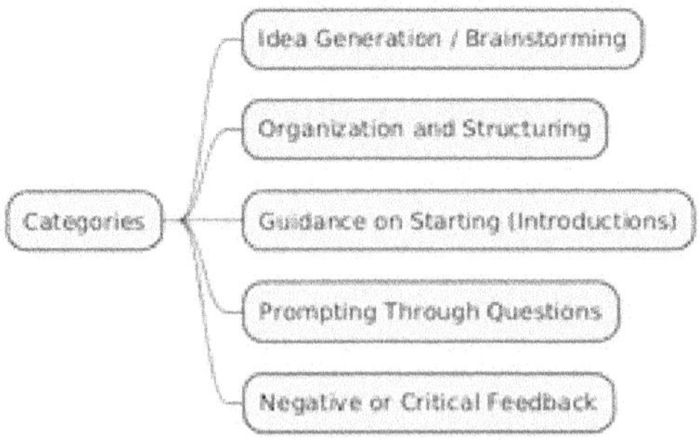

Based on these sentiment scores, most users found that AI feedback helped them gain confidence and motivation in their second-language writing. They felt more secure in trying new expressions, less worried about errors, and ultimately more engaged in the writing process. The single neutral viewpoint highlights that experiences can vary, but the overall trend is strongly positive.

Figure 10. Core categories for the question 5

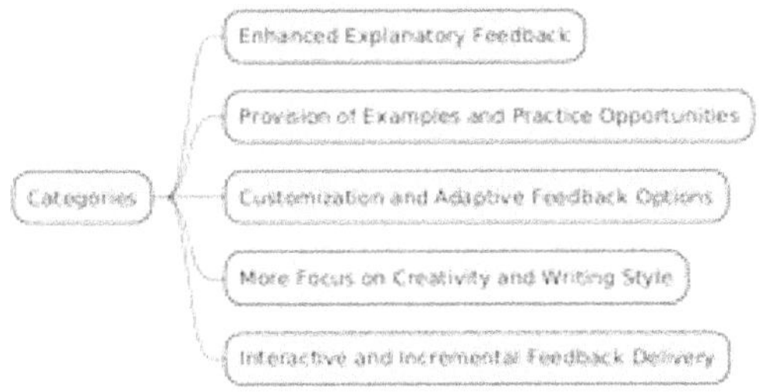

In interpreting areas related to the question, "Did the interaction with the AI affect confidence and motivation in writing in a second language? If yes, how?" several key insights emerge. The AI's ability to correct mistakes boosts confidence, as users feel reassured knowing errors will be caught, reducing their worry about making mistakes and encouraging them to write with greater assurance. Additionally, the AI's feedback serves as a motivator for writing, with its quick responses and visible progress spurring users to write more frequently, even if they might have hesitated otherwise. The interaction also alleviates discomfort and stress, transforming writing in a second language from a daunting task into a more enjoyable experience by easing fears and worries. Furthermore, people perceive improvement and progress in their skills as they observe the AI's corrections, with visible mistakes being addressed and fixed over time, reinforcing their confidence and enthusiasm as they recognize these step-ups in ability. However, some users report no effect, indicating that for them, the AI neither enhances confidence nor increases motivation for writing in a second language.

Sentiment and Qualitative Analysis for the Question as "6. Are There Any Improvements or Additional Features That Could Make the AI More Effective for Second Language Writing Support? If So, What Would You Suggest?"

While many statements from users are framed as requests for new features rather than outright complaints, the sentiment scores, which mostly range from –0.2 to +0.1, suggest that users see room for improvement without being deeply dissatisfied, offering constructive ideas to boost the AI's usefulness. A common request is for the AI to provide step-by-step or simpler explanations of corrections, rather than just pointing out errors, so users can grasp why their text is wrong and learn to avoid repeating mistakes. Many also propose a tiered feedback system—such as "basic corrections" versus "advanced suggestions"—allowing users to select the level of detail or difficulty that matches their skill level. Users frequently ask for examples and comparisons, like correct versus incorrect sentences or "real-world" usage, to better understand how to apply corrections or enhancements in context. Several statements reflect a desire for customization of tone, such as choosing between formal or informal writing modes or opting for simpler versus more advanced vocabulary, tailoring the AI's suggestions to individual goals and comfort levels. Finally, some users suggest receiving feedback in smaller, manageable chunks instead of a long list of corrections, enabling them to focus on one type of mistake at a time without feeling overwhelmed.

Figure 11. Sentiment scores for the question 6

Although the sentiment isn't strongly negative, these suggestions reveal that many learners of a second language want a more tailored and instructive approach. Explanations, examples, adjustable complexity, and tone customization are the main features they believe would make the AI significantly more helpful for their language-learning journey.

Figure 12. Core categories for the question 6

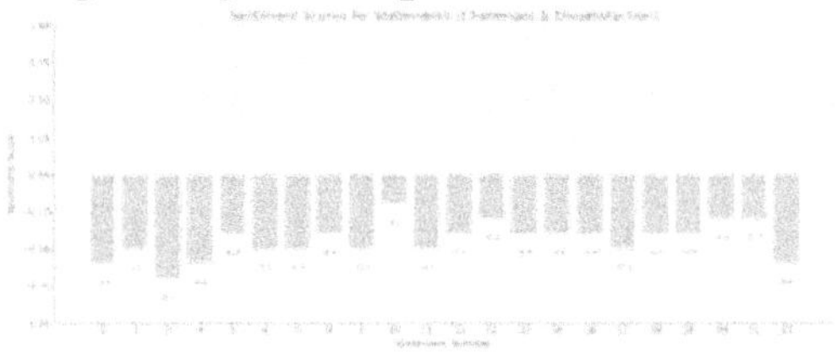

In response to a question about how to make AI better for writing in a second language, people shared several insightful ideas when asked, "Are there any improvements or new features that could help? If yes, what are they?" Here are some of their main suggestions. Many emphasized that AI should not only correct mistakes but also explain why those changes are necessary, highlighting the rules, grammar points, or reasons behind them so users can actively learn. Some users suggested that the AI should provide examples, showcasing both good and bad sentences, and include fun games or exercises for practice, offering engaging feedback to make learning enjoyable. People also expressed a desire to choose how the AI assists them, preferring options for simpler advice or more advanced guidance, starting with basic words and progressing to complex ones as their skills improve. Others noted that the AI should go beyond error correction to enhance the fun and creativity of their writing, offering tips for crafting interesting alternative sentences. Finally, some pointed out that receiving too much feedback at once can be overwhelming, suggesting instead that the AI deliver help gradually, incorporating playful elements like pretend conversations to ease the learning process.

Grounded Theory Approach the Data

Open Coding: Evolving Categories

From the first six questions, several general themes stood out. Pressing most of the users were issues revolving around idea generation and brainstorming, as the AI often provided prompts and first-sentence examples. Many of them hailed organization and structuring as the AI supplied outlines or helped plan paragraphs. Users also provided prominent testimony toward grammar and vocabulary feedback, especially when it came to corrections on syntax and word choice. Tone and formality were often associated wanting, as they should be effective factors in making language appropriate in different circumstances. There were mentions, too, about confidence and motivation being often raised, as most saw themselves more empowered and inspired-with-the assistance of the AI-to write the works. On the other hand, some respondents expressed either negative or critical viewpoints, claiming repetitiveness or high formality in their suggestions. Feeling overwhelmed or disoriented due to too many suggestions is also indicated in the users' feedback. Some others wanted more to be explained and customized, requesting stepwise rationale behind corrections and adaptable features for example, tone adjustment or graded levels of difficulty.

Axial Coding: Linking to Other Categories

It is interesting to look at the different categories and see how they interact; here, one can find the apparent tension between guidance and the potential for complications because while much of the feedback from users is positive-that they have many things to find out from the scaffold provided by this tool-others experience an overabundance of suggestions. The second major relationship identifiable directly between these concepts is confidence versus loss of personal style, in that AI corrections reassure some and encourage freer writing, while the others fear the loss of their unique tone as their writing might become homogenized in the process. Another connecting link applies to explaining compared to generic feedback, as those who have little explanation learn effectively from mistakes; those that do not learn perceive the feedback as just repetitive or superficial. Last, personalization and information returns by and large are common needs that users desire regarding customizing the AI and matching the corrections to their individual goals, skill levels, and writing conditions.

Selective Coding: The Focused Phenomenon

All these insights are condensed into one central idea: it determines AI users' experience and interaction with this tool regarding the writing process in a second language effectively, soberly balancing support with personal autonomy and meaningful explanation. When the feedback matches a learner's style, skill level, and creative objectives, this will lead to a fast improvement in grammar, structure, and, most importantly, confidence. But when feedback becomes "flabby," confusing, or overwhelming and imposes a style that feels foreign in use, it can inhibit students and dull the learning process.

The Emergent Theory

Indeed, the artificial intelligence input will mostly serve as dynamic cognitive scaffolding, providing an instructive and adaptable form of treatment from which second-language writers benefit most in the writing assistance learning of that second language.

DISCUSSION

It brings together the findings of the present research within the current evolving literature on conversational AI and its implications for second language (L2) writing. As with the previous research that shows how AI can foster such transformation in itself regarding education (Atif et al., 2021; Lin, 2022), participants in this study seem largely to report positive experiences with a conversation-based AI teaching assistant. They attributed the AI to generate their ideas, organize their thoughts, and refine their grammar and vocabulary. All these findings mirrored Tang (2025) and Chen and Gong (2025), wherein the writers emphasized that writing support through AI assistance can optimize language, increase motivation, and create a more liberating environment of learning.

One of the strongest points raised by the data is the place of the AI in alleviating the writing anxiety and boosting confidence, much like López-Minotta et al. (2025) view oral expression as significantly improved by AI conversations, and Ruan et al. (2021), who found that an AI chatbot encouraged greater engagement and fluency. The report in this study was that many respondents tended to take that to heart and feel comfortable taking the risks of trying out the language, which is quite similar to Love et al.'s (2025) interpretation that the conversational interface can enhance deeper learning by increasing students' propensity to take risks. Contextually, this confidence-building could inspire learners to go beyond perfunctory or minimal responses, to produce more authentic language.

However, there were a few limitations and complaints. A minority claimed that the AI sometimes overwhelms them with too much feedback - this phenomenon accords with Ji et al. (2022), who have their words stressing how too many comments at one time can confuse learners and make them less effective in their learning. Some critique users, saying the system fails to provide an explanation of why a certain error is wrong or how to improve over a basic fix. This mirrors calls for more educative feedback in the study of Ghafouri et al. (2024) and Duong and Chen (2025). Some of the respondents were also concerned that they might end up losing their own voice or their style as reflected in Zhang and Crosthwaite (2025), arguing that a most AI-generated text leans toward the formal or technical register, which may not necessarily reflect a student's authentic expression.

Those have shown the importance of developing AI tools with adaptive, context-sensitive models to support users. In the grounded theory analysis, personalization has emerged as a considerable user need, and future AI implementations might adopt systems that offer graded-feedback options, adjustable levels of formality, and explanations related to specific grammatical rules or stylistic conventions. This corresponds to the opinion of Li et al. (2023), who put forward stronger systems of Artificial Writing Evaluation integrating various modes of feedback. In the same vein, McAndrews and Martinez (2025) advocate for "ethical AI utilization" curricula that will include explicit instruction on understanding and interpreting AI feedback, rather than just blindly following it.

Pretty much everything about the study sets its findings in the ongoing evolving literature regarding conversational AI and its implications on writing in a second language (L2). As in the other studies that claim to highlight how AI could foster such transformation in itself concerning education (Atif et al., 2021; Lin, 2022), participants in this study seem largely to have widely positive experiences when using a conversational AI teaching assistant. They mentioned the AI to have been helpful in generating ideas, organizing thoughts, and refining grammar and vocabulary, something that mirrored Tang (2025) and Chen and Gong (2025), where the writers argued that writing support with the help of AI could be optimized regarding language, increased motivation, and creating an environment of learning that is much freer.

The strongest force in the data is how the AI alleviated writing anxiety and boosted confidence much like that of López-Minotta et al.'s (2025) discussion, wherein they claim that the oral expression of a person significantly improves when engaging in conversations led by AI and Ruan et al. (2021), who suggested that a higher engagement and fluency level is encouraged by an AI chatbot. In this study, many respondents claimed to be comfortable trying out the language, highly reflective of Love et al.'s (2025) notion that even more risk-taking and deeper learning were possible with a conversational interface. More broadly, this confidence-building could encourage students to go beyond even more formulaic or minimum responses to authentic language production.

Predominantly, most of the positive feelings turned sour to some limitations and grievance. Some of the subjects said that the AI at certain points would bombard them with feedback-most phenomenon consistent with Ji et al. (2022), who stress that too many comments at one time confuse learners and make them less effective in their learning. Some criticism by users spoke of denying an explanation by the system as to why it considered something as incorrect or how to improve without its somewhat simplistic fix, thus reiterating calls for more educative feedback in the study of Ghafouri et al. (2024) and Duong and Chen (2025). Furthermore, some respondents expressed fears about possibly losing their personal voice or style, which resonates with Zhang and Crosthwaite (2025), who argue that AI-generated text often skews toward formal or technical registers that may not reflect a student's authentic expression. .

All these difficulties highlight the need for AI tools that offer individualized, context-sensitive support. In the grounded theory analysis, personalization emerged as a central user need, suggesting that future AI could be more effective for end users by offering tiered feedback options, adjustable levels of formality, and explanations linked to specific grammatical rules or stylistic conventions. This is consistent with Li et al. (2023) who advocated stronger Artificial Writing Evaluation systems integrating various feedback modes. Along similar lines, McAndrews and Martinez (2025) argued for "ethical AI usage" curricula, which would also incorporate the direct teaching of how to read and apply AI feedback in a critical manner, rather than blindly adhering to it.

All part of the study sets its findings against the backdrop of the present emerging literature on conversational AI and its implications on writing in a second language (L2). As in other studies which claimed to stipulate how the AI could promote such transformation by itself toward education (Atif et al., 2021; Lin, 2022), participants in the study mostly reported a fair amount of positive experiences with a conversation-based AI teaching assistant. They counted the AI in helping generate their ideas, organize their thoughts, and improve their grammar and vocabulary - all of which findings mirrored Tang (2025) and Chen and Gong (2025), in which AI assisted writing support can optimize language, increase motivation, and create a freer environment of learning.

Perhaps the most dominant theme in the data is how the AI reduced writing anxiety and improved confidence, like López-Minotta et al.'s (2025) discussion that oral expression would significantly improve because of AI conversations, and Ruan et al. (2021), who found that an AI chatbot increased engagement and fluency. Many respondents then reported in this study that they found themselves being comfortable trying out the language, which is quite similar to Love et al.'s (2025) interpretation that the conversational interface can enhance deeper learning by increasing students' propensity to take risks. Such confidence may practically embolden learners to move from formulaic or minimal responses to much more genuine production in language.

CONCLUSION AND RECOMMENDATIONS

By and large were all the positive feelings turned sour to some limitations and grievance. Some of the subjects said that the AI at certain point would bombard them with feedback-the most phenomenon consistent with Ji et al. (2022), who stress that too many comments at one time confuse learners and make them less effective in their learning. Some criticism by users spoke of denying an explanation by the system as to why it considered something that an incorrect or how to improve without its somewhat simplistic fix, thus reiterating calls for more educative feedback in the study of Ghafouri et al. (2024) and Duong and Chen (2025). Furthermore, some respondents expressed fears about possibly losing their personal voice or style, which resonates with Zhang and Crosthwaite (2025), who argue that AI-generated text often skews toward formal or technical registers that may not reflect a student's authentic expression.

Such challenges point to the need for developing adaptive, context-sensitive models for AI tools that will support users. In the grounded theory analysis, personalization has emerged as a substantial user requirement, and future AI might benefit from systems where tier-level feedback options, adjustable levels of formality, and explanations related to certain grammatical rules or stylistic conventions are all available. This is comparable to Li et al. (2023), who put forward a recommendation for stronger Artificial Writing Evaluation systems integrating various modes of feedback. Along similar lines, McAndrews and Martinez (2025) argue for curricula on ethical AI use that includes explicit instructions on interpreting and applying AI feedback in a critical, rather than blind, manner.

REFERENCES

Abduljawad, S. (2025). Investigating the Impact of ChatGPT as an AI Tool on ESL Writing. *International Journal of Computer-Assisted Language Learning and Teaching, 14*(1), 1–19. DOI: 10.4018/ijcallt.367276

Alamri, W., Qasem, F., Alfotais, A., & Al Taisan, H. A. (2025). Leveraging ChatGPT AI Model in Academic Writing and Avenues for Further Development: SWOT Framework. *Forum for Linguistic Studies, 7*(2). Advance online publication. DOI: 10.30564/fls.v7i2.8218

Arighi, W. (2025). A conversation on AI, writing, and online learning with Sherri VandenAkker. *The Successful Registrar, 24*(12), 6–7. DOI: 10.1002/tsr.31407

Atif, A., Jha, M., Richards, D., & Bilgin, A. (2021). *Artificial Intelligence (AI)-enabled remote learning and teaching using Pedagogical Conversational Agents and Learning Analytics.* Intelligent Systems and Learning Data Analytics in Online Education., DOI: 10.1016/b978-0-12-823410-5.00013-9

Chen, C., & Gong, Y. (2025). The Role of AI-Assisted Learning in Academic Writing: A Mixed-Methods Study on Chinese as a Second Language Students. *Education Sciences, 15*(2), 141. DOI: 10.3390/educsci15020141

Du, Y., Wang, C., Zou, B., & Xia, Y. (2025). Personalizing AI tools for second language speaking: The role of gender and autistic traits. *Frontiers in Psychiatry, 15.* Advance online publication. DOI: 10.3389/fpsyt.2024.1464575 PMID: 39931194

Duong, T.-N.-A., & Chen, H. (2025). An AI Chatbot for EFL Writing: Students' Usage Tendencies, Writing Performance, and Perceptions. *Journal of Educational Computing Research.* Advance online publication. DOI: 10.1177/07356331241312363

Elkot, M. A., Youssif, E., & Elsheikh Hago Elmahdi, O., AbdAlgane, M., & Ali, R. (2024). Generative conversational AI: Active practices for fostering students with mild intellectual disabilities to improve English communication skills. *Contemporary Educational Technology*, *17*(1), ep549. DOI: 10.30935/cedtech/15688

Ganesh, S. V., Nayagam, M. G., Suresh, V., Rajakarunakaran, S., & Bensujin, B. (2025). Adaptive Learning Technologies: Navigating the Road from Hype to Reality. In Singh, A., & Singh, K. K. (Eds.), *Multimodal Generative AI*. Springer., DOI: 10.1007/978-981-96-2355-6_4

Ghafouri, M., Hassaskhah, J., & Mahdavi-Zafarghandi, A. (2024). From virtual assistant to writing mentor: Exploring the impact of a ChatGPT-based writing instruction protocol on EFL teachers' self-efficacy and learners' writing skill. *Language Teaching Research*. Advance online publication. DOI: 10.1177/13621688241239764

Gonda, D., & Chu, B. (2019). Chatbot as a learning resource? Creating conversational bots as a supplement for teaching assistant training course. *2019 IEEE International Conference on Engineering, Technology and Education (TALE)*, 1-5. https://doi.org/DOI: 10.1109/TALE48000.2019.9225974

Ji, H., Han, I., & Ko, Y. (2022). A systematic review of conversational AI in language education: Focusing on the collaboration with human teachers. *Journal of Research on Technology in Education*, *55*, 48–63. DOI: 10.1080/15391523.2022.2142873

Kukulska-Hulme, A., & Lee, H. (2020). Intelligent assistants in language learning: an analysis of features and limitations. *CALL for widening participation: short papers from EUROCALL 2020*. https://doi.org/.DOI: 10.14705/RPNET.2020.48.1184

Li, Q., Swanto, S., Said, N., & Din, W. (2023). Application Of Ai Writing Assistant Software In Efl Writing In China: A Review. *International Journal of Modern Education*. https://doi.org/.DOI: 10.35631/ijmoe.519023

Lin, H. (2022). Influences of Artificial Intelligence in Education on Teaching Effectiveness: The Mediating Effect of Teachers' Perceptions of Educational Technology. *International Journal of Emerging Technologies in Learning*, *17*, 144–156. DOI: 10.3991/ijet.v17i24.36037

Liu, B., Zhang, J., Lin, F., Jia, X., & Peng, M. (2025). One size doesn't fit all: A personalized conversational tutoring agent for mathematics instruction [Preprint]. arXiv. https://arxiv.org/abs/2503.02487

López-Minotta, K. L., Chiappe, A., & Mella-Noramabuena, J. (2025). Implementation of artificial intelligence to improve English oral expression. *REMIE: Multidisciplinary Journal of Educational Research, 15*(1), 43–71. DOI: 10.17583/remie.16188

Love, R., Law, E., & Cohen, P. R.. (2025). Teaching a conversational agent using natural language: Effect on learning and engagement. *International Journal of Artificial Intelligence in Education*. Advance online publication. DOI: 10.1007/s40593-025-00461-1

Madhuri, J. N., Fatma, G., Kumari, A. K., Pathak, P., Sreela, B., & Faizal, M. K. M. (2024). Creating an AI English tutor with personalized content and dynamic lessons [Paper presentation]. *2024 IEEE International Conference on Artificial Intelligence and Quantum Computation-Based Sensor Applications*, Nagpur, India.

Mananay, J. (2024). Integrating Artificial Intelligence (AI) in Language Teaching: Effectiveness, Challenges, and Strategies. *International Journal of Learning, Teaching and Educational Research*. https://doi.org/.DOI: 10.26803/ijlter.23.9.19

McAndrews, L., & Martinez, B. (2025). Friend or Fri-enemy: Teaching Approaches with AI chatbots like ChatGPT. https://doi.org/DOI: 10.31274/itaa.18685

Mills, N., Hok, H., Dressen, A., & Veillas, Q. (2025). The design and evaluation of an interactive AI companion for foreign language writing. *Foreign Language Annals*. Advance online publication. DOI: 10.1111/flan.12790

Minh, N., & Khanh, L. (2024). *Using Artificial Intelligence Tools for Developing Conversational Skills for English Majors*. European Modern Studies Journal., DOI: 10.59573/emsj.8(2).2024.40

Munni, B. E., & Rafique, R. (2025). Teachers' Experiences of Using AI-powered Technologies in Bangladeshi English Language Classrooms. *Spectrum (Lexington, Ky.)*, *18*, 89–100. DOI: 10.3329/spectrum.v18i1.76362

Naser, O. M. A., Faraj, H. A., & Elmbark, K. M. (2024). AI-Driven Conversational Interfaces: Advancements in Human-Machine Communication. *International Journal For Science Technology And Engineering*, *12*(12), 2161–2167. DOI: 10.22214/ijraset.2024.66167

Nguyen, T. H., & Hoang, T. N. H. G. (2025). Investigating the Promises and Perils of Generative AI in EFL Learning in Higher Education: A Literature Review. *AsiaCALL Online Journal*, *16*(1), 1–15. DOI: 10.54855/acoj.251611

Özdere, M. (2025). AI in Academic Writing: Assessing the Effectiveness, Grading Consistency, and Student Perspectives of ChatGPT and You.com for EFL Students. *International Journal of Technology in Education*, *8*(1), 123–154. DOI: 10.46328/ijte.1001

Ping, Q., Niu, F., Thattai, G., Chengottusseriyil, J., Gao, Q., Reganti, A., Rajagopal, P., Tur, G., Hakkani-Tür, D., & Nataraja, P. (2020). Interactive Teaching for Conversational AI. *ArXiv*, abs/2012.00958.

Ruan, S., Jiang, L., Xu, Q., Liu, Z., Davis, G., Brunskill, E., & Landay, J. (2021). EnglishBot: An AI-Powered Conversational System for Second Language Learning. *Proceedings of the 26th International Conference on Intelligent User Interfaces*. https://doi.org/DOI: 10.1145/3397481.3450648

Sakaue, J., & Yamanaka, T. (2025, March). Enhancing English proficiency through AI conversations: The impact of ChatGPT on TOEIC and Speechace performance in a project-based learning context. *English Language Teaching*, *18*(3), 1–70.

Salam, U. (2024). The Integration of ChatGPT in English for Foreign Language Course: Elevating AI Writing Assistant Acceptance. *Computers in The Schools*, •••, 1–21. DOI: 10.1080/07380569.2024.2446239

Sarfaraj, G. K., Adhvaryu, R., & Jha, A. K. (2025). A REVIEW ON INTELLIGENT TUTORING SYSTEMS: Enhancing Learning with Conversational AI. *Indian Scientific Journal Of Research In Engineering And Management*, *09*(01), 1–9. DOI: 10.55041/ijsrem40649

Tang, X. (2025). L2 Writing with AI: Perceptions and Engagement of EFL Learners in China. *English Language Teaching*, *18*(2), 68. DOI: 10.5539/elt.v18n2p68

Thakkar, A., Fentaw, A. A., & Hirpo, H. D. (2025). ChatGPT in Academia and Research: A Comprehensive Review of Integrating AI in Higher Education. In Singh, A., & Singh, K. K. (Eds.), *Multimodal Generative AI*. Springer., DOI: 10.1007/978-981-96-2355-6_10

Uwosomah, E. E., & Dooly, M. (2025). It Is Not the Huge Enemy: Preservice Teachers' Evolving Perspectives on AI. *Education Sciences*, *15*(2), 152. DOI: 10.3390/educsci15020152

Van Brummelen, J., Heng, T., & Tabunshchyk, V. (2020). Teaching Tech to Talk: K-12 Conversational Artificial Intelligence Literacy Curriculum and Development Tools., 15655-15663. https://doi.org/.DOI: 10.1609/aaai.v35i17.17844

Venter, I., Cranfield, D., Blignaut, R., Achi, S., & Tick, A. (2024). Conversational AI in Higher Education: Opportunities, Challenges, and Ethical Considerations. *2024 IEEE 28th International Conference on Intelligent Engineering Systems (INES)*, 000195-000202. https://doi.org/ DOI: 10.1109/INES63318.2024.10629104

Wang, Y., Wang, Y., Crace, K., & Zhang, Y. (2025). Understanding Attitudes and Trust of Generative AI Chatbots for Social Anxiety Support. https://doi.org/DOI: 10.1145/3706598.3714286

Xie, X. (2023). Influence of AI-driven Inquiry Teaching on Learning Outcomes. *International Journal of Emerging Technologies in Learning*, *18*, 59–70. DOI: 10.3991/ijet.v18i23.45473

Yoo, M., Jin, H., & Kim, J. (2025). *How do teachers create pedagogical chatbots?: Current practices and challenges* [Preprint]. arXiv. https://doi.org//arXiv.2503.00967DOI: 10.48550

Zhang, M., & Crosthwaite, P. (2025). More human than human? Differences in lexis and collocation within academic essays produced by ChatGPT-3.5 and human L2 writers. *International Review of Applied Linguistics in Language Teaching*. Advance online publication. DOI: 10.1515/iral-2024-0196

Zhao, X. (2022). Leveraging Artificial Intelligence (AI) Technology for English Writing: Introducing Wordtune as a Digital Writing Assistant for EFL Writers. *RELC Journal*, *54*, 890–894. DOI: 10.1177/00336882221094089

Chapter 7
Empowering Learners and Educators:
The Transformative Role of Conversational AI in Personalized Education and Student Support

M. Ruba
https://orcid.org/0000-0002-1614-7096
Velalar College of Engineering and Technology, India

G. Ashwin Prabhu
St. Joseph's College of Engineering, India

Jayashree Deka
Marathwada Mitra Mandal's Institute of Technology, India

D. Kavitha
Saveetha School of Engineering, India

S. Sathiya
https://orcid.org/0000-0002-0604-4667
Velalar College of Engineering and Technology, India

S. Pavithra
Velalar College of Engineering and Technology, India

ABSTRACT

In today's evolving educational landscape, conversational AI is emerging as a powerful ally for both learners and educators. This chapter explores how tools like chatbots, voice assistants, and virtual tutors are making

DOI: 10.4018/979-8-3373-3316-8.ch007

education more personalized, supportive, and accessible. By interacting in natural language, these AI systems offer real-time guidance, answer questions, and adapt to individual learning needs. For educators, they reduce workload by handling repetitive tasks and providing insights into student progress. The chapter also addresses important concerns around privacy, bias, and digital inclusion, and shares real-world examples of how conversational AI is creating more engaging and equitable learning environments.

1. INTRODUCTION

The rapid evolution of artificial intelligence (AI) has led to transformative changes in various sectors, with education being one of the most dynamically impacted. Among the AI-driven innovations, Conversational AI stands out for its potential to revolutionize teaching and learning processes. Conversational AI refers to technologies that enable machines to understand, process, and respond to human language in a natural, conversational manner. This includes voice assistants, chatbots, and intelligent tutoring systems powered by natural language processing (NLP), machine learning (ML), and dialogue management systems (Klopfenstein et al., 2017). In the context of 21st-century education, Conversational AI represents a powerful tool for reimagining personalized learning and student support. As educational institutions worldwide strive to make learning more inclusive, responsive, and adaptable, Conversational AI offers scalable, real-time, and intelligent interaction mechanisms (Holmes et al., 2019). These technologies can engage learners in meaningful dialogue, tailor learning experiences based on individual needs, and provide academic and emotional support on demand. The use of Conversational AI extends from virtual teaching assistants that answer questions and offer feedback to AI-driven mental health bots that support student well-being (Følstad & Brandtzaeg, 2017). Despite technological advancements and increasing digitization, educational systems continue to grapple with longstanding challenges. Personalized learning—an approach that tailors instruction to meet the unique needs, preferences, and pace of each learner—remains difficult to implement effectively at scale. Teachers often lack the resources or time to provide individualized attention, especially in large classrooms or online settings (Pane et al., 2017). Similarly, institutions struggle to provide consistent, around-the-clock student support, including academic advising, administrative assistance, and mental health resources. These challenges have been further amplified by the shift to hybrid and online learning environments. Students are now navigating complex learning pathways with minimal direct interaction with instructors. As a result, issues such as learner disengagement, lack of motivation, and academic isolation are on the rise (Means et al., 2014). Additionally, with an increasing emphasis on learner autonomy and competency-based education, there is a growing demand for tools that can guide, motivate, and support students outside the traditional classroom setting (Santhini et al., 2025).

Conversational AI has emerged as a promising solution to bridge these gaps. By simulating human-like conversations and providing context-aware, adaptive responses, AI-powered agents can offer personalized guidance, deliver targeted feedback, and assist learners in real-time (Winkler & Söllner, 2018). These systems can be integrated into learning management systems (LMS), mobile apps, or institutional portals to provide seamless and accessible support. For educators, Conversational AI can automate routine tasks, offer analytics on student performance, and act as co-facilitators in the learning process. The objectives of this chapter are threefold. First, it aims to explore the foundational concepts and technologies that underpin Conversational AI in the educational context. This includes an examination of natural language processing, speech recognition, sentiment analysis, and adaptive learning systems. Second, the chapter investigates the practical applications of Conversational AI in personalized education and student support services. Through real-world examples and case studies, it highlights how institutions are leveraging AI to enhance learning outcomes, streamline student services, and foster engagement. Third, the chapter critically analyzes the benefits, challenges, and ethical considerations surrounding the adoption of Conversational AI in education, offering insights into its future directions and policy implications. To guide readers through this comprehensive exploration, the chapter is structured as follows:

- Background and Theoretical Foundations delves into the pedagogical and technological theories that inform the design and deployment of Conversational AI in education. It provides a historical overview and discusses relevant learning theories, including constructivism, personalized learning, and dialogic learning.
- Conversational AI Technologies in Education presents an in-depth analysis of the core components of Conversational AI, such as natural language processing (NLP), automatic speech recognition (ASR), and dialogue management systems. It also reviews popular tools and platforms used in educational settings.
- Applications in Personalized Learning examines how Conversational AI supports individualized learning experiences. This includes intelligent tutoring systems, adaptive feedback mechanisms, and AI-driven content delivery tailored to learners' profiles.
- Student Support Services focuses on the non-instructional use of Conversational AI, including academic advising, career counseling, mental health support, and administrative assistance. It highlights case studies from institutions that have successfully implemented these tools.
- Benefits and Challenges offers a balanced view of the advantages and limitations of using Conversational AI in education. It addresses technical, ethical, and operational issues such as data privacy, algorithmic bias, and implementation costs.
- Future Directions and Opportunities explores emerging trends and potential innovations, such as emotion-aware AI, multilingual conversational agents, and integration with immersive technologies like AR/VR.
- Conclusion summarizes the key insights from the chapter and offers strategic recommendations for educators, policymakers, and developers to harness the full potential of Conversational AI in a responsible and student-centric manner.

Through this structure, the chapter provides a holistic understanding of how Conversational AI is transforming educational experiences for learners and educators alike. It invites stakeholders to reflect on the evolving role of AI in shaping the future of learning and to consider practical, ethical, and pedagogical strategies for its effective integration.

2. BACKGROUND AND THEORETICAL FOUNDATIONS

The foundation of any effective educational innovation lies in its theoretical underpinnings. Conversational AI, when applied in education, does not exist in a vacuum—it builds on established learning theories and advances in educational technology. Understanding these foundations helps us evaluate the pedagogical soundness and potential of AI-driven solutions. One of the key theories relevant to personalized education is constructivism, which posits that learners actively construct knowledge through experience and reflection (Piaget, 1971; Vygotsky, 1978). Constructivist approaches emphasize student-centered learning, interactive dialogue, and the scaffolding of knowledge—all principles that align well with the functioning of conversational agents. For example, an AI chatbot that prompts learners with reflective questions or adapts explanations based on the student's responses acts as a constructivist facilitator.

Personalized learning, another pivotal theory, focuses on tailoring instruction to meet the unique needs, abilities, and learning paces of individual students. This is supported by frameworks such as Universal Design for Learning (UDL) and differentiated instruction, which advocate for flexible learning environments that accommodate diverse learners (CAST, 2018). Conversational AI can operationalize personalized learning by using student data to recommend content, adjust difficulty levels, and provide individualized feedback. Another important domain is learning analytics, which involves the collection and analysis of data about learners and their contexts to improve learning outcomes. Learning analytics informs adaptive learning systems, enabling conversational agents to make data-driven decisions about when to intervene, what feedback to provide, and how to guide learners (Siemens & Long, 2011). In essence, conversational AI powered by analytics can act like a dynamic tutor that evolves with the learner. Dialogic learning, derived from the sociocultural theory of learning, is also relevant. It emphasizes learning as a result of structured dialogue and collaborative interaction (Alexander, 2008).

Conversational AI enables this kind of dialogue—albeit with a machine—through its ability to engage in natural language exchanges. While it lacks the nuance of human conversation, it can still model the dialogic process through Socratic questioning, clarification prompts, and collaborative problem-solving scenarios.

Artificial Intelligence in education (AIED) has roots in the development of Intelligent Tutoring Systems (ITS) during the 1980s and 1990s. ITS aimed to replicate the instructional processes of human tutors by providing step-by-step guidance and assessing learner responses. Early systems like SCHOLAR and GUIDON used rule-based reasoning to support medical and geographic education (Sleeman & Brown, 1982). Although effective in narrow domains, they were limited by rigid architectures and high development costs. With the rise of Natural Language Processing (NLP) and machine learning, modern conversational agents are far more flexible. Voice assistants like Apple's Siri (introduced in 2011), Amazon Alexa (2014), and Google Assistant (2016) brought conversational AI into mainstream use. These assistants understand and process user input, respond with relevant information, and learn from usage patterns. Their architectures have since inspired educational variants that support learning. Educational chatbots, such as Georgia Tech's Jill Watson, were among the early implementations in academia. Jill Watson was trained to act as a virtual teaching assistant by answering routine questions on a course discussion forum (Goel & Polepeddi, 2016). This demonstrated how conversational agents could reduce instructors' workload and enhance student engagement. Since then, AI tutors like Duolingo's chatbot (for language practice) and Carnegie Learning's MATHia (for math instruction) have expanded the scope of AI in education.

Moreover, chatbots have moved beyond cognitive support to address emotional and social dimensions of learning. For instance, mental health chatbots like Woebot and Wysa utilize conversational frameworks to provide psychological support, aligning with the affective domain of Bloom's Taxonomy. These bots draw upon cognitive-behavioral techniques and sentiment analysis to engage students in reflective, emotionally aware conversations (Fitzpatrick et al., 2017). In conclusion, the integration of conversational AI in education is deeply intertwined with existing pedagogical theories and advancements in educational technology. By building on principles of constructivism, personalized learning, learning analytics, and dialogic learning, these systems strive to replicate and enhance key aspects of human teaching. At the same time, they mark a significant evolution in the history of AI applications in education—from the static ITS of the past to the dynamic, context-aware conversational agents of today.

3. CONVERSATIONAL AI TECHNOLOGIES IN EDUCATION

Conversational AI integrates advanced computational techniques to mimic human-like dialogue, providing natural language-based interaction between machines and users. The deployment of Conversational AI in education relies on multiple underlying technologies, each playing a distinct role in enabling intelligent, responsive, and personalized learning experiences. Natural Language Processing (NLP) is the backbone of conversational systems. NLP enables machines to understand and generate human language, allowing them to interact with learners through both text and speech. Educational chatbots use NLP to analyze student queries, extract intent, and provide meaningful, context-aware responses (Jurafsky & Martin, 2023). Techniques such as part-of-speech tagging, named entity recognition, and sentiment analysis allow AI agents to comprehend language intricacies and adapt communication accordingly. Speech recognition and synthesis technologies complement NLP by facilitating spoken conversations. Automatic Speech Recognition (ASR) converts verbal input into machine-readable text, enabling hands-free interaction, especially useful in accessibility-focused and language learning environments. Text-to-Speech (TTS) systems then vocalize the AI's responses, creating a full-duplex spoken dialogue experience. Platforms like Google Speech-to-Text and Amazon Polly are widely used for such applications.

Dialogue management systems orchestrate the flow of conversation. These systems determine how the AI responds based on prior dialogue context, user intent, and available knowledge. Dialogue managers can be rule-based or data-driven, with the latter leveraging machine learning and reinforcement learning to improve over time (Serban et al., 2018). This adaptability enhances the system's responsiveness and relevance.

Sentiment analysis, another key component, involves detecting users' emotional states through linguistic cues. This helps the system tailor responses to student moods—offering encouragement during stress or modifying content delivery during confusion. Emotion-aware AI is particularly valuable in maintaining student motivation and providing empathetic support (Winkler & Söllner, 2018). Numerous platforms have emerged to support the development of Conversational AI systems tailored to educational use. OpenAI's ChatGPT, for instance, leverages the GPT architecture to enable highly contextual, free-form interactions. Educators have used ChatGPT for content generation, doubt clarification, and essay feedback. Similarly, Google Dialogflow provides an NLP engine with a graphical interface for building domain-specific chatbots. Alexa for Education enables voice-interactive learning, and IBM Watson Assistant supports enterprise-grade educational bots with data analytics integration. Each platform varies in complexity, integration support, and target use cases. For example, ChatGPT's conversational fluidity makes it ideal for open-ended discussions, while Dialogflow's intent-based design suits FAQ-style systems. Alexa's voice-first approach fits scenarios like language practice or auditory learning support. These platforms often provide APIs that allow seamless integration with Learning Management Systems (LMS), mobile apps, or institutional portals.

The architecture of a typical educational chatbot includes several layers: user input, natural language understanding (NLU), dialogue management, natural language generation (NLG), and output delivery (text or speech). User interactions trigger the NLU module, which identifies intent and entities. The dialogue manager decides the system's next action based on stored state and user history. The NLG module constructs a natural language response, which is then delivered through a user interface. This modular architecture ensures scalability, reusability, and extensibility across different subjects and educational levels (Adamopoulou & Moussiades, 2020). Educational use cases of Conversational AI are diverse and expanding. In K-12 education, AI tutors can supplement teacher efforts by providing personalized learning paths, helping students practice concepts, and clarifying doubts. Duolingo's chatbot engages users in language learning through scenario-based conversation practice. In higher education, systems like Jill Watson—developed at Georgia Tech using IBM Watson—serve as virtual teaching assistants in online forums, answering routine student queries and enhancing course participation (Goel & Polepeddi, 2016). Further applications include academic advising bots that guide students in course selection, mental health bots that offer emotional support, and administrative bots that help with enrollment, scheduling, and FAQs. Platforms such as Coursera, edX, and Moodle are increasingly integrating conversational layers to facilitate interactive learning. For example, chatbots embedded in MOOCs help learners navigate course modules and reinforce learning with adaptive quizzes.

Conversational AI can also support formative assessment. Systems can quiz students, offer feedback, and analyze performance trends. Some AI tools use reinforcement learning to optimize question sequencing based on learner proficiency. This fosters a mastery-based learning environment where students receive continuous, personalized evaluation. Challenges do remain, especially in ensuring inclusivity, minimizing algorithmic bias, and safeguarding data privacy. While conversational systems are evolving, human oversight remains essential to maintain pedagogical soundness and ethical integrity. In conclusion, the integration of Conversational AI technologies—spanning NLP, ASR, sentiment analysis, and dialogue systems—has revolutionized how educators and learners interact. Through accessible platforms and modular architectures, conversational agents can deliver scalable, adaptive, and engaging educational experiences. As these technologies mature, they promise to complement traditional pedagogies and foster more inclusive and responsive learning environments.

4. APPLICATIONS OF CONVERSATIONAL AI IN PERSONALIZED LEARNING

Conversational AI is redefining how personalized learning can be scaled and adapted to diverse learners across educational levels. It facilitates real-time interaction, adjusts instruction based on learner behavior, and supports individual learning styles through intelligent feedback and support mechanisms. The integration of conversational agents into learning environments makes the promise of truly personalized education more feasible and effective. One of the core applications of Conversational AI is in the development of Intelligent Tutoring Systems (ITS). These systems provide tailored instruction and support to learners, simulating the guidance offered by human tutors. ITS use learner modeling to track knowledge levels, learning speed, and cognitive gaps. Based on this data, conversational agents deliver customized content, provide targeted feedback, and offer hints or re-explanations when students struggle (VanLehn, 2011).

Adaptive feedback is a crucial feature enabled by Conversational AI. Unlike static e-learning modules, conversational agents can adapt their responses based on learner interactions. For example, when a student answers a question incorrectly, the chatbot can offer progressively detailed hints or explanations, scaffold learning, and recommend additional resources. This personalized guidance helps reinforce conceptual understanding and promotes a mastery-based learning approach (Roll & Wylie, 2016). Conversational AI also supports differentiated learning styles. Visual learners might benefit from agents that can provide diagrams or link to videos, while auditory learners can interact through voice-based AI systems. Kinesthetic learners, who prefer hands-on interaction, can benefit from project-based tasks and chatbot-mediated simulations. AI systems can be designed to detect and adapt to these preferences, thus making learning more inclusive (Fleming & Mills, 1992). Real-time doubt clarification is another transformative aspect of conversational agents. In traditional settings, students often hesitate to ask questions or wait long for instructor responses. AI-powered tutors eliminate these barriers by offering instant, round-the-clock support. Tools like Khan Academy's AI assistant and Coursera's discussion bots enable learners to receive immediate explanations, facilitating uninterrupted learning experiences (Yang et al., 2022).

Case studies in K-12 education reveal the positive impact of Conversational AI. For example, the use of AI chatbots in Singapore schools has improved English language acquisition by enabling daily practice through personalized dialogues. Students converse with bots in real-world scenarios, improving vocabulary retention and communication skills (Chow et al., 2017). Similarly, Duolingo's language learning chatbot engages learners in conversational practice, adjusting sentence complexity and vocabulary based on user proficiency (Settles & Meeder, 2016). In higher education, Jill Watson, the AI-powered teaching assistant developed by Georgia Tech, has demonstrated the scalability of conversational agents.

Used in a large online course, Jill answered student queries in discussion forums, reducing instructor load and improving response time without compromising quality. Students often did not realize that Jill was an AI, indicating the system's effectiveness in mimicking human interaction (Goel & Polepeddi, 2016). Massive Open Online Courses (MOOCs) have also embraced Conversational AI. Platforms like edX and FutureLearn integrate AI chatbots to help learners navigate course modules, explain key concepts, and suggest further reading. These agents act as learning companions, guiding students through complex course structures and promoting self-regulated learning (Zawacki-Richter et al., 2019).

Conversational AI can further support learning analytics and formative assessment. AI tools can track user interactions, identify misconceptions, and adjust instructional sequences accordingly. For example, Carnegie Learning's MATHia uses AI to adapt math instruction in real-time, based on learner input and performance trends. This data-driven personalization ensures that students receive targeted support precisely when they need it (Pane et al., 2017). In addition to cognitive support, conversational agents can promote motivation and engagement. Gamified AI tutors offer badges, praise, and milestones to keep learners motivated. Emotional awareness, integrated through sentiment analysis, allows AI systems to detect learner frustration or disengagement and respond empathetically. Bots like Replika and Woebot, although designed for mental health, showcase how conversational AI can foster emotional connection and support (Følstad & Brandtzæg, 2017). Despite these advancements, there are notable challenges. Bias in training data may limit the inclusivity of AI responses. For example, an English-language chatbot may not fully support multilingual learners. Moreover, over-reliance on automation might hinder the development of human communication skills. Therefore, hybrid models, where AI supports but does not replace human instructors, are emerging as best practice (Luckin et al., 2016). In conclusion, Conversational AI is a transformative force in personalized education. By enabling real-time interaction, adaptive instruction, and learner-centric design, it enhances educational access and effectiveness. With thoughtful implementation and ethical design, conversational agents can democratize education and empower both learners and educators.

5. CONVERSATIONAL AI IN STUDENT SUPPORT SERVICES

Conversational AI is increasingly playing a critical role in student support services, extending beyond instructional applications to address the holistic needs of learners. In higher education and beyond, support services such as academic advising, mental health support, enrollment assistance, and career counseling have traditionally been human-intensive, requiring significant time and staffing. Conversational AI technologies are transforming these areas by offering scalable, accessible, and often more immediate forms of support. One major area of application is academic advising. Institutions have started integrating AI-powered chatbots to answer frequently asked questions regarding course selections, degree requirements, registration deadlines, and examination schedules. For instance, the University of Murcia in Spain developed a chatbot called Lola, which assists students in understanding the academic calendar, finding the right courses, and navigating university procedures. Lola handles thousands of queries per semester, significantly reducing the workload of human advisors (Rodríguez-González et al., 2020).

Mental health support is another vital domain where Conversational AI shows great promise. Mental well-being is increasingly recognized as a determinant of academic success, and AI-powered mental health bots like Woebot and Wysa have demonstrated potential in offering cognitive-behavioral therapy (CBT) techniques through conversations. These bots provide students with a confidential, non-judgmental platform for expressing concerns and managing stress, especially when human counselors are unavailable. Studies show that these AI systems can reduce anxiety and depressive symptoms in college students, while maintaining high user satisfaction (Fitzpatrick et al., 2017). Enrollment and administrative support are also being streamlined through Conversational AI. Many universities deploy chatbots to manage inquiries during the admissions season. These bots guide prospective students through the application process, document submission, tuition payment, and scholarship eligibility. For example, Georgia State University introduced a chatbot named Pounce, which successfully reduced summer melt by over 20% by engaging admitted students and addressing their logistical concerns before enrollment (Page

& Gehlbach, 2017). Career counseling, another essential support function, is increasingly being augmented by AI tools. Conversational agents like JobPal and Mya Systems assist students in resume building, job matching, and interview preparation. These bots use NLP algorithms to parse user input and provide tailored suggestions. They also help students explore career pathways by simulating informational interviews and providing curated job market insights (Thompson, 2020).

Universities are also leveraging Conversational AI to enhance 24/7 helpdesk capabilities. Traditional support centers are limited by office hours, but AI-powered systems offer round-the-clock assistance. For instance, Ivy.ai, an AI chatbot platform, is deployed across several U.S. institutions to handle common student queries on financial aid, housing, and IT support. These bots improve response times, reduce wait periods, and enhance student satisfaction (Zhou et al., 2020). Another noteworthy implementation is Jill Watson, the AI teaching assistant at Georgia Tech, which not only supports learning but also answers logistical and procedural questions in online forums. This hybrid functionality blurs the lines between instructional and support roles, demonstrating how conversational agents can provide holistic academic assistance (Goel & Polepeddi, 2016).

Conversational AI has revolutionized how educational institutions interact with students. By mimicking human conversation through chatbots, voice assistants, and virtual agents, these systems can offer personalized, real-time support that enhances access to academic and student services. While the benefits of Conversational AI are significant across all student demographics, its role is particularly transformative for marginalized and at-risk populations who often face systemic, cultural, or logistical barriers to full participation in higher education. These student populations include, but are not limited to, first-generation college students, international students, low-income learners, individuals from racial and ethnic minority backgrounds, and those with disabilities. Marginalized and at-risk students commonly experience difficulties that more privileged students may not encounter. For example, first-generation college students may lack familiarity with higher education terminology, procedures, and expectations, placing them at a disadvantage from the outset. These students might not have the same level of familial guidance or institutional familiarity as their peers. Similarly, international students often confront linguistic challenges, cultural adjustment issues, and a lack of social support networks. Navigating academic requirements, visa regulations, and cultural norms can be overwhelming, especially in a new and unfamiliar environment. In such contexts, Conversational AI can serve as a vital intermediary between students and the institution. AI agents equipped with multilingual capabilities and culturally sensitive programming can provide guidance on enrollment procedures, campus policies, academic advising, and social integration. These systems are not just tools for information dissemination but also play a central role in fostering inclusivity and reducing the psychological burden of navigating institutional systems alone. For instance, they can offer language-specific orientation resources, connect students to culturally aligned peer mentors, and help schedule appointments with advisors or counselors in a timely and accessible manner.

One of the most compelling advantages of Conversational AI is its ability to operate 24/7, offering support regardless of time zones or institutional working hours. This is particularly beneficial for students who may be balancing education with work or family obligations and cannot access traditional support services during regular office hours. For international students living in different time zones or first-year students navigating the university landscape after hours, having a virtual assistant that can answer questions, offer reminders, and suggest next steps can significantly reduce stress and enhance the overall student experience. Moreover, these AI agents can be programmed to recognize contextual nuances and respond empathetically. For example, students who express anxiety about upcoming exams or confusion about financial aid deadlines can receive not only factual information but also reassurance and encouragement, helping to foster a sense of emotional support. While AI cannot replace human empathy, the simulation of empathetic responses can be effective in providing a first layer of comfort and reducing students' sense of isolation. This aspect of Conversational AI is particularly useful during transitional periods such as the first semester or during crises like the COVID-19 pandemic, where student anxiety levels are typically high and access to human advisors may be limited. Despite the many benefits, the deployment of Conversational AI in student support roles presents a number of significant ethical and practical challenges. One major concern is the issue of data privacy and confidentiality. As AI agents collect and process sensitive personal data, including academic records, mental health concerns, and behavioral indicators, ensuring the security of this information becomes paramount. Any breach in data security could lead to reputational damage for the institution and potentially harm the affected students.

To mitigate such risks, institutions must adhere to strict legal and ethical guidelines such as the Family Educational Rights and Privacy Act (FERPA) in the United States and the General Data Protection Regulation (GDPR) in Europe. These regulations mandate how student data can be collected, stored, and shared, and any violation can result in severe penalties. It is therefore critical that AI systems used in educational environments are designed with privacy-by-design principles and include robust encryption, anonymization, and access control mechanisms. An equally pressing concern relates to the limitations of AI in addressing emotional and psychological issues. While conversational agents can provide general advice and resources related to mental health, they lack the emotional intelligence and clinical training necessary to handle complex psychological concerns. For example, if a student expresses suicidal thoughts, an AI agent might fail to interpret the urgency of the situation or offer an inappropriate response. In such cases, the absence of human judgment can have serious consequences. To address this, institutions must incorporate escalation protocols that automatically transfer high-risk interactions to qualified human counselors. These protocols can be designed to detect specific keywords or emotional cues and route the conversation to a live support team. Additionally, AI agents should always include disclaimers and options for contacting human help when sensitive topics are being discussed. While AI can be a powerful tool for triage and support, it should never be seen as a replacement for professional mental health services.

Another limitation of Conversational AI lies in the potential for algorithmic bias. If AI systems are trained on datasets that lack cultural or linguistic diversity, they may fail to understand the needs and preferences of students from underrepresented backgrounds. For example, students who use regional dialects or non-standard English may receive less accurate or helpful responses. Similarly, culturally specific issues or concerns might be misunderstood or dismissed by an AI trained on predominantly Western norms and behaviors. This issue points to the necessity of inclusive AI design. Institutions and developers must make a concerted effort to ensure that training datasets are representative of the diverse student populations they serve. This may involve collecting input from students of different cultural, linguistic, and socioeconomic backgrounds during the design and testing phases of the AI system. Regular audits and evaluations of the AI's performance should be conducted to identify and correct biases that may emerge over time. Additionally, the overuse or over-reliance on AI in student support systems may inadvertently erode the human touch that is often critical in education. Relationships with advisors, mentors, and peers play a crucial role in student development, especially for those facing emotional, academic, or social challenges. If institutions begin to replace too many human roles with AI, they risk diminishing the relational aspects of education that foster empathy, trust, and personal growth.

To counteract this, many educational institutions are adopting hybrid models that combine the efficiency of AI with the emotional intelligence of human staff. In these models, Conversational AI handles repetitive, time-consuming tasks such as appointment scheduling, form submissions, and frequently asked questions. This allows human advisors and counselors to focus on more complex, sensitive, and high-stakes interactions that require emotional insight and nuanced understanding. By delegating routine functions to AI, institutions can free up human resources for activities that truly require human judgment, thereby improving both the efficiency and quality of student support services. Moreover, insights gained from AI interactions can inform institutional decision-making. For example, trends in student questions or complaints can highlight systemic issues in the academic process, such as unclear registration procedures or inadequate mental health resources. By analyzing these interactions, institutions can make data-driven decisions to improve policies, services, and communication strategies. In addition to immediate support, Conversational AI can be used for long-term planning and goal-setting. Some AI platforms can track a student's progress, remind them of deadlines, suggest relevant extracurricular activities, and even guide them through internship or job application processes. This form of personalized, proactive engagement is particularly beneficial for students who may not have the confidence or knowledge to seek such guidance on their own. Furthermore, Conversational AI can contribute to the creation of more inclusive educational environments. By offering services in multiple languages, recognizing different cultural holidays, or tailoring content to students' backgrounds and preferences, AI systems can help foster a sense of belonging. For students who feel alienated or marginalized in traditional academic settings, this inclusivity can make a significant difference in their motivation, engagement, and academic success. Despite these promising developments, the field is still evolving. As new technologies emerge and become integrated into educational ecosystems, the importance of ethical oversight, transparency, and stakeholder involvement will only increase. Institutions must not only invest in the technical infrastructure but also in ongoing training for staff, periodic review of AI outcomes, and mechanisms for student feedback.

In conclusion, Conversational AI holds immense promise for enhancing student support services, particularly for marginalized and at-risk populations. By providing timely, accessible, and personalized assistance, these systems can help level the playing field for students who have traditionally been underserved. However, to realize this potential fully, institutions must navigate a complex landscape of ethical, technical, and social challenges. Issues such as data privacy, emotional limitations, algorithmic bias, and the risk of diminished human interaction must be addressed through careful design, inclusive practices, and thoughtful integration. The future of educational support lies not in choosing between AI and humans but in creating a synergistic relationship where both can complement and enhance each other's strengths. Through a balanced and ethical approach, Conversational AI can become a powerful ally in building more equitable, supportive, and student-centered educational environments.

6. BENEFITS AND CHALLENGES

Conversational AI has made a significant impact on the landscape of education, particularly in enhancing both instructional delivery and student support. However, the adoption of this technology comes with both notable benefits and critical challenges that warrant careful examination. This section explores the pedagogical, technical, and accessibility benefits of Conversational AI, along with ethical concerns related to privacy, bias, trust, and data dependency. One of the primary pedagogical benefits of Conversational AI is its ability to support personalized and adaptive learning. AI-driven tutors and chatbots can adjust instructional content based on learners' previous interactions, performance, and engagement levels. This supports differentiated instruction and helps students master content at their own pace (Pane et al., 2017). Conversational agents like Duolingo's chatbot or Carnegie Learning's MATHia can deliver instant feedback, facilitate self-paced learning, and improve learner engagement by simulating human-like dialogue (Holmes et al., 2019).

From a technical standpoint, Conversational AI enhances scalability and efficiency in education. Unlike traditional one-on-one tutoring, AI-driven systems can serve thousands of students simultaneously, offering 24/7 assistance without additional human resources. This is especially beneficial in MOOCs and large university courses, where instructors cannot feasibly answer every student query. AI-powered agents can also help automate routine tasks like assignment reminders, quiz notifications, and content summarization (Winkler & Söllner, 2018). In terms of accessibility, Conversational AI reduces barriers to learning for students with disabilities or those from underserved communities. Voice-activated assistants can help visually impaired students navigate learning platforms, while multilingual chatbots can support learners from diverse linguistic backgrounds (Følstad & Brandtzaeg, 2017). Moreover, students who feel anxious about asking questions in class may find it easier to interact with a non-judgmental AI agent, fostering a more inclusive learning environment. Despite these benefits, there are significant challenges associated with the implementation of Conversational AI in education. One of the most pressing concerns is data privacy. AI systems often collect and analyze large amounts of personal data to personalize learning experiences. This raises ethical questions about data ownership, consent, and compliance with regulations like the General Data Protection Regulation (GDPR) and the Family Educational Rights and Privacy Act (FERPA) (Binns et al., 2018). Misuse or mishandling of data can lead to breaches of confidentiality and loss of student trust. Another major issue is algorithmic bias. If AI systems are trained on datasets that are not representative of diverse populations, they may reinforce existing social biases. For example, a chatbot trained primarily on English-speaking users may perform poorly when interacting with non-native speakers, leading to inequitable educational experiences

(Holstein et al., 2019). Addressing this requires inclusive dataset curation, regular audits, and involvement of diverse stakeholders in AI design.

Trust in AI is also a multifaceted challenge. Students and educators must believe that the AI systems they interact with are reliable, transparent, and fair. However, the opaque nature of some machine learning models—often referred to as "black-box" algorithms—makes it difficult to understand how decisions or recommendations are made (Zhou et al., 2020). This lack of transparency can undermine confidence in the technology and hinder adoption. Dependency on AI tools may further impact the development of critical thinking and interpersonal skills. If learners become overly reliant on AI tutors or virtual assistants, they may miss out on opportunities to engage in deeper, reflective learning or human collaboration. Moreover, AI lacks emotional intelligence and contextual sensitivity, which are crucial in mentoring and counseling roles (Fitzpatrick et al., 2017). Another concern relates to the ethical use of Conversational AI in emotionally sensitive contexts, such as mental health support. While chatbots can offer basic psychological assistance, they cannot replace trained professionals in handling severe mental health issues. In such cases, failure to recognize red flags or escalate conversations to human counselors can have serious consequences (Kim et al., 2019). To navigate these challenges, institutions are adopting hybrid models that combine the strengths of AI and human educators. Conversational AI handles routine, repetitive tasks, while human instructors manage complex, creative, or sensitive interactions. This collaborative approach not only ensures efficiency but also retains the human touch essential to education. In conclusion, while Conversational AI presents transformative opportunities for enhancing education through personalization, accessibility, and scalability, its implementation must be guided by ethical principles and inclusive practices. Institutions must invest in transparent design, robust data governance, continuous evaluation, and capacity building to ensure that AI tools support, rather than undermine, equitable and meaningful learning experiences.

7. FUTURE DIRECTIONS AND OPPORTUNITIES

As conversational AI continues to evolve, its integration into education will bring new possibilities and paradigms for teaching, learning, and student support. Emerging innovations such as emotion-aware chatbots, multilingual AI tutors, immersive technologies, and hybrid AI-human support systems are poised to redefine the educational experience in the coming years. One of the most promising advancements is the development of emotion-aware conversational agents. These systems can detect and interpret emotional cues from text, voice, or facial expressions using affective computing techniques. By understanding a student's emotional state, AI tutors can tailor their responses, provide encouragement, or escalate issues to human counselors when needed (Picard, 2010). Emotion-sensitive bots enhance the empathetic quality of learning environments, especially in online education where non-verbal cues are absent. For instance, AI-powered platforms are now being trained to recognize signs of frustration or confusion and proactively offer guidance or motivational feedback (D'Mello & Graesser, 2012). Multilingual conversational AI is another area gaining traction, particularly in regions with diverse linguistic populations. Traditional AI systems often perform optimally only in English or other dominant languages, leaving non-native speakers underserved. Advances in machine translation and multilingual natural language processing (NLP) are making it possible to build AI tutors that can interact with students in their native languages without loss of nuance or context (Conneau et al., 2020). This inclusivity fosters equitable access to education and supports a broader spectrum of learners globally.

The convergence of conversational AI with immersive technologies such as extended reality (XR), augmented reality (AR), and virtual reality (VR) is creating new opportunities for experiential learning. AI-driven avatars in virtual classrooms can simulate peer or instructor interactions, guiding learners through complex simulations in science, medicine, or engineering (Bailenson, 2018). These embodied conversational agents provide an engaging, interactive alternative to static digital learning tools. For instance, a VR-based chemistry lab with a conversational AI assistant could allow students to safely conduct virtual experiments while receiving real-time instructions and feedback. Hybrid AI-human support models are becoming increasingly popular as institutions recognize the limitations of AI in handling nuanced or emotionally complex interactions. In these models, conversational AI handles routine queries, preliminary assessments, or content delivery, while human educators manage critical thinking development, personalized mentoring, and emotional support (Holstein et al., 2020). This division of labor ensures efficiency while preserving the human touch necessary for holistic education. Innovation in educational technology (EdTech) policy and institutional strategy is also critical for the sustainable integration of conversational AI. Policies must address data governance, algorithmic transparency, and student consent. Institutions should prioritize ethical AI practices by incorporating bias audits, inclusive data practices, and open-source collaboration to ensure that AI systems serve diverse student populations (Floridi et al., 2018). Additionally, professional development for educators is essential. Teachers must be trained not only to use conversational AI tools effectively but also to interpret AI-generated insights for informed pedagogical decision-making.

Collaboration between teachers and AI systems offers a powerful pathway for augmenting human expertise. AI can analyze vast datasets on student performance, learning preferences, and engagement patterns, providing actionable insights to educators. These insights can inform personalized interventions, curriculum modifications, or targeted support strategies. Teachers, in turn, can provide contextual understanding and pedagogical nuance that AI cannot replicate. Studies have shown that when educators and AI systems collaborate effectively, student outcomes improve significantly (Luckin et al., 2016). Looking forward, there are several future-oriented research and development areas within conversational AI in education. These include:

- Emotionally adaptive chatbots that not only detect emotions but learn from them to improve over time.
- Conversational AI platforms that function as lifelong learning companions, guiding students through different education levels and career pathways.
- Integration of AI with blockchain for secure credentialing, attendance tracking, and academic records.

- Open AI ecosystems where learners and teachers can co-create content or conversational flows for custom learning experiences.

However, the journey toward widespread adoption is not without hurdles. Technical barriers, resistance to change, lack of digital infrastructure, and concerns around job displacement for educators continue to pose challenges. Addressing these will require a coordinated effort from policymakers, technologists, educators, and learners. In summary, the future of conversational AI in education is rich with potential. By embracing innovations such as emotion-aware systems, multilingual tutors, immersive learning environments, and hybrid support models, educational institutions can create more personalized, inclusive, and engaging learning experiences. The success of this transformation depends not only on technological advancement but also on thoughtful policy-making, ethical design, and the continued empowerment of educators as central figures in the learning process.

8. CONCLUSION

The integration of Conversational AI into education is reshaping how students learn, interact, and receive support. Throughout this chapter, we have examined the foundational concepts, technological underpinnings, and practical applications of Conversational AI in both personalized education and student support services. From intelligent tutoring systems to AI-powered academic advisors, conversational technologies are enabling more responsive, scalable, and adaptive learning environments. One of the most significant insights is that Conversational AI can serve as both a tutor and a mentor—supporting cognitive development while also responding to affective needs. This dual function is particularly critical in online and blended learning contexts, where traditional face-to-face interaction is limited. Emotion-aware AI systems, for example, are capable of interpreting student frustration or disengagement and providing timely, personalized support (D'Mello & Graesser, 2012; Picard, 2010). This not only enhances learning outcomes but also supports student well-being and retention.

Another key takeaway is the value of AI in broadening access and inclusivity. Multilingual conversational agents and AI systems equipped with real-time translation capabilities help break language barriers and create equitable learning opportunities for diverse populations (Conneau et al., 2020). Furthermore, the ability of AI systems to adapt content and feedback based on individual learner profiles represents a transformative step toward truly personalized education (Luckin et al., 2016). Despite the promise, successful implementation of Conversational AI requires addressing challenges around ethics, equity, and pedagogy. Issues such as data privacy, algorithmic bias, and transparency must be confronted head-on to build trust among users and stakeholders (Floridi et al., 2018). Equally important is the need for educators to be empowered as co-designers and active users of these technologies. Teachers bring irreplaceable contextual insight, empathy, and critical thinking that complement the analytical capabilities of AI systems (Holstein et al., 2020). To fully leverage the benefits of Conversational AI in education, several best practices and strategic recommendations should be considered. First, institutions should adopt a human-centered approach to AI integration—ensuring that student needs and values guide technological development. Second, policy frameworks must be established to ensure transparency, data protection, and accountability. Third, continuous professional development for educators should be prioritized, equipping them to harness AI tools meaningfully within their pedagogical practices. Finally, collaboration between technology developers, educators, students, and policymakers is essential for the ethical and sustainable advancement of Conversational AI. As the field evolves, it will be crucial to foster inclusive innovation that addresses the real challenges of education systems while remaining adaptable to future needs.

In conclusion, Conversational AI holds immense potential to empower learners and educators by personalizing instruction, expanding access, and enriching the educational experience. However, its true transformative impact will depend on thoughtful implementation, ethical governance, and the continuous involvement of educators as central agents in the learning process. By aligning AI innovation with pedagogical integrity and student well-being, we can ensure that technology acts as a catalyst for meaningful and equitable education.

REFERENCES

Adamopoulou, E., & Moussiades, L. (2020). Chatbots: History, technology, and applications. *Machine Learning with Applications*, *2*, 100006.

Alexander, R. (2008). Towards Dialogic Teaching: Rethinking Classroom Talk. *Diálogos (San José)*.

Bailenson, J. N. (2018). *Experience on Demand: What Virtual Reality Is, How It Works, and What It Can Do*. WW Norton & Company.

Binns, R., Veale, M., Van Kleek, M., & Shadbolt, N. (2018). "It's reducing a human being to a percentage": Perceptions of justice in algorithmic decisions. In *Proceedings of the 2018 CHI Conference on Human Factors in Computing Systems*.

CAST. (2018). *Universal Design for Learning Guidelines version 2.2*. https://udlguidelines.cast.org

Chow, J., Gwee, S., & Lim, L. (2017). Chatbots in language learning: Opportunities and challenges. *Educational Technology*, *57*(2), 56–60.

Conneau, A., Khandelwal, K., Goyal, N., Chaudhary, V., Wenzek, G., Guzmán, F., & Stoyanov, V. (2020). Unsupervised cross-lingual representation learning at scale. In *Proceedings of the 58th Annual Meeting of the Association for Computational Linguistics*.

D'Mello, S., & Graesser, A. (2012). AutoTutor and Affective AutoTutor: Learning by talking with cognitively and emotionally intelligent computers that talk back. [TiiS]. *ACM Transactions on Interactive Intelligent Systems*, *2*(4), 1–39.

Fitzpatrick, K. K., Darcy, A., & Vierhile, M. (2017). Delivering cognitive behavior therapy to young adults with symptoms of depression and anxiety using a fully automated conversational agent (Woebot): A randomized controlled trial. *JMIR Mental Health*, *4*(2), e19. PMID: 28588005

Fleming, N. D., & Mills, C. (1992). Not another inventory, rather a catalyst for reflection. *To Improve the Academy*, *11*(1), 137–155.

Floridi, L., Cowls, J., Beltrametti, M., Chatila, R., Chazerand, P., Dignum, V., & Vayena, E. (2018). AI4People—An ethical framework for a good AI society: Opportunities, risks, principles, and recommendations. *Minds and Machines*, *28*(4), 689–707. PMID: 30930541

Følstad, A., & Brandtzaeg, P. B. (2017). Chatbots and the new world of HCI. *Interaction*, *24*(4), 38–42.

Goel, A., & Polepeddi, L. (2016). *Jill Watson: A virtual teaching assistant for online education*. Georgia Institute of Technology.

Holmes, W., Bialik, M., & Fadel, C. (2019). *Artificial Intelligence in Education: Promises and Implications for Teaching and Learning*. Center for Curriculum Redesign.

Holstein, K., Wortman Vaughan, J., Daum, M., Dudik, M., & Wallach, H. (2019). Improving fairness in machine learning systems: What do industry practitioners need? In *Proceedings of the 2019 CHI Conference on Human Factors in Computing Systems*.

Holstein, K., Wortman Vaughan, J., Daum, M., Dudik, M., & Wallach, H. (2020). Improving fairness in machine learning systems: What do industry practitioners need? In *Proceedings of the 2020 CHI Conference on Human Factors in Computing Systems*.

Jurafsky, D., & Martin, J. H. (2023). *Speech and Language Processing* (3rd ed.). Draft.

Kim, Y., Huang, J., & Emery, S. (2019). Chatbots and college students: Conversational agents as mediators of support for marginalized students. *Journal of Student Affairs Research and Practice*, *56*(4), 392–406.

Klopfenstein, L. C., Delpriori, S., Malatini, S., & Bogliolo, A. (2017). The rise of bots: A survey of conversational interfaces, patterns, and paradigms. In *Proceedings of the 2017 Conference on Designing Interactive Systems* (pp. 555–565).

Luckin, R., Holmes, W., Griffiths, M., & Forcier, L. B. (2016). *Intelligence Unleashed: An Argument for AI in Education*. Pearson Education.

Means, B., Toyama, Y., Murphy, R., & Baki, M. (2014). The effectiveness of online and blended learning: A meta-analysis of the empirical literature. *Teachers College Record*, *116*(1), 1–47.

Page, L. C., & Gehlbach, H. (2017). How an artificially intelligent virtual assistant helps students navigate the road to college. *AERA Open*, *3*(4), 1–12.

Pane, J. F., Steiner, E. D., Baird, M. D., & Hamilton, L. S. (2017). *Informing Progress: Insights on Personalized Learning Implementation and Effects*. RAND Corporation.

Piaget, J. (1971). *Science of Education and the Psychology of the Child*. Viking Press.

Picard, R. W. (2010). Affective computing: From laughter to IEEE. *IEEE Transactions on Affective Computing*, *1*(1), 11–17.

Roll, I., & Wylie, R. (2016). Evolution and revolution in artificial intelligence in education. *International Journal of Artificial Intelligence in Education*, *26*(2), 582–599.

Santhini, C., Ruba, M., Sakthi Priya, V., & Hemalatha, R. (2025). Intercultural communication and assessment practices in the integration of AI with education. In *Generative AI approaches to sustainable development in higher education*. IGI Global.

Serban, I. V., Lowe, R., Henderson, P., Charlin, L., & Pineau, J. (2018). A survey of available corpora for building data-driven dialogue systems. *Dialogue & Discourse*, *9*(1), 1–49.

Settles, B., & Meeder, B. (2016). A trainable spaced repetition model for language learning. In *Proceedings of the 54th Annual Meeting of the Association for Computational Linguistics (*Volume 1*: Long Papers)* (pp. 1848–1858).

Siemens, G., & Long, P. (2011). Penetrating the fog: Analytics in learning and education. *EDUCAUSE Review*, *46*(5), 30–32.

Sleeman, D., & Brown, J. S. (1982). *Intelligent Tutoring Systems*. Academic Press.

VanLehn, K. (2011). The relative effectiveness of human tutoring, intelligent tutoring systems, and other tutoring systems. *Educational Psychologist*, *46*(4), 197–221.

Vygotsky, L. S. (1978). *Mind in Society: The Development of Higher Psychological Processes*. Harvard University Press.

Winkler, R., & Söllner, M. (2018). Unleashing the potential of chatbots in education: A state-of-the-art analysis. In *Academy of Management Annual Meeting Proceedings*.

Yang, J., Buechele, S., Natori, A., & Kay, J. (2022). Conversational agents in education: A systematic review. *Computers and Education: Artificial Intelligence*, *3*, 100066.

Zawacki-Richter, O., Marín, V. I., Bond, M., & Gouverneur, F. (2019). Systematic review of research on artificial intelligence applications in higher education – Where are the educators? *International Journal of Educational Technology in Higher Education*, *16*(1), 39.

Chapter 8
Safeguarding Student Data:
Privacy and Security Challenges in AI-Powered Education Tools

Md Mehedi Hasan Emon
https://orcid.org/0000-0002-6224-9552
American International University-Bangladesh, Bangladesh

Most. Sharmin Ara Chowdhury
https://orcid.org/0009-0005-1050-8283
National University Bangladesh, Bangladesh

ABSTRACT

This chapter explores the critical privacy and security challenges posed by AI-powered education tools. It examines how AI enhances student support and personalized learning while highlighting risks associated with chatbots, data collection, and processing. Ethical concerns, including consent and fairness, are discussed alongside the complexities of global regulations such as GDPR and FERPA. The chapter also addresses cybersecurity threats targeting educational AI systems and presents strategies to mitigate these risks. Emerging privacy-preserving techniques like federated learning and differential privacy are evaluated for their potential to safeguard student data. Drawing on case studies, it identifies best practices for ethical AI

DOI: 10.4018/979-8-3373-3316-8.ch008

implementation and offers actionable recommendations for educators and policymakers. Finally, this chapter underscores the need for a balanced approach that protects student privacy without stifling innovation in AI-driven education.

INTRODUCTION

Artificial intelligence (AI) is now being used more often in educational institutions and is changing how they teach, test and connect with students. The use of these technologies such as adaptive platforms and AI assistants brings great improvements in tailored help and time saved for students. At the same time, there are major worries about how student information is being handled regarding privacy, safety and governance. This chapter focuses on how to protect the personal information of students using AI at schools and why it is important. At the beginning of the chapter, the role of AI in helping students learn and supporting teachers is introduced, explaining how AI tools assist in communication, offer personal advice and encourage students to take part actively. Although these applications support education in many ways, they use a lot of data which leads to questions about its handling and security. Privacy Risks in AI-Powered Chatbots and Virtual Assistants is the section that looks at the risks that may arise when educators rely on AI chatbots and virtual assistants. Because these systems instantaneously record student data, there is a risk that this data might be used or watched by people who should not access it if the systems are not safeguarded properly. Moving forward, Data Collection, Storage and Processing in AI Education Tools discusses what happens to student data and how it is handled and points out how this could be a concern when third parties or cloud services are involved. The section discusses how institutions can be held accountable and points out the dangers caused by either amassing too much data or not being tightly regulated. The chapter afterward addresses moral issues in AI-Driven Learning Systems such as what constitutes informed consent, how algorithms can show biases, the importance of student autonomy and the threat of inequalities being reinforced by hidden computer-based decisions. Although these ethical issues were usually ignored while developing AI, they are now recognized as being very important for proper use. The next part covers global regulations and compliance for AI in education (GDPR, FERPA, etc.), giving an overview of the key policies that oversee data protection in learning. Although the General Data Protection Regulation (GDPR) and the Family Educational Rights and Privacy Act (FERPA) provide essential protection, their application to AI is not always easy and sometimes not enough, particularly in situations where the tools work across different countries or on multiple platforms. In this chapter, Cybersecurity Threats and Risk Mitigation Strategies mention the advancement of technology and how it leads to more data breaches, ransomware attacks and intruders in schools and higher education. For illustration, Case Studies and Best Practices in Ethical AI Implementation includes accounts of how universities and education institutions use secure and ethical AI in practice. The studies provide information about the ways institutions choose to operate, how students are involved in running the institution and how they comply with ethical and legal regulations. In the Consolidated Recommendations, findings are gathered and ways for educators and policymakers to move forward are suggested. The recommendations cover changes in how institutions are governed, policies for reforming regulations, what should be included in procurement and ways to support students to ensure AI is used safely and effectively. The chapter ends by making the point that these things are urgent. As AI keeps growing in schools, the need for secure student data becomes a duty, not only a challenge related to technology. The chapter provides a key intervention and main resource for academic leaders, technologists, policymakers and researchers active in both education and emerging technology areas.

THE ROLE OF AI IN STUDENT SUPPORT AND LEARNING ENHANCEMENT

The use of AI in education represents a big development in the way teaching and learning happen. AI systems are now at the center of helping education be more responsive, personalized and scalable for students. In schools and universities everywhere, AI-based tools support academic work, help students do better and reduce administrative duties. Although educational technology plays a valuable role in teaching, it also creates new difficulties connected to dealing with data, student choice and the duties of educational institutions (Zhao et al., 2023). AI can accomplish personalized education mainly because it can handle and read huge amounts of data about learners. Among all this information are learners' online movements on the LMS, the amount of time assigned to different tasks, results of assessments, use of forums and in some cases, measurements like eye-tracking and facial expressions displayed by the learners (Aly, 2024). Because of these insights, adaptive learning platforms change what and how quickly students are taught depending on their progress. For instance, Carnegie Learning's MATHia technology applies to AI so students are given the right level of practice, as well as individual tips, like tutoring done by a person.

As well as supporting adaptive learning, AI now makes academic help easier to find and faster to receive. A chatbot which is embedded onto the institution's website or LMS, can aid in answering common questions about courses, important dates and university policies. At Georgia State University, using a chatbot called "Pounce" to help incoming students reduced summer melt and resulted in more students enrolling (Peyton et al., 2025). AI writing assistants like Grammarly and Turnitin's Revision Assistant help students improve their writing by providing real-time suggestions and this helps make academic support accessible whenever needed, no matter the time. The main thing about these applications is that data is always being collected and extracted. AI is very effective in education because it can collect and process small details about students' actions and achievements. Therefore, schools and learning spaces are being changed in ways that allow for the collection of more data and surveillance. This transformation makes many people worry about telling apart helpful observation from excessive monitoring. When interaction metrics are not handled securely, they may eventually be used for algorithmic profiling and thus threaten a student's right to privacy and freedom of choice (Díaz-Rodríguez et al., 2023).

The use of algorithms in assigning things like scores and support can be very controversial, as some examples prove such as the situation in the UK in 2020, when the algorithm used to distribute grades disadvantaged students from less wealthy families (Baker & Hawn, 2022). AI technology gives students with disabilities ways to access content, convert their speech to text and get help that helps them feel included. AI tutoring systems help learners in places without many resources and can easily handle questions in certain subjects. Instead, the problem is making certain that AI is used in schools in accordance with important standards and guidelines. It is important for institutions to be more responsive and clearer when handling and managing data to obtain this balance. Initially, students should understand what information is gathered, its purpose and which people it is shared with. Secondly, people responsible for education should also be taught about the ethical sides of educational technology along with how to apply it. Thirdly, these institutions need to buy AI tools that are clear in their mechanics, easy to understand and offer users control. It requires using approaches that make it easy for students to manage and review data sharing and offering them an opportunity to give consent instead of a requirement (Shneiderman, 2020). A human-centered approach to AI in education ensures the change helps both education and students' well-being.

PRIVACY RISK'S IN AI-POWERED CHATBOTS AND VIRTUAL ASSISTANTS

Chatbots and virtual assistants have now become a common part of how students interact and get support in education. The services at these institutions operate all the time, support students with tasks related to rules, assignments and tests, give academic help and, importantly, support mental health. However, depending on conversation AI more and more has noticeable privacy consequences. At the same time as they function, using natural language and user data, these tools leave users open to their privacy being broken, their data being abused and their trust being broken. The thing that makes these risks unique is that the data chatbots work with is about individual people. Traditional education technology might only record information like grades or attendance, while chatbots regularly have extended and free-text discussions with students to invite wide-ranging details. Students might share questions about their education or more private concerns, for example, personal issues, struggles with mental health and problems within their family. When interactions are kept, reviewed and analyzed, as is usual, they create in-depth descriptions of how a student acts and feels (Hew et al., 2023).

An important risk might be introduced when organizations use secondary sources of data. AI education platforms are generally made and overseen by third-party vendors, and some may hold onto the data that their tools gather. This information may be shared, used in algorithms or applied to products and this can happen even if students do not explicitly accept it (Sanfilippo et al., 2023). Because exact details about data storage, use and sharing are not clear, the main principle of consent becomes questionable which is most serious for minors. In addition, sending data across different legal areas raises privacy issues. Educational institutions might accidentally deliver student information to servers that are not under strong privacy regulations or have no adequate data protection agreements in place. For example, if a chatbot designed in the United States is used by a school, students' personal data may be saved outside the EU, missing the stricter rules of the GDPR (Hagadone-Bedir et al., 2023). Due to these circumstances, enforcing rights is tricky and responsibility does not stay clear.

Another important problem is that it is hard to see what exact algorithms businesses use. Chatbots and virtual assistants use machine learning which grows smarter as it is exposed to information from many users. The processes used in these models to reach decisions are usually not understandable. When chatbots automatically identify students for mental health care, but the rules they use to do so are not made public or tested, this situation is risky. The use of unclear and unconfirmed data may determine whether students face interventions or are kept from using important resources (Zhai et al., 2024). The lack of transparency also influences the idea of contestability. In the traditional model, students may ask for reconsideration regarding their grades, disputes with teachers or to clarify things that were unclear. Students who use AI systems might not be aware of their personal profiling or even have a means to contest what happened to them. In these environments, users start to act mainly by creating raw data for more development of the system (Chen et al., 2023). Risks can be greater when these tools are used in compulsory education because students do not have a choice to avoid them. In these cases, consent is forced, and students are required to work with AI, even if it makes them uncomfortable because of the increased monitoring of their activities. In addition to breaking the principle of freely joining, this also brings concerns regarding children and teens' digital rights because they are specially protected in international law.

DATA COLLECTION, STORAGE, AND PROCESSING IN AI EDUCATION TOOL'S

Artificial intelligence (AI) systems used in schools depend greatly on data which involves collecting, holding and reviewing large amounts of student data. AI appeals to educators by chance to personalize lessons, make school management more efficient and provide forecasts. However, the potential of this promise hinges on collecting more data than ever before, data that goes into more detail than what traditional educational assessment used. In the process of AI transforming how schools work, it brings up significant privacy issues and challenges to managing and using data effectively and following rules. Educational AI systems record information about many aspects of students' learning. Data collected in such ways can build comprehensive profiles for students which when run by machine learning algorithms, produces recommendations for each person, detects students who may struggle and supports decisions within the institution.

The detailed checking of student actions could also lead to more personal information being gathered which was not originally necessary just for education. At first, using technology to monitor students' engagement is harmless, until the information is recycled for things other than teaching, like profiling their behavior, using it in advertisements or taking disciplinary action (Almufarreh & Arshad, 2023). A lack of specific rules about what data should be kept, its purpose and the time it is kept puts students at risk. Moreover, businesses often use third-party companies and cloud storage which also adds to security risks. While using the cloud is helpful for institutions, it means they transfer a good part of control over student data to commercial entities. In some cases, Schools and colleges share student information without carefully considering the possible risks or pushing for stronger student protections. Vendors can use the data they gather for internal purposes, like training their systems or developing products and this use may not match the original reason for data collection and therefore break the rules set by data protection laws like the GDPR. The problem becomes even more serious because of the risk of using data for profit. If there are not strong contracts and technical safeguards, student records can be seen as a commercial resource. Artificial intelligence (AI) companies might study masses of data to see how students act, what subjects they prefer, and other trends and they may share or sell these results with publishers, advertising agencies and recruiters. Also, understanding how student data is processed is difficult both for the students and to the stakeholders within the institution. Few educational institutions describe in detail how AI systems look at student data, what they discover from it or how the conclusions affect student performance. If there is little transparency in algorithms, students cannot understand or argue against decisions that are made using their data. The difficulties caused by being "black box" become most apparent in AI systems used for predictive analytics.

ETHICAL CONSIDERATION'S IN AI-DRIVEN LEARNING SYSTEMS

Educational systems using Artificial intelligence (AI) can open doors to new approaches in teaching, personalized help and managing schools. At the same time, the transformation leads to serious ethical problems that shake established principles of education and normal social values. Since the law doesn't go far enough, ethical concerns encourage institutions to carefully consider all the ways AI presence in schools can impact learners and educators (Schiff, 2022). One of the main ethical problems is dealing with informed consent, fairness, accountability, transparency and participatory governance, so each should be studied carefully. There is a major ethical concern in Artificial intelligence (AI) education regarding properly informing users and obtaining consent. Theoretically, all students should be aware of what information is being gathered, how it is managed and why. The problem is most noticeable when it takes place in schools, as using digital platforms is a mandatory requirement. When students must give consent to prevent losing access to education, the consent is not voluntary but given under coercion. These situations go against the main concepts of voluntary and autonomous action that support ethical data use.

Figure 1. Ethical Challenges in AI-Driven Education Systems

Figure 1 shows how the challenges of ethics in AI-driven education are linked together with a circular design. The most important issues in the diagram are informed consent, fairness and unintentional bias in algorithms, being transparent and accountable, unequal power and participatory governance. Ensuring that students are informed about AI's impact and that participation is completely voluntary is what informed consent stresses. Artificial intelligence (AI) can sometimes inadvertently make things worse for marginalized groups, and this issue is called fairness and algorithmic bias. The term "black box" often describes AI and transparency, and accountability aim to fix the difficulties in identifying who is responsible when an AI error occurs. Asymmetries in power mean that students may have less control over their own learning because the technologies are largely in the control of the institutions. Additionally, participatory governance states that involving many stakeholders in designing, deploying and monitoring AI is necessary for maintaining fairness in how decisions are made. As seen in Figure 1, these matters are connected and all help to determine the ethics of AI in education.

The fact that Artificial intelligence (AI) systems are not always clear about what they do makes it harder to fully consent. A lot of AI technology is not understandable to the public, since the decisions it takes depend on hidden and private algorithms. The unclear process can make students lose faith in the system, especially when they are evaluated or categorized without knowing why it happened (Stone, 2023). According to Díaz-Rodríguez et al., (2023), meaningful transparency goes beyond disclosing code or Artificial intelligence (AI) models; it guarantees that people can properly assess and even dispute results from algorithms. A further important issue is the chance that algorithms are biased and do not act ethically. Artificial intelligence (AI) systems created with old information may copy the biases and injustices that come with the original data. In this way, predictive models may highlight students from underprivileged backgrounds or ethnic minorities as a possible risk, not due to the students' actual problems, but just because of the patterns found in prior success or failure of similar groups (Arizmendi et al., 2022). These biases can become part of the system's logic and in doing so, they might look objective to users. This has the potential to single out students as a risk and further strengthen existing inequalities in education in the name of making decisions based on evidence. Fairness in AI concerns the just way results and technologies are allocated, not only the accuracy of those results. Who is helped by improvements from AI in education and who suffers from the mistakes made by AI? According to studies, AI-assisted personalization is mostly helpful to students who have strong digital skills and excellent technological support, but it may not serve all types of students well (Arora et al., 2025). Therefore, it is ethically important to develop AI systems that are open, appropriate for different cultures and reach all users on the Internet.

It is also extremely important to focus on accountability. As decisions influenced by AI become more common, figuring out who is responsible for problems becomes harder. Which person or group is responsible for the algorithm, the company supplying it, the school putting it into action or the teachers spending time on it? According to Farsi et al., (2021), this situation where responsibility is spread leaves students with very little opportunity to raise complaints. Therefore, the organizations responsible for Artificial intelligence (AI) in education should accept full responsibility for the systems they involve, setting up ethical reviews and keeping human involvement. There is often a significant imbalance in power between students and the institutions which adds to the ethical problems. AI-based education systems are usually established and used in places where students do not participate much in decision-making. The situation could change education so that it relies heavily on data and monitoring rather than on collaboration and people. Therefore, associations in Artificial intelligence (AI) education should look for ways beyond simple compliance with the law, choosing instead to actively involve people and think ahead. Involving students, teachers and others in the designing and deploying of AI in education allows the systems created to reflect what is important to the community. By adopting this approach, employees become accountable and feel responsible for their decisions which may highlight areas that are unclear or raise ethical problems for developers or administrators.

Figure 2. Ethical Governance Model (AI in Education)

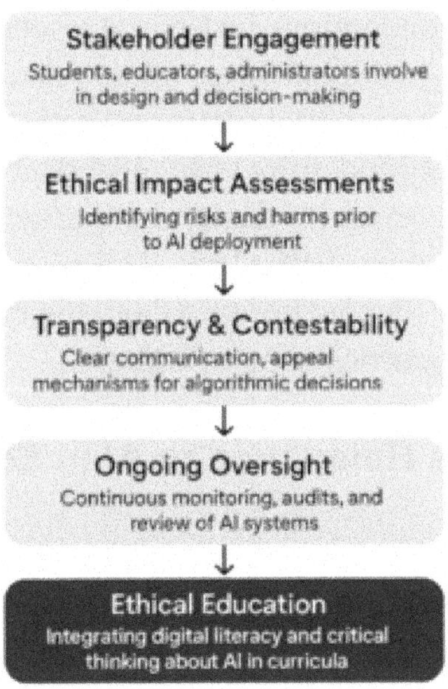

A structured flowchart called Ethical Governance Model for AI in Education is presented to visualize how ethics and AI should be managed and applied in education. The priority is Stakeholder Engagement, making sure students, educators and administrators are involved in designing and making decisions. At the following level, Ethical Impact Assessments aim to spot possible risks and harm immediately before Artificial intelligence (AI) is used. Next, Transparency & Contestability calls for openness and ways to review and challenge the outcomes made by algorithms. In Ongoing Oversight, there is constant monitoring, checking and reviewing of AI systems in place. The last layer, Ethical Education, points out how digital literacy and considering AI should be part of what is taught in schools. Figure 2 shows a process where AI in education is used thoughtfully and cooperatively.

GLOBAL REGULATION'S AND COMPLIANCE FOR AI IN EDUCATION

AI in schools is growing, so it is now more important than ever to keep student data secure. The adoption of AI-based resources, for learning, tutoring and admin tasks, typically involves a lot of data gathering, processing and analysis. This shift to digital platforms calls for strong standards to look after privacy, safety and proper use of student data. Although GDPR and FERPA define important protections and principles, using them in AI for education presents many difficulties. This section discusses aspects of these regulations, how they matter to AI and the emerging problems that institutions in other countries need to address.

The GDPR and Its Relevance to AI in Education

The GDPR which came into effect in 2018, is seen as the top standard for data protection legislation worldwide. If personal data of people in the EU is processed by a company, it must follow the GDPR even if the company is not based in Europe. The principles of data minimization, purpose limitation, transparency and accountability form the basis for any talk about AI in education (Bogina et al., 2022). GDPR requires that companies only gather personal information if it is required for a clear and legitimate reason and only the amount necessary. This principle confronts AI systems which often require access to a large amount of data. Adaptive learning platforms may collect small behavioral details, biometric information or emotions to understand what a student needs. Any data gathered under the GDPR needs justification beforehand by legal objectives and must be given with free and full consent. Additionally, GDPR recognizes important rights for people using data which matters for students using Artificial intelligence (AI) technology. These are access to their data, to correct any inaccuracies, to object to processing and the "right to be forgotten" through a data erasure request (Berendt et al., 2020). Educational institutions should ensure these rights are carried out in AI systems, although this may be difficult since AI algorithms and automated decisions are difficult to fully understand. According to the regulation, data protection is required by design and by default, so businesses must consider privacy when they design and use their technologies (Quach et al., 2022). As part of using AI education tools, programmers and institutions should take advance steps like limited data use, encryption and restricted access to ensure privacy is not compromised.

FERPA: Protecting Student Education Records in the U.S.

Since 1974, the FERPA has been the main law that ensures student education records are protected in the United States. In contrast to GDPR which covers many areas of data protection, FERPA applies only to educational records at institutions receiving federal aid in the U.S. (Cohen et al., 2024). Federal law allows parents (and students over 18) to see and change information in their education records and keeps disclosure private, except for allowed special conditions. Therefore, edtech tools that deal with educational data must comply closely with FERPA rules if they want to let a third party receive this data (Zimmerle, 2021). FERPA also protects categories of education records that directly involve a student and are kept by an educational agency or institution. AI-made data such as analytics reports and behavior data are now involved which raises issues related to how AI vendors secure and manage this data in accordance with FERPA.

Challenges in Defining Roles: Data Controllers and Processors

Among the many challenges in AI education, figuring out who is responsible for guiding decisions concerning data is a major one. The regulation separates data controllers, who set the guidelines and data processors, whose job is to carry out the processing under the controller's control.

Figure 3. Data Controller vs. Data Processor in AI-Enhanced Education Systems

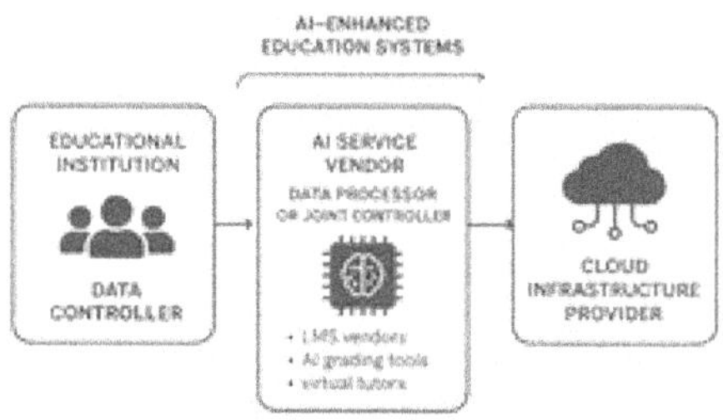

Figure 3 shows the regular roles and relationships between main participants involved in AI-enhanced education. Data processing in schools is handled by the institution which determines both the reasons and the methods. The role of Artificial intelligence (AI) service vendors such as LMS platforms, AI grading products and virtual tutors can vary, so they may process information or determine its use, making them controllers or data processors. Cloud infrastructure providers are regularly chosen by these companies to manage and handle educational data. The figure displays directional arrows to illustrate how data passes and what compliance tasks are assigned by law such as under the GDPR.

The use of third-party AI tools by schools is often uncertain about who oversees student data. Those handling data within AI platforms supplied by vendors might use it for improvement, studies or business, crossing the original goals set by the school (Shtayyat et al., 2025). Because of this uncertainty, it becomes challenging to enforce standards and hold people accountable which could expose organizations to criticism from regulators. In the same way, FERPA gives education institutions the authority to guard student records, but third parties might have different duties based on their agreements and the data they can see. A proper legal review is needed to properly unite the practices of an institution with the actions of its vendors and clear policies for data governance should be put in place.

Cross-Border Data Transfers and Jurisdictional Complexities

AI education platforms are usually run across boundaries, supported by cloud services and data centers all over the world. Different countries have their own privacy laws and ways of enforcing them, so transferring data internationally leads to more compliance complications (Rong et al., 2025). A university in an EU country using an AI vendor from the United States is required to make sure data transfer processes are in line with GDPR through measures such as Standard Contractual Clauses or other suitable choices. After the Privacy Shield framework was suspended in 2020, transferring information to the US became more difficult. This led institutions to re-examine how they comply with data protection laws (Okoli & Yekini, 2023). If data protection laws are not comprehensive in some countries, schools may mistakenly expose student data to less careful safeguards. This leads to a mix of regulations that require administrators to pay more attention to risks and prevent problems before they arise.

The Regulatory Gap: Emerging AI-Specific Challenges

Laws such as GDPR and FERPA already were not written to manage issues around AI. The time it takes to make new rules causes problems with understanding and following the law, especially since AI changes rapidly. For instance, GDPR places limits on automated decisions that solely rely on computer processing and result in significant impacts (Article 22). However, it is still an open question what a "significant effect" should mean for educational uses of AI such as grading and adapting courses (Khan & Mer, 2023). Moreover, most existing laws are not made to deal with the AI-related risks related to bias in algorithms, fairness and predictive use of student data. Therefore, educational institutions sometimes must find new ways to follow the regulations, and they tend to set stricter internal rules than is legally required.

Institutional Policies and Codes of Practice

Since legal and ethical issues related to AI keep changing, many schools are writing AI policies and codes to follow along with existing laws. These frameworks describe guidelines for data ethics, privacy, transparency and accountability designed for schools.

Policies in this category generally underline the following areas:

- Carrying out privacy impact assessments ahead of using AI in business.
- Informing students and parents clearly about the reasons for collecting and using their data.
- Ensuring that approval, selection and management of vendors are all subject to thorough due diligence.
- Ensuring there are human checks on decisions made with algorithms for students.
- Ensuring people have ways to address issues if their data is used improperly.

Figure 4. Institutional Compliance Roadmap for Responsible AI Use (AI in Education)

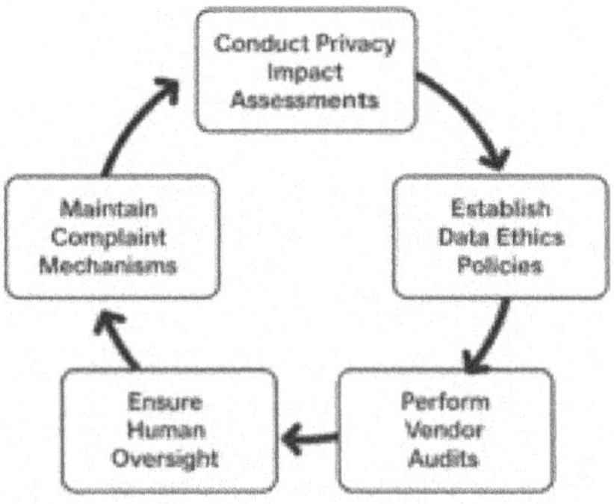

The circle map highlights five basic steps institutions need to follow to use AI properly in schools and universities. Figure 4 demonstrates that the process starts by performing privacy impact assessments, next is to create data ethics policies, run audits on vendors, monitor the actions of employees and provide complaint mechanisms. Every component is connected by directional arrows which indicate that compliance and oversight in institutions are done on an ongoing basis.

The role of data protection officers and ethics committees in organizations is significant because they help oversee following these guidelines and create a positive AI usage culture.

CYBERSECURITY THREAT'S AND RISK MITIGATION STRATEGIE'S IN AI-POWERED EDUCATION TOOL'S

Artificial intelligence (AI) has rapidly been added to schools and education systems, changing teaching approaches, student learning and daily administrative roles. However, the changes cause new cybersecurity problems to arise. AI-based educational tools manage lots of sensitive data such as PII, reports, analytics and even biometrics, making them appeal to cybercriminals. Strong networks with many active components and third-party extensions, typically hosted on cloud infrastructure, unfortunately create more risks. It is very important to learn the types of threats that can affect education and build effective prevention strategies for them so that trust with stakeholders can be preserved.

The Cybersecurity Threat Landscape in AI Education

AI systems that are used in education face a range of cyber threats which often take advantage of their special features and work environments. Phishing is a well-known risk in which tricky emails or messages are sent to educators, students or administrators to persuade them to reveal their login details or to download dangerous software. The rising need for remote learning during and after the COVID-19 pandemic has made the situation worse, because users access various online resources remotely instead of in school networks (Babu & Simon P., 2023). AI-based educational systems are highly at risk from ransomware attacks. Cybercriminals may secure important information and require a ransom to restore it which can stop schools and universities from functioning properly. Due to pressing operational needs and important information kept by schools, they are elite targets for ransomware attacks all over the world. There is also a major concern about unauthorized data being extracted from an organization. A lot of the data in AI systems contains personally identifying information, details from educational background and information on user behavior. Data stored in these repositories are prone to theft which attackers may use for committing identity theft, blackmail or listing them for sale on hidden web markets. There is also a threat from inside the company, because not everyone using the system is careful or happy which can allow data breaches to happen (Vayyala, 2025). API integration and the use of cloud services make AI tools more powerful, though this leads to a bigger attack surface. Any service outside the organization can create a risk that attackers break in without permission. Problems with cloud configurations are known to cause a lot of data breaches, putting schools and universities at risk of penalties and negative public perception (Neal Joshua et al., 2022).

Layered Security Architecture's: A Holistic Approach

Eliminating cybersecurity risks means organizations should implement security solutions that operate at different levels together. It is commonly referred to as "defense in depth" because it means different security controls are working together to protect the system (Lekkala & Gurijala, 2024). On the fundamental level, IAM systems are necessary. IAM prevents unauthorized people from accessing company data or important systems. The approach must be taken to give users only as much access to resources as they need to carry out their duties. In schools, where AI tools are used by students, faculty and administrators with different levels of access, RBAC are particularly significant (J. A. Khan, 2024). Enabling MFA makes it much more difficult for someone to take control of your account. MFA, which relies on passwords along with other methods like hardware tools or fingerprints, is more difficult for attackers to hack (Suleski et al., 2023). Both data at rest and data in transit are secure mainly due to encryption.

End-to-end encryption stops anyone from interfering with or getting access to information being sent between users and AI software. Also, encrypting all stored data and backups stops thieves and anyone not authorized from accessing storage systems (Nadji, 2024). Real-time monitoring and detection of anomalies in the network back up these controls by showing what is happening in the system. AI-powered advanced monitoring tools can observe unusual access patterns, data circulation and rise in traffic and report that as a potential cyber threat. Prompt identification of the problem helps deal with it early and prevents more damage (Cevallos-Salas et al., 2024).

Figure 5. Layered Security Architecture for AI-Powered Education Systems

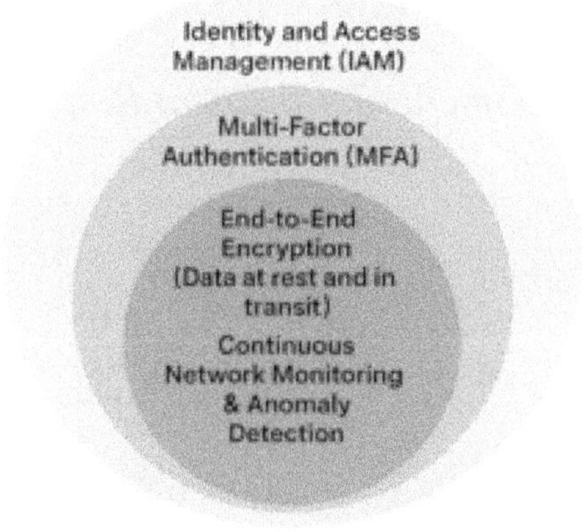

Figure 5 shows a security architecture with different layers, resembling concentric rings, to properly secure AI-powered educational systems. The diagram shows every important component of security as a separate layer. At the outer layer, the overall process dark security combines IAM, MFA, encryption and ongoing surveillance with anomaly detection. This way of displaying information emphasizes that each additional security step is designed to complement the previous ones to produce an effective and strong defense.

Incident Response and Recovery Planning

Despite all the work being put into security, it is still possible for breaches to happen, so robust plans for incident response are needed. The safety of students and minimal disruption to their schoolwork should guide the plans and they must fit the school's unique situation. It is necessary to have set approaches for finding and limiting breaches, to immediately tell people involved and to work with law enforcement and regulatory bodies where required. A well-organized incident response team made up of IT authorities, lawyers, public relations experts and educators is important to deal with the problem. It is important to keep an open line of communication with students, parents and teachers to make sure people trust the institution during a crisis (Izumi et al., 2021).

Figure 6. Security Assessment and Incident Response Cycle (AI in Education)

Figure 6 demonstrates how cybersecurity management must go through a continuous cycle to preserve strong security in AI education organizations. The first step is a Security Audit and a review of vulnerabilities, then comes Penetration Testing and finally Incident Detection takes place. After a cybersecurity incident is discovered, you must deal with Containment and Remediation next, followed by Notification and Communication and end with Post-Incident Review and Improvement. It highlights how it is important to work proactively and iteratively to keep the organization safe and reliable in the long run.

Cybersecurity Education and Awareness

Cybersecurity cannot be entirely assured just by technology. Human factors are major areas to threaten security, as phishing and social engineering attacks target user habits. Consequently, every faculty, administrator and student must receive thorough cybersecurity training. Training should explain correct password procedures, how to distinguish between suspicious and genuine emails, safe dealing with sensitive information and the risks involved with data within AI platforms. Teaching cyber security to employees as a habit encourages them to be careful and helps prevent accidental data theft (Armas & Taherdoost, 2025). In addition, encouraging people to feel responsible makes them more likely to report security incidents which benefit the whole school community.

Figure 7. Cybersecurity Awareness and Education Framework (AI in Education)

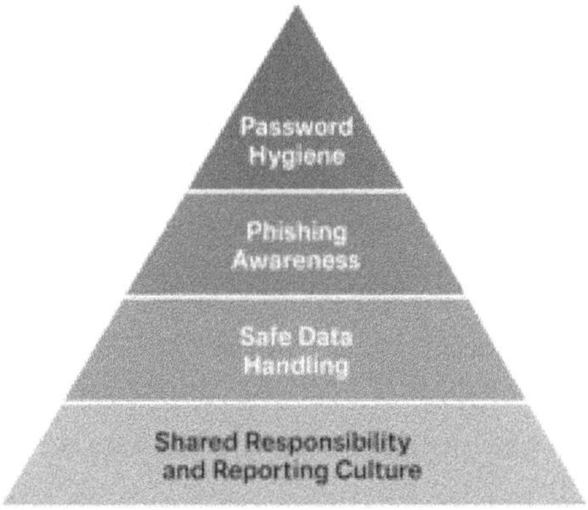

The framework shows a pyramid representing the most important aspects of a strong cybersecurity education. It includes ways to work with passwords, dangers of phishing, correct data handling and has an emphasis on responsibility and reporting. All layers come together to show that building a strong human firewall relies on basic knowledge and practices. The emphasis is on every person taking shared responsibility, since cybersecurity works best when individual actions are combined with proper support from within the organization. Figure 7 clearly highlights that including human aspects with technical tools is crucial for making an organization's cybersecurity strong.

PRIVACY-PRESERVING AI TECHNIQUES: FEDERATED LEARNING AND DIFFERENTIAL PRIVACY

The increase in Artificial intelligence (AI) in healthcare and education has made people debate more about the protection of privacy and data. The need for AI to use a lot of different data often goes against the requirement to preserve people's privacy. In this situation, machine learning methods focused on preserving privacy such as federated learning and differential privacy, have received a lot of attention. These methods focus on maintaining the privacy of people as AI extracts information, making AI more trustworthy.

Federated Learning: Decentralizing AI Model Training

Federated learning makes a big change to the usual centralized model training process by letting AI models learn directly from the devices or servers where the data is stored, rather than sending everything to a central data center. By spreading the data to many computers instead of just one central server, the risks from data breaches are greatly reduced (Choudhary et al., 2024). The core idea behind federated learning is that local nodes be they smartphones, edge Federated learning is based on nodes like phones, edge devices or servers at institutions each developing their own version of the model using their private data. It is only the updated parameters or gradients that travel to the central aggregator and these updates help the global model become better. This process keeps going until the model performs as desired. A major positive aspect of federated learning is that it helps preserve data sovereignty, which is becoming more worrying, given regulations such as the GDPR. Businesses such as educational institutions, healthcare providers or banks may store their sensitive information safely internally and still be part of broader AI movements. In this way, hospitals can work together on diagnostic AI which helps protect patient data from leaving their secure systems and saves them from many compliance rules (Cirillo et al., 2025). Even though there are many pluses, federated learning comes with its own set of difficulties. It is important to orchestrate such a system with many devices, each using different amounts of processing power, data storage and with limited or unlimited network connections. Model performance can be affected by these heterogeneities in terms of speed and how accurately it fits the data (Mora et al., 2024). Also, federated learning systems are at risk from threats such as model poisoning, where the participants intentionally update the model with false information. Thus, strong procedures for checking participant identities and finding suspicious activities are required.

Differential Privacy: Protecting Individual Information in Aggregate Data

Differential privacy introduces carefully chosen noise to the data or model, so that the impact of including or excluding any one person's data is reduced. Adversaries are not allowed to confidently recognize individuals by using this statistical guarantee, even if they are given aggregate outputs or models (Hathaliya et al., 2022). The process that makes differential privacy possible is plain even though it is mathematically well-defined. A small amount of noise, randomly picked from Laplace or Gaussian distributions, is put into datasets to blur the effect of each record during queries. The amount of noise used in differential privacy shows how much information can be learned from the data at the cost of privacy. Differential privacy allows certain privacy guarantees for AI models while they learn or share their predictions. A good example is Google adding differential privacy in Chrome which controls the release of data about each user's browsing activity to protect their privacy (Ye & Hu, 2020)). At the same time, including noisy data can harm the performance of AI systems which makes balancing the situation necessary. If the environment is too noisy, machine learning models will not be reliable, but if the environment is too quiet, their privacy guarantees are broken. People are still researching how to find the right privacy budget for every application and possible threat level.

Practical and Technical Challenges in Implementation

In theory, these privacy-preserving techniques look very good, but putting them into practice is still quite difficult. Large investments in communication networks, edge computing and secure aggregation protocols are needed for federated learning. The struggle happens most in places that lack resources, advanced infrastructure or both such as rural schooling and less-developed regions (Poleto et al., 2023). Another major issue is having the right technical skills on the team. Federated learning systems and differentially private models need to be developed, kept updated and verified using skills from machine learning, cryptography and data governance. The fact that businesses' technology resources are not always enough often leads them to lean on outside vendors, further increasing worries about privacy and compliance.

CASE STUDIES AND BEST PRACTICES IN ETHICAL AI IMPLEMENTATION

When AI is used in education, it requires careful thinking about ethical matters, especially related to handling data; being honest about what happens; and working together with all people involved. The use of AI in education is growing, so institutions are being urged to put in place privacy, fairness and accountability frameworks. Several notable cases show how clear ethical guidelines can be included in AI at work and school, making these methods easy to imitate by others.

University of Edinburgh: Embedding Ethical Review and Student Participation

A clear example of the University of Edinburgh addressing ethics' in AI governance is their comprehensive DPIA framework. While traditional DPIAs concentrate mainly on following rules such as GDPR, Edinburgh's solution includes both ethical and technical considerations when carrying out DPIAs (Fawns et al., 2021).

Figure 8. Ethical AI Governance Framework (University of Edinburgh)

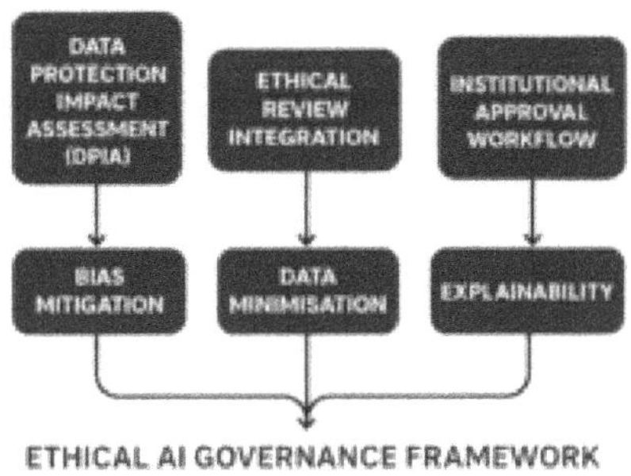

Figure 8 illustrates how the University of Edinburgh carries out its ethical AI governance system. The system brings together four main features: DPIA, Ethical Review Integration, Institutional Approval Workflow and Student Consultation Process (as part of the institutional workflow). All these components support the main ethical principles of AI: Bias Mitigation, Data Minimisation and Explainability. The figure explains that these key elements make sure AI development and use remain responsible by having institutions in charge, engaging stakeholders and sticking to ethical standards.

It is important in this structure that students are involved in guiding and reviewing the curriculum. The university first seeks input from student representatives to learn about their issues and expectations regarding privacy, fairness and effects on their learning experience of using AI tools with their data. Not only does this make things clearer, but it also helps AI projects reflect the lives and needs of those who are mainly influenced by algorithms. All AI systems at the University are required to go through thorough ethical scrutiny before being approved institutionally and project teams are expected to tackle bias, minimize the collected data and clearly explain how the AI reaches its decisions. This approach to governance manages risks in advance, showing how a solid and ethical process to AI should be used (Molina-Carmona & García-Peñalvo, 2025).

The Open University: Transparency through Learning Analytics Dashboards

At the Open University in the United Kingdom, they built learning analytics dashboards to encourage students to make informed choices. The dashboards give students instant AI-based predictions about their grades, how involved they are and useful tips for improving their learning (Susnjak et al., 2022). Open University students can view the forecasts and discuss or reject them which helps to maintain a "humanized" loop in the algorithm. This way, students find out how their data is analyzed and used, addressing the usual complaint that AI systems are not easy to understand. When there is such transparency, students believe in the system and are encouraged to take part actively in their education, as learning algorithms in education may strongly affect their achievements (Tychola et al., 2024). The success at the Open University proves that explaining AI tools simply is crucial for people with different tech knowledge. The institution uses clean and simple user interfaces with helpful notes, decreases confusion and lets users make smart decisions about their data.

Core Themes from Studie's: Institutional Leadership and Stakeholder Engagement

Together, these cases highlight the main point necessary for ethical AI use. The most important role is that of strong institutional leadership. It is important for ethical AI that the culture within an organization supports ethical ideas along with following legal requirements. A leader should support transparency, inclusivity and accountability as main values, as this creates the foundation for ethical actions across the whole institution. In addition, engaging stakeholders plays a key role in making something happen. When students, faculty, IT specialists, legal advisors and outside experts join the effort early on, a wide range of ethical problems can be found, and AI can be aligned with what the community wants and needs. The involvement of different teams reduces the risk of missing significant details because teams are working together rather than separately.

Figure 9. Core Themes for Ethical AI Implementation (AI in Education)

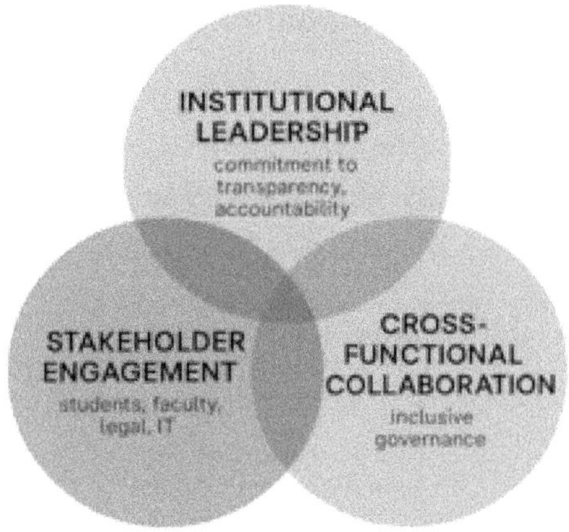

In this Venn diagram, the three main themes required for ethical AI in education are Institutional Leadership, Stakeholder Engagement and Cross-Functional Collaboration. The circles highlight the main pillars of education committing to openness and responsibility (Institutional Leadership); including students, faculty, legal teams and IT (Stakeholder Engagement); and having an inclusive method of governance (Cross-Functional Collaboration). Figure 9 highlights the way all these factors help build a balanced and ethical setup for using AI in education.

Best Practice's: Vendor Due Diligence and Algorithmic Audit's

Due to many schools and colleges using outside vendors for AI, choosing the right vendor is now a mandatory practice. It requires reviewing how vendors safeguard data, keep things transparent and match up to ethical standards. The agreement should clearly state that privacy, data minimization and being able to explain decisions are expected and there must be regular checks for accountability. Algorithmic audits play an important role as additional protection. An independent review of AI algorithms can uncover biased choices, types of discrimination or unexpected side effects that might not be clear to those using or creating the software. Nowadays, educational institutions often join forces with external auditors or make their own internal review boards to hold such reviews on a regular basis. This process needs to have technical checks as well as assessments for equity and fairness.

Figure 10. Best Practice's for Ethical AI Deployment

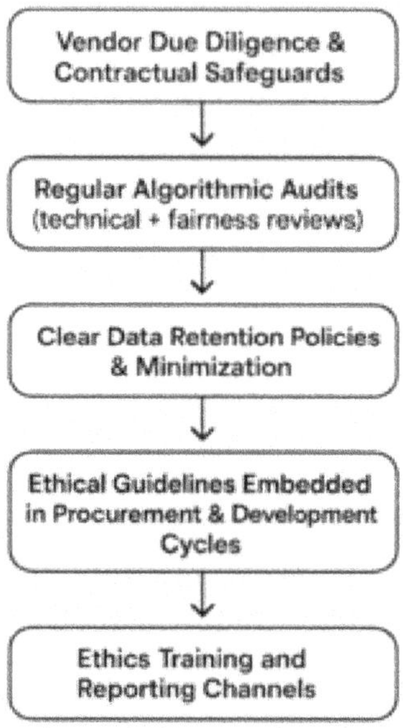

The figure shows a clear flowchart with five main best practices for using AI ethically. It starts with checking vendors and setting up contract terms, then performs regular checks (both technical and for fairness), has clear data storage guidelines and minimization, focuses on ethics in procurement and development and finishes with giving ethics training and ensuring reporting channels are in place. In Figure 10, actionable suggestions are provided for institutions to guarantee responsible AI management remains a core part of their activities.

RECOMMENDATIONS FOR EDUCATOR'S AND POLICYMAKER'S

When AI is used more extensively in schools worldwide, people making educational decisions should always balance advancements with the security and data privacy rights of students. AI can greatly improve educational performance and administrative work; still, if security systems are not set in place, these technologies may reinforce differences, harm privacy rights and threaten trust. The following recommendations to support ethical and responsible use of AI in education are supported by recent studies and cases.

Mandate Transparency and Accountability: Ethical use of AI depends first on being transparent. Adopting AI, schools should make sure that vendors clearly describe how student data is obtained, stored, analyzed and given to others. Mechanisms for accountability should be set up to allow AI-driven outcomes from vendors and institutions to be checked. This requires contracts for data protection, regular testing of algorithms and steps for reporting any incidents.

Enhance Legal and Ethical Literacy: There is a significant but often missed issue in AI adoption related to data privacy laws and ethical matters not being well understood by educators and administration staff. Educational courses should be provided to these stakeholders so that they fully comprehend laws like GDPR, FERPA and those that deal with AI.

Embed Privacy by Design: The idea of privacy by design is that privacy and security need to be part of the system from the start, rather than added on later. Technical tools including end-to-end encryption, anonymization, federated learning and differential privacy should be used by developers to protect the privacy of student information.

Strengthening Regulatory Oversight: AI is advancing more rapidly than laws and educational guidelines in these areas which means there are gaps in what is monitored and managed. Therefore, policymakers need to update legal rules to specifically consider potential difficulties brought by AI in schools and universities.

Promote Student Agency: Ethical AI in education is centered on giving power to students to take an active role instead of being just the data the system uses. Students should be given an opportunity to participate in how their data is managed, to promote transparency and shared leadership.

CONCLUSION

AI being used in schools marks a major change in how student support and learning assistance are thought of and delivered. AI tools like adaptive learning systems and chatbots give learners and schools improved learning experiences and quicker administration processes. This chapter has pointed out the different aspects of such difficulties. Easy-to-use chatbots and virtual assistants can collect large amounts of student personal information. It becomes a major privacy issue when students are not informed about the kinds of information collected or how it is being used. Data collection, storage and processing using these systems are often hidden, which makes it difficult to maintain transparency and trust. It is very important to consider ethics when putting AI into learning systems. Consent, fairness and accountability are not only conceptual; they directly play a part in affecting student experiences and their outcomes. If AI applications are not carefully managed, they may promote current biases, make unequal outcomes worse and damage the reasons for education. The large difference in power between those in authority and students in some cases, followed by uneven digital skills, requires education institutions to focus on student involvement and inclusive decision-making. The GDPR and FERPA are valuable and important regulations on a global level, but they sometimes fail to address all the problems that arise with AI. As AI changes, schools and policymakers should keep changing and adapting these laws and create new AI-related policies and ethics to cover any gaps in the regulations.

Cybersecurity risks increase these issues since AI tools are appealing to bad actors because they handle sensitive data. Firms should use multiple security measures which involve encryption, identity check-ups, security reviews and clear plans to react to incidents. Additionally, it is important for all parties interested in AI such as students and educators, to be educated about cybersecurity to ensure the systems work smoothly. New methods such as federated learning and differential privacy can help deal with the conflict between using data and keeping it private. This approach can change AI systems' approach to student data, stopping the risks of breaches and misuse. However, making these systems work requires a high level of expertise and paying close attention to accuracy as well as personal privacy. According to the case studies and best practices in the chapter, implementing AI ethically is both possible and should always be practiced. A look at successful cases shows the significance of strong leadership, clear data, involved stakeholders and strict management of vendors. These are good examples for schools and teaching institutions to follow as they deal with the ethics and technology involved in adopting AI. At the end, the recommendations point out the importance of involving different groups to work together on these subjects. Educators should treat transparency, education, privacy-by-design, adapting to new regulations and putting students in charge as the main elements of adding responsible AI to education.

REFERENCES

Almufarreh, A., & Arshad, M. (2023). Promising Emerging Technologies for Teaching and Learning: Recent Developments and Future Challenges. *Sustainability*, *15*(8), 6917. DOI: 10.3390/su15086917

Aly, M. (2024). Revolutionizing online education: Advanced facial expression recognition for real-time student progress tracking via deep learning model. *Multimedia Tools and Applications*, *84*(13), 12575–12614. DOI: 10.1007/s11042-024-19392-5

Arizmendi, C. J., Bernacki, M. L., Raković, M., Plumley, R. D., Urban, C. J., Panter, A. T., Greene, J. A., & Gates, K. M. (2022). Predicting student outcomes using digital logs of learning behaviors: Review, current standards, and suggestions for future work. *Behavior Research Methods*, *55*(6), 3026–3054. DOI: 10.3758/s13428-022-01939-9 PMID: 36018483

Armas, R., & Taherdoost, H. (2025). Building a Cybersecurity Culture in Higher Education: Proposing a Cybersecurity Awareness Paradigm. *Information (Basel)*, *16*(5), 336. DOI: 10.3390/info16050336

Arora, A. K., Kumar, A., Tyagi, R., Sharma, S., Kumar, A., & Kumar, S. (2025). Future of Education With AI-. *Assistive Technology*, •••, 169–190. DOI: 10.4018/979-8-3693-9395-6.ch008

Babu, C. V. S., & Simon, P. A. (2023). *Adaptive AI for Dynamic Cybersecurity Systems.*, DOI: 10.4018/979-8-3693-0230-9.ch003

Baker, R. S., & Hawn, A. (2022). Algorithmic Bias in Education. *International Journal of Artificial Intelligence in Education*, *32*(4), 1052–1092. DOI: 10.1007/s40593-021-00285-9

Berendt, B., Littlejohn, A., & Blakemore, M. (2020). AI in education: Learner choice and fundamental rights. *Learning, Media and Technology*, *45*(3), 312–324. DOI: 10.1080/17439884.2020.1786399

Bogina, V., Hartman, A., Kuflik, T., & Shulner-Tal, A. (2022). Educating Software and AI Stakeholders About Algorithmic Fairness, Accountability, Transparency and Ethics. *International Journal of Artificial Intelligence in Education*, *32*(3), 808–833. DOI: 10.1007/s40593-021-00248-0

Cevallos-Salas, D., Estrada-Jiménez, J., & Guamán, D. S. (2024). Application layer security for Internet communications: A comprehensive review, challenges, and future trends. *Computers & Electrical Engineering*, *119*, 109498. DOI: 10.1016/j.compeleceng.2024.109498

Chen, Y., Jensen, S., Albert, L. J., Gupta, S., & Lee, T. (2023). Artificial Intelligence (AI) Student Assistants in the Classroom: Designing Chatbots to Support Student Success. *Information Systems Frontiers*, *25*(1), 161–182. DOI: 10.1007/s10796-022-10291-4

Choudhary, S. K., Kar, A. K., & Dwivedi, Y. K. (2024). How does Federated Learning Impact Decision-Making in Firms: A Systematic Literature Review. *Communications of the Association for Information Systems*, *54*, ●●●. https://www.scopus.com/inward/record.uri?eid=2-s2.0-85186765994&partnerID=40&md5=9ce5200161d256be6d150d6edad43207

Cirillo, F., De Santis, M., & Esposito, C. (2025). *Applications of Solid Platform and Federated Learning for Decentralized Health Data Management*., DOI: 10.1007/978-3-031-70775-9_6

Cohen, B., Hu, A., Patino, D., & Coffman, J. (2024). This Is Going on Your Permanent Record: A Legal Analysis of Educational Data in the Cloud. *ACM Journal on Responsible Computing*, *1*(3), 1–27. DOI: 10.1145/3675230

Díaz-Rodríguez, N., Del Ser, J., Coeckelbergh, M., López de Prado, M., Herrera-Viedma, E., & Herrera, F. (2023). Connecting the dots in trustworthy Artificial Intelligence: From AI principles, ethics, and key requirements to responsible AI systems and regulation. *Information Fusion*, *99*, 101896. DOI: 10.1016/j.inffus.2023.101896

Farsi, Z., Sajadi, S. A., Afaghi, E., Fournier, A., Aliyari, S., Ahmadi, Y., & Hazrati, E. (2021). Explaining the experiences of nursing administrators, educators, and students about education process in the COVID-19 pandemic: A qualitative study. *BMC Nursing*, *20*(1), 151. DOI: 10.1186/s12912-021-00666-4 PMID: 34416886

Fawns, T., Gallagher, M., & Bayne, S. (2021). *Institutional Contexts in Supporting Quality Online Postgraduate Education: Lessons Learned from Two Initiatives at the University of Edinburgh* (pp. 197–215). https://doi.org/DOI: 10.1007/978-3-030-77673-2_11

Hagadone-Bedir, M., Voithofer, R., & Kulp, J. T. (2023). Contextualizing privacy with wearable data in higher education. *British Journal of Educational Technology*, *54*(6), 1619–1635. DOI: 10.1111/bjet.13378

Hathaliya, J. J., Tanwar, S., & Sharma, P. (2022). Adversarial learning techniques for security and privacy preservation: A comprehensive review. *Security and Privacy*, *5*(3). Advance online publication. DOI: 10.1002/spy2.209

Hew, K. F., Huang, W., Du, J., & Jia, C. (2023). Using chatbots to support student goal setting and social presence in fully online activities: Learner engagement and perceptions. *Journal of Computing in Higher Education*, *35*(1), 40–68. DOI: 10.1007/s12528-022-09338-x PMID: 36101883

Izumi, T., Sukhwani, V., Surjan, A., & Shaw, R. (2021). Managing and responding to pandemics in higher educational institutions: Initial learning from COVID-19. *International Journal of Disaster Resilience in the Built Environment*, *12*(1), 51–66. DOI: 10.1108/IJDRBE-06-2020-0054

Khan, F., & Mer, A. (2023). *Embracing Artificial Intelligence Technology: Legal Implications with Special Reference to European Union Initiatives of Data Protection* (pp. 119–141). https://doi.org/DOI: 10.1108/S1569-375920230000111C007

Khan, J. A. (2024). *Role-Based access Control (RBAC) and Attribute-Based Access Control*. ABAC., DOI: 10.4018/979-8-3693-1431-9.ch005

Lekkala, S., & Gurijala, P. (2024). *Security and Privacy for Modern Networks*. Apress., DOI: 10.1007/979-8-8688-0823-4

Molina-Carmona, R., & García-Peñalvo, F. J. (2025). *Safeguarding Knowledge: Ethical Artificial Intelligence Governance in the University Digital Transformation* (pp. 201–220). https://doi.org/DOI: 10.1007/978-3-031-71530-3_14

Mora, A., Bujari, A., & Bellavista, P. (2024). Enhancing generalization in Federated Learning with heterogeneous data: A comparative literature review. *Future Generation Computer Systems*, *157*, 1–15. DOI: 10.1016/j.future.2024.03.027

Nadji, B. (2024). *Data Security*. Integrity, and Protection., DOI: 10.1007/978-3-031-61117-9_4

Neal Joshua, E. S., Bhattacharyya, D., & Rao, N. T. (2022). Managing information security risk and Internet of Things (IoT) impact on challenges of medicinal problems with complex settings. In *Multi-Chaos, Fractal and Multi-Fractional Artificial Intelligence of Different Complex Systems* (pp. 291–310). Elsevier. https://doi.org/DOI: 10.1016/B978-0-323-90032-4.00007-9

Okoli, C. S. A., & Yekini, A. (2023). Implied jurisdiction agreements in international commercial contracts: A global comparative perspective. *Journal of Private International Law*, *19*(3), 321–361. DOI: 10.1080/17441048.2023.2294615

Peyton, K., Unnikrishnan, S., & Mulligan, B. (2025). A review of university chatbots for student support: FAQs and beyond. *Discover Education*, *4*(1), 21. DOI: 10.1007/s44217-025-00397-7

Poleto, T., Nepomuceno, T. C. C., de Carvalho, V. D. H., Friaes, L. C. B. de O., de Oliveira, R. C. P., & Figueiredo, C. J. J. (2023). Information Security Applications in Smart Cities: A Bibliometric Analysis of Emerging Research. *Future Internet*, *15*(12), 393. DOI: 10.3390/fi15120393

Quach, S., Thaichon, P., Martin, K. D., Weaven, S., & Palmatier, R. W. (2022). Digital technologies: Tensions in privacy and data. *Journal of the Academy of Marketing Science*, *50*(6), 1299–1323. DOI: 10.1007/s11747-022-00845-y PMID: 35281634

Rong, K., Ling, Y., Yang, T., & Huang, C. (2025). Cross-border data transfer: Patterns and discrepancies. *Journal of International Business Policy*, *8*(1), 10–32. DOI: 10.1057/s42214-025-00209-7

Sanfilippo, M. R., Apthorpe, N., Brehm, K., & Shvartzshnaider, Y. (2023). Privacy governance not included: Analysis of third parties in learning management systems. *Information and Learning Science, 124*(9/10), 326–348. DOI: 10.1108/ILS-04-2023-0033

Schiff, D. (2022). Education for AI, not AI for Education: The Role of Education and Ethics in National AI Policy Strategies. *International Journal of Artificial Intelligence in Education, 32*(3), 527–563. DOI: 10.1007/s40593-021-00270-2

Shneiderman, B. (2020). Bridging the Gap Between Ethics and Practice. *ACM Transactions on Interactive Intelligent Systems, 10*(4), 1–31. DOI: 10.1145/3419764

Shtayyat, A., Gawanmeh, A., & Mashaleh, A. (2025). *Risk Analysis of AI Integration in Educational Systems.*, DOI: 10.4018/979-8-3373-0832-6.ch017

Stone, A. (2023). Student Perceptions of Academic Integrity: A Qualitative Study of Understanding, Consequences, and Impact. *Journal of Academic Ethics, 21*(3), 357–375. DOI: 10.1007/s10805-022-09461-5 PMID: 36466717

Suleski, T., Ahmed, M., Yang, W., & Wang, E. (2023). A review of multi-factor authentication in the Internet of Healthcare Things. *Digital Health, 9*. Advance online publication. DOI: 10.1177/20552076231177144 PMID: 37252257

Susnjak, T., Ramaswami, G. S., & Mathrani, A. (2022). Learning analytics dashboard: A tool for providing actionable insights to learners. *International Journal of Educational Technology in Higher Education, 19*(1), 12. DOI: 10.1186/s41239-021-00313-7 PMID: 35194560

Tychola, K. A., Vrochidou, E., & Papakostas, G. A. (2024). *Emotional Learning Analytics in Education.*, DOI: 10.4018/979-8-3693-2663-3.ch004

Vayyala, R. (2025). Data Lineage. In *Data Governance, DevSecOps, and Advancements in Modern Software* (pp. 73–98). IGI Global., DOI: 10.4018/979-8-3373-0365-9.ch004

Ye, Q., & Hu, H. (2020). *Local Differential Privacy: Tools*. Challenges, and Opportunities., DOI: 10.1007/978-981-15-3281-8_2

Zhai, C., Wibowo, S., & Li, L. D. (2024). The effects of over-reliance on AI dialogue systems on students' cognitive abilities: A systematic review. *Smart Learning Environments*, *11*(1), 28. DOI: 10.1186/s40561-024-00316-7

Zhao, Y., Zhao, M., & Shi, F. (2023). Integrating Moral Education and Educational Information Technology: A Strategic Approach to Enhance Rural Teacher Training in Universities. *Journal of the Knowledge Economy*, *15*(3), 15053–15093. DOI: 10.1007/s13132-023-01693-z

Zimmerle, J. C. (2021). Safe, Sound, and Private: Promoting Data Protection for Students. *Computers in the Schools*, *38*(1), 1–18. DOI: 10.1080/07380569.2021.1882203

KEY TERMS AND DEFINITIONS

Artificial Intelligence (AI): The use of technology and machines to imitate human thought for education, logical thinking and solving problems.

Chatbots: AI-based agents help educational staff respond to student questions immediately via text or voice.

Cybersecurity: The practice of securing systems, networks and data against any threats, illegal entry or harm in the digital world.

Data Privacy: The ability for people to guide how their personal data is collected, stored and distributed.

Differential Privacy: A method that adds fake data to private information, making it useless, while useful parts of the data can still be accessed.

Federated Learning: A system of learning that does not involve sharing raw data, by training on different decentralized devices.

FERPA: A federal law ensuring that student education records are kept private and stating when they may be disclosed.

GDPR: A European privacy law that instructs how to protect and manage personal data.

Chapter 9
The Role of Generative AI in Curriculum Development and Its Impact on Well-Being

Hayatullah Niazai
Ahmad Shah Abdali Medical College, Afghanistan

Wali Khan Monib
https://orcid.org/0000-0002-9575-9305
Shaikh Zayed University, Afghanistan

ABSTRACT

This chapter explores the integration of Generative AI (GenAI) in curriculum development and its impact on students' well-being. The chapter used Taba curriculum development model, discussing GenAI role in diagnosis of needs, formulation of objectives, selection of content, organization of content, selection of learning experiences, organization of learning activities and evaluation. The analysis indicates that GenAI can be valuable and helpful at the various stages of curriculum development with teacher agency and oversight. Moreover, it can have positive and negative impacts on students' health and psychological well-being depending on its usage.

DOI: 10.4018/979-8-3373-3316-8.ch009

It is not GenAI technology itself, but the manner of its use that determines its impact. The chapter underscores the need for its effective integration to promote quality education and safeguard learner mental health.

1. INTRODUCTION

GenAI has quickly become a disruptive innovation in any education system worldwide. It can autonomously generate novel content, including text, images, audio, video, simulations, or computer code. GenAI is increasingly being considered an assistant tool and a partner that can help redesign personalized learning (Monib, Qazi, Apong, Azizan, et al., 2024; Shimizu et al., 2023). There is a growing research interest in AI tools such as ChatGPT in various fields, including education (Monib, Qazi, Jain, et al., 2025). Traditionally, curriculum development has been a complex task comprising many stakeholders, such as educators, policymakers, students, and accrediting bodies. This is resource-intensive, bound by context, and time (Padovano & Cardamone, 2024). The uptake of GenAI into the learning environment offers quite different affordances: rapid generation of content, individualized pathways for learning, and dynamic strategies for assessment. These can be quite innovative in reducing the instructional workload, increasing access to the content, and supporting differentiated instruction aligned with the diversity of learner profiles.

The implementation of GenAI in education does not come above board. An ongoing conversation on the issues of biased algorithms, privacy of data, ownership, authorship, and academic integrity is still very much alive among researchers and practitioners (Monib, Qazi, & Mahmud, 2025). Even though there is currently expertise simulation possible with GenAI, it is provided without pedagogical intentionality and the enormous emotional intelligence and ethics that are held by human teachers (Chan & Tsi, 2024). These tensions create urgent issues about the proper place of GenAI in formal education on such a level as concerns the curricula and learning. This chapter aims to discuss GenAI in curriculum development and its impact on students' health and psychological well-being.

1.1 Organization of the Chapter

The chapter is organized into six sections. After this introduction, Section 2 reviews the relevant literature on GenAI in education and GenAI in curriculum development, as well as presents the conceptual framework, the Taba Model. Section 3, thereafter, provides an outline of the methodology used to carry out this comprehensive literature review. Section 4 is about results and discussion. Section 5 is about future recommendations, and Section 6 is the conclusion.

2. LITERATURE REVIEW

2.1 GenAI in Education

Artificial Intelligence (AI) was coined by John McCarthy as applying to systems that emulate human thinking, often using large language models and generative adversarial networks (Dashkevych & Portnov, 2024; Haupt et al., 2022). One of the most recent innovations in education, which is bound to transform the very processes of knowledge creation, knowledge delivery, and personalization, is GenAI like ChatGPT (Monib, Qazi, Silva, et al., 2024). Undoubtedly, its capabilities promise content that is highly interactive, that simulates individual activity, fostering environments that are adaptive and learner-centered (Monib, Qazi, Silva, et al., 2024; Ng et al., 2025). The very known among them, though, work on the rapid production of personalized lesson plans and teaching aids as part of GenAI content, large language models. This decreases the effort required of instructors while making the curricula steadier and more flexible. But the integration of GenAI in education raises critical challenges. The ethical concerns, including the bias in AI-generated content, and also the data privacy protection, intellectual property rights, and safeguarding academic integrity, need careful governance. Responsible AI deployment should prioritize transparency, fairness, and also inclusivity to not exacerbate existing inequities. As such, technology such as GenAI evolves, its influence will be seen not only in the curriculum but also in knowledge dissemination, learner assessment, and pedagogical innovation, thus calling for constant research in its impacts and also its ethical implications in education.

2.2 GenAI in Curriculum Development

Curriculum, as the structural backbone of formal education, has been conceptualized through multiple lenses and definitions: curriculum, therefore, is a structured plan for achieving learning objectives; it is the totality of learner experiences; it is an academic field or subject matter; it is content, and it is the framework for organizing content (Hunkins & Ornstein, 2018). This chapter works with curriculum being defined as a deliberate and goal-oriented sequence of learning experiences that allows it to be measured with outcomes and standards, which typically are educational system standards. When applied to curriculum development, GenAI helps to enhance the efficiency of content development and responsiveness by generating, autonomously and just in time, specific learning materials, according to pedagogical aims and the learner context. Design is undertaken based on large-scale data analysis so as to enable the curriculum developers to design responsively to ever more precise learner profiles, metrics of performance, and demands of context. In this way, GenAI enables scaled curriculum personalization and hence differentiated instruction as well as inclusive access.

Likewise, GenAI improves formative assessment practices. In monitoring real-time engagement and comprehension by students, the AI-driven system would consequently offer adaptive feedback loops and targeted interventions. Such new pedagogic systems would be more supportive of the requirements of modern curriculum that, among many other things, propose flexibility, the agency of the learner, and cultural responsiveness in teaching. Noteworthy, such personalization can, provided help when there is transparency and proper oversight by the teaching staff, help remedy the attainment inequities. The chapter employs a theoretical framework for GenAI integration into the curriculum.

2.3 Theoretical Framework

This review adopts the Taba Model as a guiding analytical framework to examine how GenAI can be integrated into curriculum development processes. Developed by Hilda Taba, the model offers a structured, inductive, and teacher-centered approach to curriculum design (Asuncion et al., 2023). It comprises seven sequential stages: (1) Diagnosis of Needs, (2) Formulation of Objectives, (3) Selection of Content, (4) Organization of Content, (5) Selection of Learning Experiences, (6) Organization of Learning Experiences, and (7) Evaluation and Revision (Asuncion et al., 2023). These stages provide a systematic lens to analyze how GenAI technologies can support or transform each phase of curriculum development. Figure 1 outlines the model structure. In this review, the Taba Model is operationalized as a conceptual framework for synthesizing the literature. Rather than presenting a linear account of AI applications, the model enables a staged analysis of GenAI's contribution to curriculum theory and design.

Figure 1. Taba Model of Curriculum Development

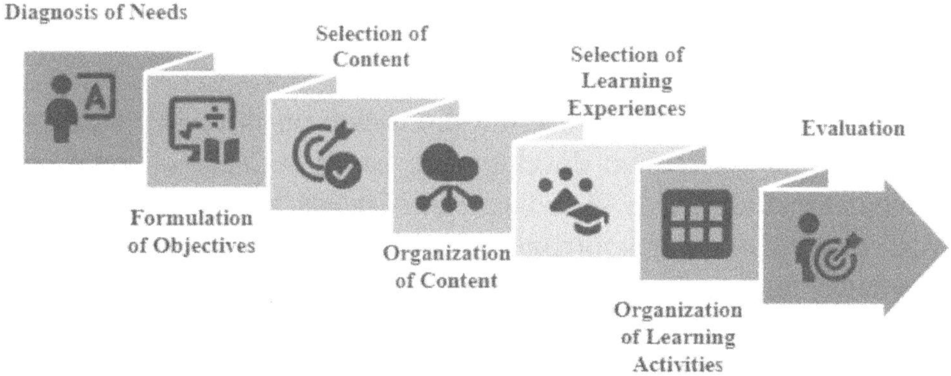

3. METHOD

This chapter adopts a comprehensive review of relevant literature on the role of GenAI in curriculum development and its impact on students' well-being. Unlike systematic reviews that follow narrowly defined inclusion criteria, the comprehensive approach allows for the inclusion of diverse literature (Monib, Qazi, Apong, Azizan, et al., 2024). Literature was identified through targeted searches across Scopus, Web of Science, and Google Scholar using keywords such as Generative AI, GenAI, GenAI tools, AND curriculum development, Taba model, student well-being, psychological impact, and mental impact. Sources were also searched based on curriculum development stages, particularly keywords that are outlined in Taba's grassroots model (diagnosis of needs, formulation of objectives, content selection, learning experience design, activity organization, and evaluation). In reviewing the selected literature, emphasis was placed on identifying not only opportunities but also critical tensions, particularly in relation to teacher agency, equity, and the pedagogical assumptions embedded in AI-driven content.

4. RESULTS AND DISCUSSION

This section presents results and discussion on three key areas: (1) GenAI role in curriculum development, based on Taba's model with subthemes including GenAI in diagnosis of needs, formulation of objectives, selection of content, organization of content, selection of learning experiences, organization of learning activities, as well as evaluation and means of evaluation. (2) GenAI's impact on students' health and psychological well-being, addressing both benefits and risks. (3) case studies as illustrations of practical application. Further details are presented below.

4.1 GenAI in Curriculum Development

4.1.1 GenAI in Diagnosis of Needs

GenAI holds very transformative potential in the "Diagnosis of Needs" stage, which centers on identifying learners' existing knowledge, interests, and contextual circumstances to inform curriculum development. This relies on teachers' observational insights, assessments, and feedback. While it is valuable, it is often time-intensive, reactive, and limited in scope. However, with the integration of GenAI, a deeper, data-driven understanding of learner profiles through real-time analysis of diverse educational data sources can be gained. For example, AI-powered learning management systems can aggregate and interpret students' performance metrics, behavioral engagement (e.g., time-on-task, navigation paths). These systems can then generate descriptive and predictive insights—such as identifying knowledge gaps, patterns of disengagement, or recurring misconceptions—that surpass the capacity of manual teacher observation. For example, AI techniques can be used to analyze student interactions learning materials to know their learning behaviors and preferences, which can inform personalized content (Sharma et al., 2024). Similarly, machine learning algorithms analyze student data to predict academic performance and identify at-risk students, enabling timely interventions (Sunandar et al., 2024).

Moreover, AI-supported learning analytics can be benefited in incorporate multimodal data, including written assignments, speech inputs, and emotion detection (with ethical safeguards), offering nuanced portrayals of learners' emotional, cognitive, and motivational states. Through these capabilities, GenAI can dynamically cluster learners with similar needs or preferences and recommend differentiated instructional strategies. In their study, Liu and Wang (2025) introduced a real-time emotion-aware learning system that leverages facial expression recognition to support personalized education and dynamic instructional adjustments and the system identifies key emotional states—happy, sad, angry, surprised, disgusted, neutral, and fearful—with an overall recognition accuracy of 82.5%. In multilingual or multicultural settings, GenAI can translate learner inputs or that it can identify language-specific learning needs, thereby enhancing linguistic inclusivity. The classification algorithms like Support Vector Machines (SVM), decision trees, and clustering methods might be used to group students based on their abilities and learning styles (Betty et al., 2024).

Needs diagnosis with GenAI can be beneficial for a systemic disparities illuminating across gender, socioeconomic status, and geographic location, such as by detecting consistent underperformance or those with limited access to learning resources within subgroups. This allows teachers and institutions to address inequalities proactively by tailoring interventions. However, the use of GenAI must align with ethical AI principles, including transparency, data privacy, and bias mitigation, to ensure the tools do not replicate or reinforce existing educational inequities. AI systems can detect biases and performance disparities in educational outcomes related to gender and intersectional categories such as race-gender and race-income. Techniques like adversarial learning have been shown to enhance fairness for these intersectional groups (Mangal & Pardos, 2024). Contextually, in underserved educational systems—such as rural areas in low-income countries—AI-driven mobile assessments or conversational agents can democratize needs diagnosis by extending reach to learners beyond traditional classroom boundaries. Prioritizing transparency, ethical design, and inclusive implementation, AI can be a powerful force for democratizing education and preparing students for a future deeply shaped by technological innovation (Bello & Aubert, 2025).

4.1.2 GenAI in Formulation of Objectives.

The formulation of learning objectives is a deliberate, learner-centered process that stems from diagnosed needs. GenAI can be used to tailor learning objectives to student needs, relevant and achievable for students. AI tools can be used to level-appropriate learning objectives, including cognitive, affective, and psychomotor domains. For example, based on aggregated learner input and diagnostic analytics, AI might be used to suggest objectives of lower-order thinking, such as targeting knowledge and comprehension, or higher-order thinking, such as targeting critical thinking skills. However, while AI can formulate or adapt objectives, teacher agency remains central in the validation and selection process. Teachers play a critical role in assessing the appropriateness and feasibility of the objectives since they bring professional and expert judgment, contextual awareness, and pedagogical insight that AI lacks, especially in aligning objectives with community values, school ethos, and real-world relevance. This highlights the importance of teacher agency in enhancing learning outcomes. GenAI can therefore serve as a collaborative co-designer—offering multiple options or refinements based on curriculum alignment and learner needs—while teachers retain decision-making authority to endorse, adapt, or reject those suggestions. Furthermore, AI can support inclusive and responsive goal-setting by identifying disparities in learner readiness, interests, and access. For instance, it can scaffold objectives for students with learning difficulties based on their level of understanding. It can help suggest culturally relevant examples for multilingual learners, thus aligning with SDG 4 and SDG 5 on eliminating disparity in gender and disability.

4.1.3 GenAI in the Selection of Content

The content selection follows the formulated objectives and anchored in the principles of validity, relevance, and significance. The objectives shape and justify the inclusion of content, ensuring alignment between what is intended to teach. GenAI can enhance this process to create and help in selecting content (Monib, Qazi, & Apong, 2025) that are intellectually appropriate level and contextually meaningful in alignment with formulated objectives. By curating materials from vast resources, GenAI tools such as ChatGPT can assist in identifying content that supports the achievement of specific learning objectives efficiently. However, as Taba emphasized, content need be teacher-validated for developmental appropriateness and conceptual significance. Studies show that when teachers have the autonomy to override AI-generated content, it positively impacts student outcomes. For instance, in a study conducted in Kenya, teachers who could apply their pedagogical judgment to modify system-generated content saw higher digital scores among their students compared to those who relied solely on AI-generated content (Sun et al., 2024). GenAI offers options but does not determine what is ultimately selected; teachers retain epistemic authority and responsibility to ensure that the chosen content reflects subject integrity and learner relevance. Ravarini et al. (2024), in their study framing educators as designers and co-creators, position GenAI as a facilitative and utilitarian tool.

4.1.4 GenAI in the Organization of Content

Taba distinguished content organization from content selection, emphasizing the need for logical sequencing based on conceptual relationships and disciplinary structures. At this stage, teacher organizes the content into a sequence, taking into consideration learners' maturity, academic achievement, and interests (Ornstein & Hunkins, 2017). GenAI can support teachers by modeling content progressions that move from simple to complex, concrete to abstract, or foundational to advanced. For instance, an AI tool could generate a concept map or learning trajectory that helps structure how ideas should unfold over time, reinforcing vertical coherence and horizontal integration. Al-Ma'arif et al. (2024) presented an AI-driven curriculum personalization system using the K-Nearest Neighbors (K-NN) algorithm to tailor content based on students' psychological profiles and interests by clustering learners through psychometric data. The system delivers personalized, engaging content aligned with individual learning styles and motivations. The AI can be used to sequence can assist teachers in planning coherence while maintaining fidelity to subject logic. Importantly, GenAI supports content structuring without dictating pedagogy, thus remaining aligned with Taba's distinction between knowledge sequencing and instructional method.

4.1.5 GenAI in the Selection of Learning Experiences

The teacher selects instructional methods that engage the students with the content (Ornstein & Hunkins, 2017). Engagement, along with other content-related factors, is essential for improving learning outcomes (Monib, Qazi, Apong, & Mahmud, 2024). Learning experiences should be deliberately selected to enable students to interact meaningfully with content and to achieve specified objectives. GenAI can assist teachers in identifying and tailoring learning experiences that are suited to specific learner profiles, instructional contexts, and content domains. For example, AI tools can propose simulations, inquiry tasks, project-based learning ideas, or hands-on investigations that are aligned with the selected content. A study by Swan et al. (2025) reported that AI-enabled mannequins in nursing education have been found to be effective and acceptable for teaching complex scenarios like opioid overdose responses. GenAI should not replace pedagogical judgment but expand the range of possibilities, allowing teachers to make informed choices based on the intersection of objective, content, and learner diversity.

4.1.6 GenAI in the Organization of Learning Activities

Taba viewed the organization of learning experiences as central to learning. A teacher organizes the learning activities into a sequence, often determined by the content and keeping in mind the particular students who will be taught (Ornstein & Hunkins, 2017). GenAI can support this by helping the teacher structure learning activities in ways that build systematically. GenAI can analyze curriculum standards, learning objectives, and prior learner data to generate a pedagogically sound sequence of tasks. For instance, by using Natural Language Processing (NLP) and pattern recognition algorithms, GenAI systems identify concept hierarchies and cognitive demand levels. Based on this, GenAI can propose exploratory tasks (e.g., brainstorming or simulations) to activate prior knowledge, followed by guided instruction (e.g., scaffolded explanations or step-by-step walkthroughs), and conclude with performance tasks (e.g., project-based assessments or case studies). This sequencing aligns with established instructional design models such as Bloom's Taxonomy and backward design, ensuring coherence and cumulative learning. The AI-generated sequence is not arbitrary—it leverages learner analytics to adjust pacing and difficulty, and applies instructional alignment principles to ensure each task builds meaningfully on the last. This results in learning pathways that enhance retention (by spaced repetition and scaffolding), transfer (by contextualized practice), and engagement (by cognitive congruence and motivational design). Here, GenAI functions as a planning assistant, helping educators maintain coherent activity structure without overstepping into content selection or decision-making.

4.1.7 GenAI in Evaluation and Means of Evaluation

The evaluation should be tied directly to instructional objectives. GenAI can aid this process, generating assessment tools—such as objective tests, performance tasks, and rubrics—that align with the specific goals identified earlier in the planning process. AI tools can also assist in creating formative checks for understanding and suggesting feedback strategies tailored to the student's performance level (Niazai & Monib, 2025). For example, GenAI such as ChatGPT might be used to draft reflective prompts for self-assessment or create differentiated quizzes based on diagnostic patterns. However, consistent with Taba's view, evaluation remains a teacher-driven process where AI-generated assessments serve as drafts subject to professional review, ensuring that evaluation is not only technically aligned but also ethically and contextually appropriate.

4.2 GenAI Impact on Health and Psychological Well-Being

The integration of GenAI into curriculum development presents both promising opportunities and significant risks for learners' health and psychological well-being. On the positive side, GenAI enables personalized and adaptive learning experiences that reduce academic stress and anxiety by tailoring content to individual learner pacing and cognitive readiness. For example, Han et al. (2025) studied that how GenAI can generate content tailored to students' proficiency levels using a deep learning model, reducing teacher workload and enhancing student motivation, which can contribute to effective learning outcomes for all. In another study, Yang (2025) reported that GenAI significantly enhances students' cognitive and emotional engagement, motivation, learning retention, and reward sensitivity.

Moreover, these personalized systems also can help improve health literacy and well-being, especially when AI-curated content delivers accessible, reliable and relevant—a key contribution to both access to health information and education for sustainable development. In the context of physical health, AI-designed High-Intensity Interval Training programs have demonstrated improvements in mental health metrics, such as reduced anxiety and depression scores, and increased quality of life (Fan et al., 2025). This suggests that AI-driven personalized interventions can positively impact mental health. AI tools can also help improve students' emotional management and coping strategies (Klimova & Pikhart, 2025). Shahzad et al. (2025) examined the effects of ChatGPT-4 and social media on academic performance and psychological well-being among 441 Chinese university students. They found both technologies positively influenced outcomes, but collaborative learning negatively mediated the relationship between GenAI and academic/psychological well-being, while positively mediating the effect of social media. This suggests that although GenAI enhances individual performance, it may disrupt collaborative dynamics, highlighting the need for pedagogical frameworks that integrate AI without undermining social learning processes.

However, it can at the same time cause psychological issues if not used in a balanced and effective way. The psychological risks associated with AI integration in curricula must not be ignored. Huang et al. (2025) highlight that GenAI may cause psychological harm that is difficult to quantify and poorly addressed by current legal frameworks. Their qualitative study proposes remedies such as emotional distress compensation, regulatory standards, and AI liability insurance. Excessive reliance on AI tools can lead to digital fatigue, cognitive overload, and social isolation, particularly when AI-driven learning replaces collaborative or interpersonal learning. Over-reliance on AI can lead to technostress and digital fatigue, negatively impacting students' mental health and social interactions (Klimova & Pikhart, 2025). Similarly, Bobrytska et al. (2025) conducted a systematic review on how digitalization in higher education affects students' health, cognition, and social interaction. The study found that fully digital models were associated with high levels of digital fatigue, stress, and cognitive overload. Blended learning reduced these effects but still caused Zoom fatigue. Traditional classroom settings supported better social interaction and sustained cognitive engagement. AI-enhanced systems offered personalised learning benefits (Monib, Qazi, Silva, et al., 2024) but risked fragmenting deep learning. Furthermore, emotional dependency on system-generated feedback may diminish students' resilience and critical thinking, undermining the goals of learner empowerment central to SDG 4. Additionally, algorithmic bias and misinformation pose significant threats, especially in medical or health-related content. Inaccurate AI-generated outputs can mislead learners and reinforce harmful stereotypes if not rigorously validated by educators. Ravarini et al. (2024) stress the importance of educators maintaining their dual role as designers and facilitators to ensure GenAI serves as a co-creative tool rather than an authoritative source. Lastly, the digital divide remains a persistent equity issue. In under-resourced settings, such as rural schools, unequal access to AI infrastructure can exacerbate psychological stress and marginalization. Studies such as Sun et al. (2024) highlight that teacher agency in modifying AI-generated content significantly improves learning outcomes, reaffirming the importance of human-centered design and equitable access to educational technology. Similarly, technological skills are essential for students (Monib, 2023). It can be said that while GenAI can have positive and negative impacts. These dual imperatives call for policies that prioritize teacher autonomy, learner dignity and well-being, and inclusive digital futures.

4.3 Case Studies

Case studies offers in-depth illustrations of GenAI's role in curriculum development and its impact on students' well-being, providing contextualized evidence of how GenAI functions in practice. For example, Cosar (2024) explored the application of AI-supported learning analytics using the eXtreme Gradient Boosting (XGBoost) algorithm to enhance educational prediction and personalization. The study aimed to develop a predictive model to predict students' final exam scores by analyzing factors such as age, participation rates, and previous exam scores. The findings highlight the practical value of AI-based analytics in identifying students at risk, supporting differentiated instruction, and contributing to more personalized and adaptive learning environments. The study affirms the potential of machine learning models, particularly XGBoost, to enhance data-informed educational decision-making and optimize student outcomes across diverse learning contexts.

Jauhiainen and Garagorry Guerra (2024) investigated the use of GenAI, specifically ChatGPT-3.5 and 4, for dynamic personalization of instructional content in primary school classrooms. The study involved 110 students aged 8 to 14 across two schools in Uruguay and explored how GenAI can adapt educational materials in real-time during lessons. The AI-generated texts, illustrations, and exercises were aligned with national curriculum goals and adjusted based on individual pupil knowledge levels. Findings showed that AI-driven personalization enhanced cognitive ergonomics, increased student motivation, and improved academic performance. The authors conclude that GenAI offers a promising solution for tailoring school learning materials to meet diverse learner needs and support curriculum-aligned instruction in primary education. Moreover, Sun et al. (2024) investigated teacher–AI collaboration in digital personalised learning (DPL) among 562 pre-primary learners across 45 classrooms. Teachers who were in the experimental group were allowed to use pedagogical judgment to modify AI-suggested content, while those in the control group followed system-generated recommendations exclusively. Results revealed that learners in the experimental group achieved significantly higher digital learning scores, indicating the positive impact of teacher agency on learning outcomes. Additionally, teacher agency—measured by the frequency and diversity of content overrides—was found to influence learner device engagement, though not lesson plan usage or final scores. Similarly, Cordero and Cordero-Castillo (2025) examined the opportunities, challenges, and best practices for integrating GenAI (GenAI) into higher education. Based on a series of professional development courses for university professors, the study explored how large language models (e.g., ChatGPT, Copilot, Gemini, Claude) enhance teaching practices and resource development. Using literature review, interviews, surveys, and collaborative activities, the authors found that GenAI improves teacher productivity, supports lesson planning, and facilitates the creation of instructional materials. However, concerns were raised regarding ethical use, AI-generated content detection, and the necessity of institutional policies. The study recommends teacher training, development of task-specific prompts, and fostering student critical thinking to ensure ethical and effective GenAI integration. The authors propose a practical guide for responsibly embedding GenAI in classroom settings. These underscore the critical role of human-in-the-loop instructional design and the need for AI systems that preserve and enhance teacher decision-making, particularly in low and middle-income contexts. Similarly, Chun et al. (2025) conducted a comparative study on the use of GenAI-powered textbooks (based on

LLama 3.1) versus traditional printed materials in a university health sciences course. While no significant differences were found in academic performance, learning time, or satisfaction between groups, qualitative data highlighted the AI textbook's strengths in promoting self-regulated learning and personalized content delivery. The study also identified key challenges, including digital equity, algorithmic bias, and data privacy. The authors stress the need for educator training, ethical frameworks, and scalable strategies to responsibly integrate AI in higher education.

Regarding well-being, a study by Yang and Rui (2025) examined the relationship between AI-enhanced learning environments and emotional health among EFL university students. The study focused on how depression and anxiety influence engagement. Using data from 673 participants and employing statistical analyses including correlation, regression, and structural equation modeling, the study found a significant link between emotional well-being and student engagement in AI-supported settings. While personalized feedback and adaptive learning tools helped reduce some emotional distress, the study also identified potential negative effects—such as increased anxiety and frustration—when students felt overwhelmed or unsupported. Emotional fluctuations were shown to directly affect participation, motivation, and focus. Students with higher levels of depression and anxiety demonstrated lower engagement, while those with stronger emotional health were more actively engaged. Similarly, Yang (2025) examined the impact of GenAI on student learning through the lens of Reinforcement Theory, involving 487 undergraduates from seven North China universities. The study found strong positive effects of AI tools on cognitive and emotional engagement, learning retention, reward sensitivity, and motivation. Frequent interaction with AI-generated content enhanced comprehension, emotional connection, and motivational engagement, reinforcing both intrinsic and extrinsic learning behaviors. The findings emphasize the potential of AI-driven environments to personalize learning, improve retention, and foster adaptive, motivated learners in higher education.

5. FUTURE RECOMMENDATIONS

The future of GenAI in education includes the integration of immersive technologies like Virtual Reality (VR) and predictive analytics, which can further enhance personalized learning experiences (Yadav et al., 2025). Moreover, ongoing research and randomized controlled trials (RCTs) are necessary to evaluate the long-term impacts of AI-based educational tools and to develop adaptive frameworks that balance technological advancements with human-centered education (Chun et al., 2025). Future research should also explore how GenAI tools perform across different subject domains and learner profiles, particularly in relation to mental health and engagement metrics. Mixed-methods studies evaluating AI-enhanced instructional design, adaptive learning systems, and teacher-student-AI interaction dynamics would provide deeper insight.

6. CONCLUSION

This chapter explored the GenAI integration into curriculum development and its impact on students' well-being. The findings suggest that GenAI has significant potential to support the curriculum process when used with appropriate teacher oversight. It also highlights that student psychological outcomes are highly contingent on implementation strategies—beneficial when GenAI enhances personalization and engagement, but potentially detrimental if it introduces cognitive overload, bias, or misalignment with learning needs. The analysis further indicates that AI is dependent on student usage, as they use it. The results underscore the importance of effective strategies for integrating GenAI in curriculum development. The chapter emphasizes that effective deployment of AI requires not only technical infrastructure but also pedagogical frameworks that ensure transparency, ethical use, and instructional relevance. Teacher agency is discussed as a key factor in both the benefits and risks of GenAI-supported learning environments. GenAI's contribution to the curriculum will depend on sustained, evidence-based integration efforts that align technological capabilities with sound pedagogical practices.

REFERENCES

Al-Ma'arif, D. M. N., Maulana, A., Aidha, R., Sanjaya, I., & Fergina, A. (2024, December). AI-Driven Curriculum Personalization System Using K-Nearest Neighbors Algorithm Based on Psychological Profiles and Interests. In 2024 10th International Conference on Computing, Engineering and Design (ICCED) (pp. 1-6). IEEE.

Asuncion, A. C., de Vera Asuncion, A., Macalipis, J. G., Borromeo, C. M. T., Rivera, J. C., & Limon, M. R. (2023). Weaving gaps in garments education technology: Crafting a skill-based E-toolkit based on Taba's curriculum development model. *Social Sciences & Humanities Open*, *8*(1), 100656. DOI: 10.1016/j.ssaho.2023.100656

Bello, L., & Aubert, L. (2025). Artificial intelligence in the classroom: Democratizing knowledge and transforming education [Article]. *Seminars in Medical Writing and Education*, *4*, 469. Advance online publication. DOI: 10.56294/mw2025469

Betty, M., Efendi, S., Zarlis, M., & Suwilo, S. (2024). Differentiated e-learning models based on needs and abilities of students with artificial intelligence. [Article]. *ICIC Express Letters*, *18*(11), 1201–1210. DOI: 10.24507/icicel.18.11.1201

Bobrytska, V. I., Krasylnykova, H. V., Protska, S. M., Skyrda, T. S., Krasylnykov, S. R., & Chkhalo, O. M. (2025). Digitalisation in Higher Education: A Systematic Review of its Impact on Health, Cognition, and Social Interaction [Review]. *International Journal of Learning. Teaching and Educational Research*, *24*(5), 339–359. DOI: 10.26803/ijlter.24.5.18

Chan, C. K. Y., & Tsi, L. H. Y. (2024). Will generative AI replace teachers in higher education? A study of teacher and student perceptions. *Studies in Educational Evaluation*, *83*, 101395. DOI: 10.1016/j.stueduc.2024.101395

Chun, J., Kim, J., Kim, H., Lee, G., Cho, S., Kim, C., Chung, Y., & Heo, S. (2025). A Comparative Analysis of On-Device AI-Driven, Self-Regulated Learning and Traditional Pedagogy in University Health Sciences Education [Article]. *Applied Sciences (Switzerland)*, *15*(4), 1815. Advance online publication. DOI: 10.3390/app15041815

Cordero, J., & Cordero-Castillo, A. (2025). Exploring the Potential of Generative AI in Education: Opportunities, Challenges, and Best Practices for Classroom Integration [Conference paper]. *Communications in Computer and Information Science, 2261 CCIS*, 252-265. https://doi.org/ DOI: 10.1007/978-3-031-85930-4_23

Cosar, M. (2024). Utilizing the eXtreme Gradient Boosting Algorithm for Artificial Intelligence-supported Learning Analytics Application [Conference paper]. *Eurasia Proceedings of Science, Technology, Engineering and Mathematics, 28*, 277-285. https://doi.org/DOI: 10.55549/epstem.1521844

Dashkevych, O., & Portnov, B. A. (2024). How can generative AI help in different parts of research? An experiment study on smart cities' definitions and characteristics. *Technology in Society*, *77*, 102555. DOI: 10.1016/j.techsoc.2024.102555

Fan, M., Lipowski, M., Wang, X., & Liu, T. (2025). The effectiveness of healthcare interventions for high-intensity interval training under generative artificial intelligence technology [Article]. *Journal of Mechanics in Medicine and Biology*, *25*(5), 2540033. Advance online publication. DOI: 10.1142/S0219519425400330

Han, X., Li, Z., Zhang, W., & Fan, W. (2025). Generative AI in Education: Developing Personalized Learning Experiences with Hyperspherical Variational Self-Attention Autoencoder [Conference paper]. *Proceedings of 2024 3rd International Conference on Artificial Intelligence and Education, ICAIE 2024*, 670-674. https://doi.org/DOI: 10.1145/3722237.3722354

Haupt, S. E., Gagne, D. J., Hsieh, W. W., Krasnopolsky, V., McGovern, A., Marzban, C., Moninger, W., Lakshmanan, V., Tissot, P., & Williams, J. K. (2022). The History and Practice of AI in the Environmental Sciences. *Bulletin of the American Meteorological Society*, *103*(5), E1351–E1370. DOI: 10.1175/BAMS-D-20-0234.1

Huang, X., Nor, M. Z. B. M., Yusoff, Z. M., & Liang, Z. (2025). Psychological harm induced by generative AI and its legal remedies [Article]. *Environment and Social Psychology*, *10*(3), 3554. Advance online publication. DOI: 10.59429/esp.v10i3.3554

Hunkins, F. P., & Ornstein, A. C. (2018). *Curriculum: Foundations, principles, and issues*. Pearson Education London.

Jauhiainen, J. S., & Garagorry Guerra, A. (2024). Generative AI and education: Dynamic personalization of pupils' school learning material with ChatGPT [Article]. *Frontiers in Education*, *9*, 1288723. Advance online publication. DOI: 10.3389/feduc.2024.1288723

Klimova, B., & Pikhart, M. (2025). Exploring the effects of artificial intelligence on student and academic well-being in higher education: A mini-review [Short survey]. *Frontiers in Psychology*, *16*, 1498132. Advance online publication. DOI: 10.3389/fpsyg.2025.1498132 PMID: 39963679

Liu, M., & Wang, W. (2025). Design and Implementation of an Emotion-Aware Learning System Based on Facial Expression Recognition [Conference paper]. *Proceedings of 2024 3rd International Conference on Artificial Intelligence and Education, ICAIE 2024*, 154-159. https://doi.org/DOI: 10.1145/3722237.3722264

Mangal, M., & Pardos, Z. A. (2024). Implementing equitable and intersectionality-aware ML in education: A practical guide [Article]. *British Journal of Educational Technology*, *55*(5), 2003–2038. DOI: 10.1111/bjet.13484

Monib, W. K. (2023). Implementation of 21st Century Skills in EFL Classroom: Perceptions of Lecturers and Students. [IJonSES]. *International Journal on Social & Education Sciences*, *5*(3), 536–559. DOI: 10.46328/ijonses.544

Monib, W. K., Qazi, A., & Apong, R. A. (2025). Microlearning beyond boundaries: A systematic review and a novel framework for improving learning outcomes [Article]. *Heliyon*, *11*(2), e41413. Advance online publication. DOI: 10.1016/j.heliyon.2024.e41413 PMID: 39882484

Monib, W. K., Qazi, A., Apong, R. A., Azizan, M. T., De Silva, L., & Yassin, H. (2024). Generative AI and future education: A review, theoretical validation, and authors' perspective on challenges and solutions. *PeerJ. Computer Science*, *10*, e2105. DOI: 10.7717/peerj-cs.2105 PMID: 39650462

Monib, W. K., Qazi, A., Apong, R. A., & Mahmud, M. M. (2024). Investigating learners' perceptions of microlearning: Factors influencing learning outcomes. *IEEE Access : Practical Innovations, Open Solutions*, *12*, 1–17. DOI: 10.1109/ACCESS.2024.3472113

Monib, W. K., Qazi, A., Jain, J., & Ponniah, L. (2025). A Comprehensive Scientometric Analysis of ChatGPT Research Global Trends and Future Prospects. *TechTrends*. Advance online publication. DOI: 10.1007/s11528-025-01110-z

Monib, W. K., Qazi, A., & Mahmud, M. M. (2025). Exploring learners' experiences and perceptions of ChatGPT as a learning tool in higher education. *Education and Information Technologies*, *30*(1), 917–939. DOI: 10.1007/s10639-024-13065-4

Monib, W. K., Qazi, A., Silva, L. D., & Mahmud, M. M. (2024). Exploring Learners' Experiences with ChatGPT in Personalized Learning. *2024 6th International Workshop on Artificial Intelligence and Education (WAIE)*, 66-70. https://doi.org/DOI: 10.1109/WAIE63876.2024.00019

Ng, D. T. K., Chan, E. K. C., & Lo, C. K. (2025). Opportunities, challenges and school strategies for integrating generative AI in education. *Computers and Education: Artificial Intelligence*, *8*, 100373. DOI: 10.1016/j.caeai.2025.100373

Niazai, H., & Monib, W. K. (2025). AI for Personalized Learning in Medical Education. In Martínez Asanza, D. (Ed.), *Teaching in the Age of Medical Technology* (pp. 91–122). IGI Global Scientific Publishing., DOI: 10.4018/979-8-3373-1519-5.ch004

Ornstein, A. C., & Hunkins, F. P. (2017). *Curriculum: Foundations, principles, and issues* (7th ed.). Pearson.

Padovano, A., & Cardamone, M. (2024). Towards human-AI collaboration in the competency-based curriculum development process: The case of industrial engineering and management education. *Computers and Education: Artificial Intelligence*, *7*, 100256. DOI: 10.1016/j.caeai.2024.100256

Ravarini, A., Canavesi, A., & Passerini, K. (2024). From Users to Allies: Exploring Educator and Generative AI Roles in Shaping the Future of Higher Education [Conference paper]. *International Conference on Higher Education Advances*, 312-319. https://doi.org/DOI: 10.4995/HEAd24.2024.17345

Shahzad, M. F., Xu, S., Liu, H., & Zahid, H. (2025). Generative Artificial Intelligence (ChatGPT-4) and Social Media Impact on Academic Performance and Psychological Well-Being in China's Higher Education [Article]. *European Journal of Education*, *60*(1), e12835. Advance online publication. DOI: 10.1111/ejed.12835

Sharma, S. K., Dixit, R. J., Rai, D., & Mall, S. (2024). Artificial intelligence and machine learning in smart education. In *Infrastructure Possibilities and Human-Centered Approaches With Industry 5.0* (pp. 86–106). IGI Global., DOI: 10.4018/979-8-3693-0782-3.ch006

Shimizu, I., Kasai, H., Shikino, K., Araki, N., Takahashi, Z., Onodera, M., Kimura, Y., Tsukamoto, T., Yamauchi, K., Asahina, M., Ito, S., & Kawakami, E. (2023). Developing Medical Education Curriculum Reform Strategies to Address the Impact of Generative AI: Qualitative Study. *JMIR Medical Education*, *9*. Advance online publication. DOI: 10.2196/53466 PMID: 38032695

Sun, C., Major, L., Daltry, R., Moustafa, N., & Friedberg, A. (2024). Teacher-AI Collaboration in Content Recommendation for Digital Personalised Learning among Pre-primary Learners in Kenya [Conference paper]. *L@S 2024 - Proceedings of the 11th ACM Conference on Learning @ Scale*, 346-350. https://doi.org/DOI: 10.1145/3657604.3664662

Sunandar, E., Purnama, A., Arribathi, A. H., Yusuf, D. A., & Daeli, O. P. M. (2024). Strategies and Consequences of AI-Enhanced Predictive Models for Early Identification of Students at Risk [Conference paper]. *2024 3rd International Conference on Creative Communication and Innovative Technology, ICCIT 2024*. https://doi.org/DOI: 10.1109/ICCIT62134.2024.10701122

Swan, B. A., Febres-Cordero, S., Steiger, L., Lisenby, A., Getz, T., Hudson, J., Cole, K., Branch, R., McDermott, C., Fugate, K., & Giordano, N. A. (2025). Feasibility and acceptability of incorporating artificial intelligence into simulation education [Article]. *Clinical Simulation in Nursing*, *104*, 101739. Advance online publication. DOI: 10.1016/j.ecns.2025.101739

Yadav, R., Huzooree, G., Yadav, M., & Gangodawilage, D. S. K. (2025). Generative AI for personalized learning content creation. In *Transformative AI Practices for Personalized Learning Strategies* (pp. 107–130). IGI Global., DOI: 10.4018/979-8-3693-8744-3.ch005

Yang, H. (2025). Harnessing generative AI: Exploring its impact on cognitive engagement, emotional engagement, learning retention, reward sensitivity, and motivation through reinforcement theory [Article]. *Learning and Motivation*, *90*, 102136. Advance online publication. DOI: 10.1016/j.lmot.2025.102136

Yang, H., & Rui, Y. (2025). Transforming EFL students' engagement: How AI-enhanced environments bridge emotional health challenges like depression and anxiety [Article]. *Acta Psychologica*, *257*, 105104. Advance online publication. DOI: 10.1016/j.actpsy.2025.105104 PMID: 40413880

Compilation of References

Abduljawad, S. (2025). Investigating the Impact of ChatGPT as an AI Tool on ESL Writing. *International Journal of Computer-Assisted Language Learning and Teaching*, *14*(1), 1–19. DOI: 10.4018/ijcallt.367276

Adamopoulou, E., & Moussiades, L. (2020). Chatbots: History, technology, and applications. *Machine Learning with Applications*, *2*, 100006.

Aggarwal, S., Wright, J., Morgan, A., Patton, G., & Reavley, N. (2023). Religiosity and spirituality in the prevention and management of depression and anxiety in young people: A systematic review and meta-analysis. *BMC Psychiatry*, *23*(1), 729. DOI: 10.1186/s12888-023-05091-2 PMID: 37817143

Ahmed, N., & Hassan, S. (2024). The Impact of Conversational AI on Student Mental Health: A Comparative Study. *Journal of Educational Technology & Society*, *27*(2), 33–47. DOI: 10.1016/j.jets.2024.02.003

Ajayi, R. (2025). AI-powered innovations for managing complex mental health conditions and addiction treatments. *International Research Journal of Modernization in Engineering Technology and Science*, •••, 1–18.

AlAjmi, M. K. (2022). The impact of digital leadership on teachers' technology integration during the COVID-19 pandemic in Kuwait. *International Journal of Educational Research*, *112*, 101928. DOI: 10.1016/j.ijer.2022.101928 PMID: 35153373

Alamri, W., Qasem, F., Alfotais, A., & Al Taisan, H. A. (2025). Leveraging ChatGPT AI Model in Academic Writing and Avenues for Further Development: SWOT Framework. *Forum for Linguistic Studies*, *7*(2). Advance online publication. DOI: 10.30564/fls.v7i2.8218

Alenezi, H. S., & Faisal, M. H. (2020). Utilizing crowdsourcing and machine learning in education: Literature review. *Education and Information Technologies*, *25*(4), 2971–2986.

Alexander, R. (2008). Towards Dialogic Teaching: Rethinking Classroom Talk. *Diálogos (San José)*.

Alhasani, M., & Orji, R. (2025). Promoting Stress Management among Students in Higher Education: Evaluating the Effectiveness of a Persuasive Time Management Mobile App. *International Journal of Human-Computer Interaction*, *41*(1), 219–241. DOI: 10.1080/10447318.2023.2297330

Ali, M., & Rahman, F. (2023). Integrating AI Chatbots into University Counseling Services: Benefits and Challenges. *Journal of University Counseling*, *29*(3), 150–165. DOI: 10.1016/j.juc.2023.03.009

Alison, C. S. M., Kyoko, U., & Hironari, N. (2019, July). Student Learning Space: The Integration of Curriculum and Technology in Singapore. In *Proceedings of the 3rd International Conference on Education and Multimedia Technology* (pp. 37-40).

Al-Ma'arif, D. M. N., Maulana, A., Aidha, R., Sanjaya, I., & Fergina, A. (2024, December). AI-Driven Curriculum Personalization System Using K-Nearest Neighbors Algorithm Based on Psychological Profiles and Interests. In 2024 10th International Conference on Computing, Engineering and Design (ICCED) (pp. 1-6). IEEE.

Almadani, N. (2024). *Emotional Intelligence*., DOI: 10.4018/979-8-3693-7372-9.ch004

Almarzooqi, F. M. A., & Abouassar, P. (2024). Strategic Leadership and Effective Management in Implementing an AI-Enhanced Online Parent-Teacher Communication System for a Primary School in the UAE. *Journal of Research in Curriculum Instruction and Educational Technology*, *10*(2), 39–64.

Almeida, D., & Barr, N. (2025). Innovations in Health Data Protection Ethical, Legal, and Technological Perspectives in a Global Context. In *Navigating Privacy, Innovation, and Patient Empowerment Through Ethical Healthcare Technology* (pp. 171–196). IGI Global. https://doi.org/DOI: 10.4018/979-8-3693-7630-0.ch007

Almufarreh, A., & Arshad, M. (2023). Promising Emerging Technologies for Teaching and Learning: Recent Developments and Future Challenges. *Sustainability*, *15*(8), 6917. DOI: 10.3390/su15086917

Al-Sayed, S., Assayed, S. K., Alkhatib, M., & Shaalan, K. (2024). Impact of Artificial Intelligence Chatbots on Student Well-being and Mental Health: A Systematic Review. *People and Behavior Analysis*, *2*(2), 10–31098.

Aly, M. (2024). Revolutionizing online education: Advanced facial expression recognition for real-time student progress tracking via deep learning model. *Multimedia Tools and Applications*, *84*(13), 12575–12614. DOI: 10.1007/s11042-024-19392-5

American Counseling Association (ACA). (2021). *Why Counseling is Important*. Retrieved from www.counseling.org

American Psychological Association. (2023). AI in psychology: Promise, pitfalls, and potential. https://www.apa.org/news/press/releases/2023/09/artificial-intelligence-psychology

Anand, S., Miglani, S., & Anand, R. (2025). *Multimodal AI for Enhanced Emotional Intelligence in the Cloud Computing Era.*, DOI: 10.4018/979-8-3693-9694-0.ch008

Ansari, D. (2022). An accumulation of distress: Grief, loss, and isolation among healthcare providers during the COVID-19 pandemic. *SSM. Mental Health*, *2*, 100146. DOI: 10.1016/j.ssmmh.2022.100146 PMID: 36104985

Ansari, G., Gupta, S., & Singhal, N. (2021). Natural Language Processing in Online Reviews. In *Natural Language Processing for Global and Local Business* (pp. 40–64). IGI Global Scientific Publishing.

Aravind, K., & Arun, S. (2024). *S., I. R., & Pazhamalai, V.* Transforming Healthcare., DOI: 10.4018/979-8-3693-1243-8.ch002

Arighi, W. (2025). A conversation on AI, writing, and online learning with Sherri VandenAkker. *The Successful Registrar, 24*(12), 6–7. DOI: 10.1002/tsr.31407

Arizmendi, C. J., Bernacki, M. L., Raković, M., Plumley, R. D., Urban, C. J., Panter, A. T., Greene, J. A., & Gates, K. M. (2022). Predicting student outcomes using digital logs of learning behaviors: Review, current standards, and suggestions for future work. *Behavior Research Methods, 55*(6), 3026–3054. DOI: 10.3758/s13428-022-01939-9 PMID: 36018483

Armas, R., & Taherdoost, H. (2025). Building a Cybersecurity Culture in Higher Education: Proposing a Cybersecurity Awareness Paradigm. *Information (Basel), 16*(5), 336. DOI: 10.3390/info16050336

Arora, A. K., Kumar, A., Tyagi, R., Sharma, S., Kumar, A., & Kumar, S. (2025). Future of Education With AI-. *Assistive Technology*, •••, 169–190. DOI: 10.4018/979-8-3693-9395-6.ch008

Assayed, S. K., Alkhatib, M., & Shaalan, K. (2024b). A Comparative Study of ChatGPT and Seq2Seq Chatbot for Effective Students Advising. *ChatGPT and Global Higher Education: Using Artificial Intelligence in Teaching and Learning*, 148.

Assayed, S. K., Alkhatib, M., Shaalan, K. F., & Alsayed, S. A. (2025, April). HSGAdviser: AI Speech Assistant for Enabling Sustainable Education Solutions. In *2025 1st International Conference on Computational Intelligence Approaches and Applications (ICCIAA)* (pp. 1-6). IEEE.

Assayed, S. K., Alkhatib, M., & Shaalan, K. (2024a). The key challenges in educational advising chatbot dialogue system. In *Innovation in the University 4.0 System based on Smart Technologies* (pp. 74–82). Chapman and Hall/CRC.

Assayed, S., Shaalan, K., Al-Sayed, S., & Alkhatib, M. (2023). Psychological emotion recognition of students using machine learning based chatbot. [IJAIA]. *International Journal of Artificial Intelligence & Applications, 14*(2).

Asuncion, A. C., de Vera Asuncion, A., Macalipis, J. G., Borromeo, C. M. T., Rivera, J. C., & Limon, M. R. (2023). Weaving gaps in garments education technology: Crafting a skill-based E-toolkit based on Taba's curriculum development model. *Social Sciences & Humanities Open, 8*(1), 100656. DOI: 10.1016/j.ssaho.2023.100656

Athavale, V. A., Selvakumar, P., Poorani, S., Anand, T., & Rathore, D. S. (2025). Designing Chatbots for Educational Leadership. In Musundire, A. (Ed.), *Chatbots in Educational Leadership and Management* (pp. 181–204). IGI Global Scientific Publishing., DOI: 10.4018/979-8-3693-8734-4.ch008

Atif, A., Jha, M., Richards, D., & Bilgin, A. (2021). *Artificial Intelligence (AI)-enabled remote learning and teaching using Pedagogical Conversational Agents and Learning Analytics.* Intelligent Systems and Learning Data Analytics in Online Education., DOI: 10.1016/b978-0-12-823410-5.00013-9

Avasthi, S., Sanwal, T., Sareen, P., & Tripathi, S. L. (2022). *Augmenting Mental Healthcare With Artificial Intelligence.* Machine Learning, and Challenges in Telemedicine., DOI: 10.4018/978-1-7998-8786-7.ch005

Awodiji, O. A., & Naicker, S. R. (2023). *Preparing school leaders for the fourth industrial revolution: An assessment of their continuous professional development needs.* Social Sciences &amp. *Humanities Open, 8*(1), 100521. DOI: 10.1016/j.ssaho.2023.100521

Babu, C. V. S., & Simon, P. A. (2023). *Adaptive AI for Dynamic Cybersecurity Systems.*, DOI: 10.4018/979-8-3693-0230-9.ch003

Bailenson, J. N. (2018). *Experience on Demand: What Virtual Reality Is, How It Works, and What It Can Do.* WW Norton & Company.

Baker, R. S., & Hawn, A. (2022). Algorithmic Bias in Education. *International Journal of Artificial Intelligence in Education, 32*(4), 1052–1092. DOI: 10.1007/s40593-021-00285-9

Barr, N., Lopes, D. G., Schwendinger, M., & Gafaro, S. (2025). Ethical Implications and Patient-Centered Innovations in Digital Healthcare. In *Navigating Privacy, Innovation, and Patient Empowerment Through Ethical Healthcare Technology* (pp. 107–138). IGI Global. https://doi.org/ DOI: 10.4018/979-8-3693-7630-0.ch005

Baumhauer, J., Mortenson, L. Y., Rion, E., & Hong, V. (2025). Management of College Student Mental Health Emergencies. *Current Psychiatry Reports, 27*(5), 337–346. DOI: 10.1007/s11920-025-01603-x PMID: 40097778

Beck, A. T. (1979). *Cognitive therapy of depression*. Guilford Press.

Bello, L., & Aubert, L. (2025). Artificial intelligence in the classroom: Democratizing knowledge and transforming education [Article]. *Seminars in Medical Writing and Education, 4*, 469. Advance online publication. DOI: 10.56294/mw2025469

Benta, D., Bologa, G., & Dzitac, I. (2014). E-learning platforms in higher education. Case study. *Procedia Computer Science, 31*, 1170–1176.

Berendt, B., Littlejohn, A., & Blakemore, M. (2020). AI in education: Learner choice and fundamental rights. *Learning, Media and Technology, 45*(3), 312–324. DOI: 10.1080/17439884.2020.1786399

Bernadas, J. M. A. C., Soriano, C. R., Cabañes, J. V. A., & Tarroja, M. C. H. (2025). Ambivalent visibilities : Social media bullying and disconnective practice of the youth. *Convergence (London)*. Advance online publication. DOI: 10.1177/13548565251328774

Betty, M., Efendi, S., Zarlis, M., & Suwilo, S. (2024). Differentiated e-learning models based on needs and abilities of students with artificial intelligence. [Article]. *ICIC Express Letters, 18*(11), 1201–1210. DOI: 10.24507/icicel.18.11.1201

Bhatt, S. (2024). Digital Mental Health: Role of Artificial Intelligence in Psychotherapy. *Indian Journal of Psychological Medicine*, *46*(1), 12–19. DOI: 10.1177/02537176231221612:contentReference[oaicite:2]{index=2} PMID: 39544658

Binns, R., Veale, M., Van Kleek, M., & Shadbolt, N. (2018). "It's reducing a human being to a percentage": Perceptions of justice in algorithmic decisions. In *Proceedings of the 2018 CHI Conference on Human Factors in Computing Systems*.

Blease, C., Kaptchuk, T. J., Bernstein, M. H., Mandl, K. D., Halamka, J. D., & DesRoches, C. M. (2019). Artificial Intelligence and the Future of Psychiatry: Insights From a Global Physician Survey. *NPJ Digital Medicine*, *2*(1), 1–6.

Blease, C., Kaptchuk, T. J., Bernstein, M. H., Mandl, K. D., Halamka, J. D., & DesRoches, C. M. (2019). Artificial Intelligence and the future of psychiatry: Insights from a global physician survey. npj. *Digital Medicine*, *2*(1), 1–6. DOI: 10.1038/s41746-019-0182-7

Bobrytska, V. I., Krasylnykova, H. V., Protska, S. M., Skyrda, T. S., Krasylnykov, S. R., & Chkhalo, O. M. (2025). Digitalisation in Higher Education: A Systematic Review of its Impact on Health, Cognition, and Social Interaction [Review]. *International Journal of Learning. Teaching and Educational Research*, *24*(5), 339–359. DOI: 10.26803/ijlter.24.5.18

Bogina, V., Hartman, A., Kuflik, T., & Shulner-Tal, A. (2022). Educating Software and AI Stakeholders About Algorithmic Fairness, Accountability, Transparency and Ethics. *International Journal of Artificial Intelligence in Education*, *32*(3), 808–833. DOI: 10.1007/s40593-021-00248-0

Bolia, I. K., Savvidou, O. D., Kang, H. P., Chatzichristodoulou, N., Megaloikonomos, P. D., Mitsiokapa, E., Mavrogenis, A. F., & Papagelopoulos, P. J. (2021). Cross-cultural adaptation and validation of the Musculoskeletal Tumor Society (MSTS) scoring system and Toronto Extremity Salvage Score (TESS) for musculoskeletal sarcoma patients in Greece. *European Journal of Orthopaedic Surgery & Traumatology*, *31*(8), 1631–1638. DOI: 10.1007/s00590-021-02921-5 PMID: 33721082

Bora, N., & Thokan, S. (2023). Relationship of Conversational Artificial Intelligence with Academic Anxiety and Academic Motivations in Indian Students. *International Journal of Indian Psychology*, *11*(4), 1988–2005. DOI: 10.25215/1104.183:contentReference[oaicite:5]{index=5}

Boucher, E. M., Harake, N. R., Ward, H. E., Stoeckl, S. E., Vargas, J., Minkel, J., Parks, A. C., & Zilca, R. (2021). Artificially Intelligent Chatbots in Digital Mental Health Interventions: A Review. *Expert Review of Medical Devices*, *18*(1), 37–49. DOI: 10.1080/17434440.2021.1876638:contentReference[oaicite:32]{index=32} PMID: 34872429

Braslow, J. (2023). *Mental ills and bodily cures: psychiatric treatment in the first half of the twentieth century* (Vol. 8). Univ of California Press.

Brown, T., & Green, M. (2023). Chatbots in Higher Education: Assessing Their Role in Student Mental Health Support. *Journal of College Student Development*, *64*(1), 12–27. DOI: 10.1353/csd.2023

CAST. (2018). *Universal Design for Learning Guidelines version 2.2.* https://udlguidelines.cast.org

Cevallos-Salas, D., Estrada-Jiménez, J., & Guamán, D. S. (2024). Application layer security for Internet communications: A comprehensive review, challenges, and future trends. *Computers & Electrical Engineering*, *119*, 109498. DOI: 10.1016/j.compeleceng.2024.109498

Chan, C. K. Y., & Tsi, L. H. Y. (2024). Will generative AI replace teachers in higher education? A study of teacher and student perceptions. *Studies in Educational Evaluation*, *83*, 101395. DOI: 10.1016/j.stueduc.2024.101395

Chen, C., & Gong, Y. (2025). The Role of AI-Assisted Learning in Academic Writing: A Mixed-Methods Study on Chinese as a Second Language Students. *Education Sciences*, *15*(2), 141. DOI: 10.3390/educsci15020141

Chen, L., Chen, P., & Lin, Z. (2020). Artificial intelligence in education: A review. *IEEE Access : Practical Innovations, Open Solutions*, *8*, 75264–75278.

Chen, Y., Jensen, S., Albert, L. J., Gupta, S., & Lee, T. (2023). Artificial Intelligence (AI) Student Assistants in the Classroom: Designing Chatbots to Support Student Success. *Information Systems Frontiers*, *25*(1), 161–182. DOI: 10.1007/s10796-022-10291-4

Chen, Y., & Zhao, L. (2024). The Impact of AI Chatbots on Student Anxiety and Depression: A Meta-Analysis. *Journal of Affective Computing*, *15*(2), 210–225. DOI: 10.1109/JAFFC.2024.3056789

Choudhary, S. K., Kar, A. K., & Dwivedi, Y. K. (2024). How does Federated Learning Impact Decision-Making in Firms: A Systematic Literature Review. *Communications of the Association for Information Systems*, *54*, •••. https://www.scopus.com/inward/record.uri?eid=2-s2.0-85186765994&partnerID=40&md5=9ce5200161d256be6d150d6edad43207

Chow, J., Gwee, S., & Lim, L. (2017). Chatbots in language learning: Opportunities and challenges. *Educational Technology*, *57*(2), 56–60.

Chundru, S., & Whig, P. (2024). *Future of Emotional Intelligence in Technology*., DOI: 10.4018/979-8-3693-7011-7.ch024

Chun, J., Kim, J., Kim, H., Lee, G., Cho, S., Kim, C., Chung, Y., & Heo, S. (2025). A Comparative Analysis of On-Device AI-Driven, Self-Regulated Learning and Traditional Pedagogy in University Health Sciences Education [Article]. *Applied Sciences (Switzerland)*, *15*(4), 1815. Advance online publication. DOI: 10.3390/app15041815

Cirillo, F., De Santis, M., & Esposito, C. (2025). *Applications of Solid Platform and Federated Learning for Decentralized Health Data Management*., DOI: 10.1007/978-3-031-70775-9_6

Cohen, B., Hu, A., Patino, D., & Coffman, J. (2024). This Is Going on Your Permanent Record: A Legal Analysis of Educational Data in the Cloud. *ACM Journal on Responsible Computing*, *1*(3), 1–27. DOI: 10.1145/3675230

Colizzi, M., Lasalvia, A., & Ruggeri, M. (2020). Prevention and early intervention in youth mental health: Is it time for a multidisciplinary and trans-diagnostic model for care? *International Journal of Mental Health Systems, 14*(1), 23. DOI: 10.1186/s13033-020-00356-9 PMID: 32226481

Conneau, A., Khandelwal, K., Goyal, N., Chaudhary, V., Wenzek, G., Guzmán, F., & Stoyanov, V. (2020). Unsupervised cross-lingual representation learning at scale. In *Proceedings of the 58th Annual Meeting of the Association for Computational Linguistics.*

Cordero, J., & Cordero-Castillo, A. (2025). Exploring the Potential of Generative AI in Education: Opportunities, Challenges, and Best Practices for Classroom Integration [Conference paper]. *Communications in Computer and Information Science, 2261 CCIS*, 252-265. https://doi.org/ DOI: 10.1007/978-3-031-85930-4_23

Corey, G. (2016). *Theory and Practice of Counseling and Psychotherapy* (10th ed.). Cengage Learning.

Cosar, M. (2024). Utilizing the eXtreme Gradient Boosting Algorithm for Artificial Intelligence-supported Learning Analytics Application [Conference paper]. *Eurasia Proceedings of Science, Technology, Engineering and Mathematics, 28*, 277-285. https://doi.org/DOI: 10.55549/epstem.1521844

Crawford, J., Allen, K.-A., Pani, B., & Cowling, M. (2024). When artificial intelligence substitutes humans in higher education: The cost of loneliness, student success, and retention. *Studies in Higher Education, 49*(5), 883–897. DOI: 10.1080/03075079.2024.2326956

D'Alfonso, S. (2020). AI in mental health. *Current Opinion in Psychology, 36*, 112–117. PMID: 32604065

D'Mello, S., & Graesser, A. (2012). AutoTutor and Affective AutoTutor: Learning by talking with cognitively and emotionally intelligent computers that talk back. [TiiS]. *ACM Transactions on Interactive Intelligent Systems, 2*(4), 1–39.

Dai, R., Thomas, M. K. E., & Rawolle, S. (2024). The roles of AI and educational leaders in AI-assisted administrative decision-making: A proposed framework for symbiotic collaboration. *Australian Educational Researcher*. Advance online publication. DOI: 10.1007/s13384-024-00771-8

Daisy, A. (2024). Digital Mental. *Health Education*, •••, 143–180. DOI: 10.4018/979-8-3693-8242-4.ch006

Dashkevych, O., & Portnov, B. A. (2024). How can generative AI help in different parts of research? An experiment study on smart cities' definitions and characteristics. *Technology in Society*, *77*, 102555. DOI: 10.1016/j.techsoc.2024.102555

Delen, D., Davazdahemami, B., & Rasouli Dezfouli, E. (2024). Predicting and Mitigating Freshmen Student Attrition: A Local-Explainable Machine Learning Framework. *Information Systems Frontiers*, *26*(2), 641–662. DOI: 10.1007/s10796-023-10397-3 PMID: 37361887

Denecke, K., Abd-Alrazaq, A., & Househ, M. (2021). *Artificial Intelligence for Chatbots in Mental Health: Opportunities and Challenges* (pp. 115–128). https://doi.org/DOI: 10.1007/978-3-030-67303-1_10

Dhinakaran, D., Kumar, N. J., & Ponnuviji, N. P. (2025). Safeguarding confidentiality and privacy in cloud-enabled healthcare systems with spectrasafe encryption and dynamic k-anonymity algorithm. *Expert Systems with Applications*, *279*, 127584.

Díaz-Rodríguez, N., Del Ser, J., Coeckelbergh, M., López de Prado, M., Herrera-Viedma, E., & Herrera, F. (2023). Connecting the dots in trustworthy Artificial Intelligence: From AI principles, ethics, and key requirements to responsible AI systems and regulation. *Information Fusion*, *99*, 101896. DOI: 10.1016/j.inffus.2023.101896

Duong, T.-N.-A., & Chen, H. (2025). An AI Chatbot for EFL Writing: Students' Usage Tendencies, Writing Performance, and Perceptions. *Journal of Educational Computing Research*. Advance online publication. DOI: 10.1177/07356331241312363

Du, Y., Wang, C., Zou, B., & Xia, Y. (2025). Personalizing AI tools for second language speaking: The role of gender and autistic traits. *Frontiers in Psychiatry, 15*. Advance online publication. DOI: 10.3389/fpsyt.2024.1464575 PMID: 39931194

Elkot, M. A., Youssif, E., & Elsheikh Hago Elmahdi, O., AbdAlgane, M., & Ali, R. (2024). Generative conversational AI: Active practices for fostering students with mild intellectual disabilities to improve English communication skills. *Contemporary Educational Technology*, *17*(1), ep549. DOI: 10.30935/cedtech/15688

Ellis, R. A. (2024). *The Education Leadership Challenges for Universities in a Postdigital Age*. Postdigital Science and Education., DOI: 10.1007/s42438-024-00461-9

Emon, M. M. H., Khan, T., Rahman, M. A., Hamid, A. B. A., & Yaakub, N. I. (2025). GreenTech Revolution: Navigating Challenges and Seizing Opportunities. In *AI and Green Technology Applications in Society* (pp. 63–90). IGI Global Scientific Publishing. https://doi.org/DOI: 10.4018/979-8-3693-9879-1.ch003

Engelbrecht, J., Oates, G., & de Carvalho Borba, M. (2025). Artificial intelligence and social media in mathematics education. In *social media in the changing mathematics classroom* (pp. 43-65). Cham: Springer Nature Switzerland.

Fan, M., Lipowski, M., Wang, X., & Liu, T. (2025). The effectiveness of healthcare interventions for high-intensity interval training under generative artificial intelligence technology [Article]. *Journal of Mechanics in Medicine and Biology*, *25*(5), 2540033. Advance online publication. DOI: 10.1142/S0219519425400330

Farsi, Z., Sajadi, S. A., Afaghi, E., Fournier, A., Aliyari, S., Ahmadi, Y., & Hazrati, E. (2021). Explaining the experiences of nursing administrators, educators, and students about education process in the COVID-19 pandemic: A qualitative study. *BMC Nursing*, *20*(1), 151. DOI: 10.1186/s12912-021-00666-4 PMID: 34416886

Fawns, T., Gallagher, M., & Bayne, S. (2021). *Institutional Contexts in Supporting Quality Online Postgraduate Education: Lessons Learned from Two Initiatives at the University of Edinburgh* (pp. 197–215). https://doi.org/DOI: 10.1007/978-3-030-77673-2_11

Fengchao, X., & Mingchi, J. (2023). School leadership and management innovation in the Internet+ education era. *International Journal of New Developments in Education*, *5*(12), 28–34. DOI: 10.25236/IJNDE.2023.051205

Fitzpatrick, K. K., Darcy, A., & Vierhile, M. (2017). Delivering cognitive behavior therapy to young adults with symptoms of depression and anxiety using a fully automated conversational agent (Woebot): A randomized controlled trial. *JMIR Mental Health*, *4*(2), e19. DOI: 10.2196/mental.7785 PMID: 28588005

Fleming, N. D., & Mills, C. (1992). Not another inventory, rather a catalyst for reflection. *To Improve the Academy*, *11*(1), 137–155.

Floridi, L., Cowls, J., Beltrametti, M., Chatila, R., Chazerand, P., Dignum, V., & Vayena, E. (2018). AI4People—An ethical framework for a good AI society: Opportunities, risks, principles, and recommendations. *Minds and Machines*, *28*(4), 689–707. PMID: 30930541

Følstad, A., & Brandtzaeg, P. B. (2017). Chatbots and the new world of HCI. *Interaction*, *24*(4), 38–42.

Freud, S. (1910). *Five Lectures on Psychoanalysis*. Norton.

Fullam, E. (2025). How Does a Mental Health Chatbot Work? A 'Conversation Design' Concept of Mental Health Intervention. *Health*, *29*(1), 3–19. DOI: 10.1177/09526951241305274:contentReference[oaicite:8]{index=8} PMID: 38407179

Fulmer, R., Joerin, A., Gentile, B., Lakerink, L., & Rauws, M. (2018). Using psychological artificial Intelligence (Tess) to relieve symptoms of depression and anxiety: Randomized controlled trial. *JMIR Mental Health*, *5*(4), e64. DOI: 10.2196/mental.9782 PMID: 30545815

Fusarelli, B. C., & Fusarelli, L. D. (2024). Leadership for the Future: Enhancing Principal Preparation through Standards and Innovation. *Education Sciences*, *14*(12), 1403. DOI: 10.3390/educsci14121403

Gaffney, H., Mansell, W., & Tai, S. (2019). Conversational Agents in the Treatment of Mental Health Problems: Mixed-Method Systematic Review. *JMIR Mental Health*, *6*(10), e14166. PMID: 31628789

Gambhir, A., Jain, N., & Pandey, M., & Simran. (2024). Beyond the Code: Bridging Ethical and Practical Gaps in Data Privacy for AI-Enhanced. *Health Care Systems*, •••, 37–65. DOI: 10.1007/978-981-97-6790-8_2

Ganesan, I., Ponnuviji, N. P., Kumar, A. S., Nithya, M., Jambulingam, U., & Lalitha, S. D. (2024). Real-Time Event Detection and Predictive Analytics Using IoT and Deep Learning. In Industry Applications of Thrust Manufacturing: Convergence with Real-Time Data and AI (pp. 1-41). IGI Global Scientific Publishing.

Ganesan, A. (2025). *Transforming Wellness.*, DOI: 10.4018/979-8-3693-9521-9.ch018

Ganesh, S. V., Nayagam, M. G., Suresh, V., Rajakarunakaran, S., & Bensujin, B. (2025). Adaptive Learning Technologies: Navigating the Road from Hype to Reality. In Singh, A., & Singh, K. K. (Eds.), *Multimodal Generative AI*. Springer., DOI: 10.1007/978-981-96-2355-6_4

Gao, Y. (2025). The impact and application of artificial intelligence technology on mental health counseling services for college students. *Journal of Computational Methods in Sciences and Engineering*, *25*(2), 1686–1701. DOI: 10.1177/14727978241302641

Garcia, M. E., & Lopez, R. (2024). The Effectiveness of AI Chatbots in Addressing Student Mental Health Issues: A Longitudinal Study. *Journal of Educational Psychology*, *116*(4), 456–470. DOI: 10.1037/edu0000765

Ghafouri, M., Hassaskhah, J., & Mahdavi-Zafarghandi, A. (2024). From virtual assistant to writing mentor: Exploring the impact of a ChatGPT-based writing instruction protocol on EFL teachers' self-efficacy and learners' writing skill. *Language Teaching Research*. Advance online publication. DOI: 10.1177/13621688241239764

Ghamrawi, N., Shal, T., & Ghamrawi, N. A. R. (2023). Exploring the impact of AI on teacher leadership: Regressing or expanding? *Education and Information Technologies*, *29*(7), 8415–8433. DOI: 10.1007/s10639-023-12174-w

Ghosh, S., & Dey, A. (2023). AI Chatbots in Higher Education: A Study on Student Mental Health Support. *International Journal of Educational Technology*, *10*(2), 45–58. DOI: 10.1016/j.ijet.2023.02.005

Gkinko, L., & Elbanna, A. (2022). Hope, tolerance and empathy: Employees' emotions when using an AI-enabled chatbot in a digitalised workplace. *Information Technology & People*, *35*(6), 1714–1743. DOI: 10.1108/ITP-04-2021-0328

Goel, A., & Polepeddi, L. (2016). *Jill Watson: A virtual teaching assistant for online education*. Georgia Institute of Technology.

Gonda, D., & Chu, B. (2019). Chatbot as a learning resource? Creating conversational bots as a supplement for teaching assistant training course. *2019 IEEE International Conference on Engineering, Technology and Education (TALE)*, 1-5. https://doi.org/DOI: 10.1109/TALE48000.2019.9225974

Hagadone-Bedir, M., Voithofer, R., & Kulp, J. T. (2023). Contextualizing privacy with wearable data in higher education. *British Journal of Educational Technology*, *54*(6), 1619–1635. DOI: 10.1111/bjet.13378

Haikalis, M., Doucette, H., Meisel, M. K., Birch, K., & Barnett, N. P. (2022). Changes in College Student Anxiety and Depression From Pre- to During-COVID-19: Perceived Stress, Academic Challenges, Loneliness, and Positive Perceptions. *Emerging Adulthood*, *10*(2), 534–545. DOI: 10.1177/21676968211058516 PMID: 35382515

Han, X., Li, Z., Zhang, W., & Fan, W. (2025). Generative AI in Education: Developing Personalized Learning Experiences with Hyperspherical Variational Self-Attention Autoencoder [Conference paper]. *Proceedings of 2024 3rd International Conference on Artificial Intelligence and Education, ICAIE 2024*, 670-674. https://doi.org/DOI: 10.1145/3722237.3722354

Hathaliya, J. J., Tanwar, S., & Sharma, P. (2022). Adversarial learning techniques for security and privacy preservation: A comprehensive review. *Security and Privacy*, *5*(3). Advance online publication. DOI: 10.1002/spy2.209

Haupt, S. E., Gagne, D. J., Hsieh, W. W., Krasnopolsky, V., McGovern, A., Marzban, C., Moninger, W., Lakshmanan, V., Tissot, P., & Williams, J. K. (2022). The History and Practice of AI in the Environmental Sciences. *Bulletin of the American Meteorological Society*, *103*(5), E1351–E1370. DOI: 10.1175/BAMS-D-20-0234.1

Health, I. T. gov. (2021). Benefits of health IT for behavioral health. https://www.healthit.gov/topic/health-it-health-care-settings/behavioral-health

Hew, K. F., Huang, W., Du, J., & Jia, C. (2023). Using chatbots to support student goal setting and social presence in fully online activities: Learner engagement and perceptions. *Journal of Computing in Higher Education*, *35*(1), 40–68. DOI: 10.1007/s12528-022-09338-x PMID: 36101883

Hilbert, S., Coors, S., Kraus, E., Bischl, B., Lindl, A., Frei, M., & Stachl, C. (2021). Machine learning for the educational sciences. *Review of Education*, *9*(3), e3310.

Holmes, W., Bialik, M., & Fadel, C. (2019). *Artificial Intelligence in Education: Promises and Implications for Teaching and Learning*. Center for Curriculum Redesign.

Holstein, K., Wortman Vaughan, J., Daum, M., Dudik, M., & Wallach, H. (2019). Improving fairness in machine learning systems: What do industry practitioners need? In *Proceedings of the 2019 CHI Conference on Human Factors in Computing Systems.*

Holstein, K., Wortman Vaughan, J., Daum, M., Dudik, M., & Wallach, H. (2020). Improving fairness in machine learning systems: What do industry practitioners need? In *Proceedings of the 2020 CHI Conference on Human Factors in Computing Systems*.

Holt-Quick, C., Warren, J., Stasiak, K., Williams, R., Christie, G., Hetrick, S., Hopkins, S., Cargo, T., & Merry, S. (2020). A Chatbot Architecture for Promoting Youth Resilience. *arXiv preprint arXiv:2005.07355*. https://doi.org/DOI: 10.48550/arXiv.2005.07355arXiv

Huang, X., Nor, M. Z. B. M., Yusoff, Z. M., & Liang, Z. (2025). Psychological harm induced by generative AI and its legal remedies [Article]. *Environment and Social Psychology*, *10*(3), 3554. Advance online publication. DOI: 10.59429/esp.v10i3.3554

Hunkins, F. P., & Ornstein, A. C. (2018). *Curriculum: Foundations, principles, and issues*. Pearson Education London.

IBM. (2023). How AI is transforming mental health care. https://www.ibm.com/blog/how-ai-is-transforming-mental-health-care

Inkster, B., Sarda, S., & Subramanian, V. (2018). An empathy-driven, conversational artificial intelligence agent (Wysa) for digital mental well-being: Real-world data evaluation. *JMIR mHealth and uHealth*, *6*(11), e12106. DOI: 10.2196/12106 PMID: 30470676

Iyamu, T. (2018). Collecting qualitative data for information systems studies: The reality in practice. *Education and Information Technologies*, *23*(5), 2249–2264. DOI: 10.1007/s10639-018-9718-2

Izumi, T., Sukhwani, V., Surjan, A., & Shaw, R. (2021). Managing and responding to pandemics in higher educational institutions: Initial learning from COVID-19. *International Journal of Disaster Resilience in the Built Environment*, *12*(1), 51–66. DOI: 10.1108/IJDRBE-06-2020-0054

Jauhiainen, J. S., & Garagorry Guerra, A. (2024). Generative AI and education: Dynamic personalization of pupils' school learning material with ChatGPT [Article]. *Frontiers in Education*, *9*, 1288723. Advance online publication. DOI: 10.3389/feduc.2024.1288723

Ji, H., Han, I., & Ko, Y. (2022). A systematic review of conversational AI in language education: Focusing on the collaboration with human teachers. *Journal of Research on Technology in Education, 55*, 48–63. DOI: 10.1080/15391523.2022.2142873

Johnson, A. P., & Lester, R. J. (2022). Mental health in academia: Hacks for cultivating and sustaining wellbeing. *American Journal of Human Biology, 34*(S1). Advance online publication. DOI: 10.1002/ajhb.23664 PMID: 34357661

Jurafsky, D., & Martin, J. H. (2021). *Speech and language processing* (3rd ed. draft). https://web.stanford.edu/~jurafsky/slp3/

Jurafsky, D., & Martin, J. H. (2023). *Speech and Language Processing* (3rd ed.). Draft.

Karakose, T., & Tulubas, T. (2025). The Role of Educational Leaders in the Age of Artificial Intelligence (AI).

Karakose, T., & Tulubas, T. (2024). School Leadership and Management in the Age of Artificial Intelligence (AI): Recent Developments and Future Prospects. *Educational Process International Journal, 13*(1). Advance online publication. DOI: 10.22521/edupij.2024.131.1

Khan, A. A., Laghari, A. A., & Awan, S. A. (2021). Machine learning in computer vision: A review. *EAI Endorsed Transactions on Scalable Information Systems, 8*(32).

Khan, F., & Mer, A. (2023). *Embracing Artificial Intelligence Technology: Legal Implications with Special Reference to European Union Initiatives of Data Protection* (pp. 119–141). https://doi.org/DOI: 10.1108/S1569-375920230000111C007

Khan, J. A. (2024). *Role-Based access Control (RBAC) and Attribute-Based Access Control*. ABAC., DOI: 10.4018/979-8-3693-1431-9.ch005

Kim, J., & Wargo, E. (2025). Empowering educational leaders for AI integration in rural STEM education: Challenges and strategies. *Frontiers in Education, 10.* Advance online publication. DOI: 10.3389/feduc.2025.1567698

Kim, K., & Kwon, K. (2023). Exploring the AI competencies of elementary school teachers in South Korea. *Computers and Education: Artificial Intelligence*, *4*, 100137. DOI: 10.1016/j.caeai.2023.100137

Kim, S., & Choi, J. (2023). Exploring the Role of AI Chatbots in Enhancing Student Resilience and Coping Mechanisms. *Computers & Education*, *182*, 104456. DOI: 10.1016/j.compedu.2023.104456

Kim, Y., Huang, J., & Emery, S. (2019). Chatbots and college students: Conversational agents as mediators of support for marginalized students. *Journal of Student Affairs Research and Practice*, *56*(4), 392–406.

Klimova, B., & Pikhart, M. (2025). Exploring the effects of artificial intelligence on student and academic well-being in higher education: A mini-review [Short survey]. *Frontiers in Psychology*, *16*, 1498132. Advance online publication. DOI: 10.3389/fpsyg.2025.1498132 PMID: 39963679

Klopfenstein, L. C., Delpriori, S., Malatini, S., & Bogliolo, A. (2017). The rise of bots: A survey of conversational interfaces, patterns, and paradigms. In *Proceedings of the 2017 Conference on Designing Interactive Systems* (pp. 555–565).

Klos, M. C., Escoredo, M., Joerin, A., Lemos, V. N., Rauws, M., & Bunge, E. L. (2021). Artificial Intelligence–Based Chatbot for Anxiety and Depression in University Students: Pilot Randomized Controlled Trial. *JMIR Formative Research*, *5*(8), e20678. DOI: 10.2196/20678 PMID: 34092548

Kukulska-Hulme, A., & Lee, H. (2020). Intelligent assistants in language learning: an analysis of features and limitations. *CALL for widening participation: short papers from EUROCALL 2020.* https://doi.org/.DOI: 10.14705/RPNET.2020.48.1184

Kumar, A., & Gupta, D. (2021). Sentiment analysis as a restricted NLP problem. In *Natural language processing for global and local business* (pp. 65–96). IGI Global.

Kusal, S., Patil, S., Choudrie, J., Kotecha, K., Vora, D., & Pappas, I. (2023). A systematic review of applications of natural language processing and future challenges with special emphasis in text-based emotion detection. *Artificial Intelligence Review, 56*(12), 15129–15215. DOI: 10.1007/s10462-023-10509-0

Lee, C. (2021). Patient loyalty to health services: The role of communication skills and cognitive trust. *International Journal of Healthcare Management, 14*(4), 1254–1264. DOI: 10.1080/20479700.2020.1756111

Lee, H. J., & Park, S. Y. (2023). The Role of AI Chatbots in Reducing Academic Stress Among University Students. *Computers in Human Behavior, 137*, 106852. DOI: 10.1016/j.chb.2023.106852

Lekkala, S., & Gurijala, P. (2024). *Security and Privacy for Modern Networks*. Apress., DOI: 10.1007/979-8-8688-0823-4

Li, Q., Swanto, S., Said, N., & Din, W. (2023). Application Of Ai Writing Assistant Software In Efl Writing In China: A Review. *International Journal of Modern Education*. https://doi.org/.DOI: 10.35631/ijmoe.519023

Lin, H. (2022). Influences of Artificial Intelligence in Education on Teaching Effectiveness: The Mediating Effect of Teachers' Perceptions of Educational Technology. *International Journal of Emerging Technologies in Learning, 17*, 144–156. DOI: 10.3991/ijet.v17i24.36037

Liu, M., & Wang, W. (2025). Design and Implementation of an Emotion-Aware Learning System Based on Facial Expression Recognition [Conference paper]. *Proceedings of 2024 3rd International Conference on Artificial Intelligence and Education, ICAIE 2024*, 154-159. https://doi.org/DOI: 10.1145/3722237.3722264

Liu, B., Zhang, J., Lin, F., Jia, X., & Peng, M. (2025). One size doesn't fit all: A personalized conversational tutoring agent for mathematics instruction [Preprint]. arXiv. https://arxiv.org/abs/2503.02487

Lopes, R. M., Silva, A. F., Rodrigues, A. C. A., & Melo, V. (2024). Chatbots for Well-Being: Exploring the Impact of Artificial Intelligence on Mood Enhancement and Mental Health. *European Psychiatry : the Journal of the Association of European Psychiatrists*, *67*(S1), S1143. DOI: 10.1192/j.eurpsy.2024.1143

López-Minotta, K. L., Chiappe, A., & Mella-Noramabuena, J. (2025). Implementation of artificial intelligence to improve English oral expression. *REMIE: Multidisciplinary Journal of Educational Research*, *15*(1), 43–71. DOI: 10.17583/remie.16188

Love, R., Law, E., & Cohen, P. R.. (2025). Teaching a conversational agent using natural language: Effect on learning and engagement. *International Journal of Artificial Intelligence in Education*. Advance online publication. DOI: 10.1007/s40593-025-00461-1

Luckin, R., Holmes, W., Griffiths, M., & Forcier, L. B. (2016). *Intelligence Unleashed: An Argument for AI in Education*. Pearson Education.

Madanchian, M., Taherdoost, H., Vincenti, M., & Mohamed, N. (2024). Transforming Leadership Practices through Artificial Intelligence. *Procedia Computer Science*, *235*, 2101–2111.

Madhuri, J. N., Fatma, G., Kumari, A. K., Pathak, P., Sreela, B., & Faizal, M. K. M. (2024). Creating an AI English tutor with personalized content and dynamic lessons [Paper presentation]. *2024 IEEE International Conference on Artificial Intelligence and Quantum Computation-Based Sensor Applications*, Nagpur, India.

Mananay, J. (2024). Integrating Artificial Intelligence (AI) in Language Teaching: Effectiveness, Challenges, and Strategies. *International Journal of Learning, Teaching and Educational Research*. https://doi.org/.DOI: 10.26803/ijlter.23.9.19

Mangal, M., & Pardos, Z. A. (2024). Implementing equitable and intersectionality-aware ML in education: A practical guide [Article]. *British Journal of Educational Technology*, *55*(5), 2003–2038. DOI: 10.1111/bjet.13484

McAndrews, L., & Martinez, B. (2025). Friend or Fri-enemy: Teaching Approaches with AI chatbots like ChatGPT. https://doi.org/DOI: 10.31274/itaa.18685

Means, B., Toyama, Y., Murphy, R., & Baki, M. (2014). The effectiveness of online and blended learning: A meta-analysis of the empirical literature. *Teachers College Record, 116*(1), 1–47.

Mehta, A. K., Yashoda, L., Selvakumar, P., Mishra, B. R., Das, A., & C. T. C., M. (2025). Teaching Methods: Techniques for Disadvantaged Learners. In S. Hai-Jew (Ed.), *Mitigating Learner Disadvantages in Teaching and Learning* (pp. 181-206). IGI Global Scientific Publishing. https://doi.org/DOI: 10.4018/979-8-3693-8623-1.ch007

Mills, N., Hok, H., Dressen, A., & Veillas, Q. (2025). The design and evaluation of an interactive AI companion for foreign language writing. *Foreign Language Annals*. Advance online publication. DOI: 10.1111/flan.12790

Milton, J., & Al-Busaidi, A. (2023). *New Role of Leadership in AI Era: Educational Sector. SHS Web of Conferences,* 156, 09005. https://doi.org/DOI: 10.1051/shsconf/202315609005

Miner, A. S., Haque, A., Fries, J. A., Fleming, S. L., Wilfley, D. E., Terence Wilson, G., & Shah, N. H. (2020). Assessing the accuracy of automatic speech recognition for psychotherapy. *NPJ Digital Medicine*, *3*(1), 82. PMID: 32550644

Minh, N., & Khanh, L. (2024). *Using Artificial Intelligence Tools for Developing Conversational Skills for English Majors*. European Modern Studies Journal., DOI: 10.59573/emsj.8(2).2024.40

Mohamed Jasim, K., Malathi, A., Bhardwaj, S., & Aw, E. C.-X. (2025). A systematic review of AI-based chatbot usages in healthcare services. *Journal of Health Organization and Management*. Advance online publication. DOI: 10.1108/JHOM-12-2023-0376 PMID: 39865955

Molina-Carmona, R., & García-Peñalvo, F. J. (2025). *Safeguarding Knowledge: Ethical Artificial Intelligence Governance in the University Digital Transformation* (pp. 201–220). https://doi.org/DOI: 10.1007/978-3-031-71530-3_14

Monib, W. K., Qazi, A., Silva, L. D., & Mahmud, M. M. (2024). Exploring Learners' Experiences with ChatGPT in Personalized Learning. *2024 6th International Workshop on Artificial Intelligence and Education (WAIE)*, 66-70. https://doi.org/DOI: 10.1109/WAIE63876.2024.00019

Monib, W. K. (2023). Implementation of 21st Century Skills in EFL Classroom: Perceptions of Lecturers and Students. [IJonSES]. *International Journal on Social & Education Sciences*, *5*(3), 536–559. DOI: 10.46328/ijonses.544

Monib, W. K., Qazi, A., & Apong, R. A. (2025). Microlearning beyond boundaries: A systematic review and a novel framework for improving learning outcomes [Article]. *Heliyon*, *11*(2), e41413. Advance online publication. DOI: 10.1016/j.heliyon.2024.e41413 PMID: 39882484

Monib, W. K., Qazi, A., Apong, R. A., Azizan, M. T., De Silva, L., & Yassin, H. (2024). Generative AI and future education: A review, theoretical validation, and authors' perspective on challenges and solutions. *PeerJ. Computer Science*, *10*, e2105. DOI: 10.7717/peerj-cs.2105 PMID: 39650462

Monib, W. K., Qazi, A., Apong, R. A., & Mahmud, M. M. (2024). Investigating learners' perceptions of microlearning: Factors influencing learning outcomes. *IEEE Access : Practical Innovations, Open Solutions*, *12*, 1–17. DOI: 10.1109/ACCESS.2024.3472113

Monib, W. K., Qazi, A., Jain, J., & Ponniah, L. (2025). A Comprehensive Scientometric Analysis of ChatGPT Research Global Trends and Future Prospects. *TechTrends*. Advance online publication. DOI: 10.1007/s11528-025-01110-z

Monib, W. K., Qazi, A., & Mahmud, M. M. (2025). Exploring learners' experiences and perceptions of ChatGPT as a learning tool in higher education. *Education and Information Technologies*, *30*(1), 917–939. DOI: 10.1007/s10639-024-13065-4

Mora, A., Bujari, A., & Bellavista, P. (2024). Enhancing generalization in Federated Learning with heterogeneous data: A comparative literature review. *Future Generation Computer Systems*, *157*, 1–15. DOI: 10.1016/j.future.2024.03.027

Munir, H., Vogel, B., & Jacobsson, A. (2022). Artificial intelligence and machine learning approaches in digital education: A systematic revision. *Information (Basel)*, *13*(4), 203.

Munni, B. E., & Rafique, R. (2025). Teachers' Experiences of Using AI-powered Technologies in Bangladeshi English Language Classrooms. *Spectrum (Lexington, Ky.)*, *18*, 89–100. DOI: 10.3329/spectrum.v18i1.76362

Nadji, B. (2024). *Data Security*. Integrity, and Protection., DOI: 10.1007/978-3-031-61117-9_4

Naser, O. M. A., Faraj, H. A., & Elmbark, K. M. (2024). AI-Driven Conversational Interfaces: Advancements in Human-Machine Communication. *International Journal For Science Technology And Engineering*, *12*(12), 2161–2167. DOI: 10.22214/ijraset.2024.66167

Naslund, J. A., Aschbrenner, K. A., Marsch, L. A., & Bartels, S. J. (2017). The future of mental health care: Peer-to-peer support and social media. *Epidemiology and Psychiatric Sciences*, *25*(2), 113–122. PMID: 26744309

Neal Joshua, E. S., Bhattacharyya, D., & Rao, N. T. (2022). Managing information security risk and Internet of Things (IoT) impact on challenges of medicinal problems with complex settings. In *Multi-Chaos, Fractal and Multi-Fractional Artificial Intelligence of Different Complex Systems* (pp. 291–310). Elsevier. https://doi.org/DOI: 10.1016/B978-0-323-90032-4.00007-9

Nelson, J., Kaplan, J., Simerly, G., Nutter, N., Edson-Heussi, A., Woodham, B., & Broman-Fulks, J. (2025). The balance and integration of artificial intelligence within cognitive behavioral therapy interventions. *Current Psychology (New Brunswick, N.J.)*, *44*(9), 7847–7857. DOI: 10.1007/s12144-025-07320-1

Nepal, S., Pillai, A., Campbell, W., Massachi, T., Heinz, M. V., Kunwar, A., Choi, E. S., Xu, O., Kuc, J., Huckins, J., Holden, J., Preum, S. M., Depp, C., Jacobson, N., Czerwinski, M., Granholm, E., & Campbell, A. T. (2024). MindScape Study: Integrating LLM and Behavioral Sensing for Personalized AI-Driven Journaling Experiences. *arXiv preprint arXiv:2409.09570*. https://doi.org//arXiv.2409.09570:contentReference[oaicite:26]{index=26}DOI: 10.48550

Ng, D. T. K., Chan, E. K. C., & Lo, C. K. (2025). Opportunities, challenges and school strategies for integrating generative AI in education. *Computers and Education: Artificial Intelligence*, *8*, 100373. DOI: 10.1016/j.caeai.2025.100373

Nguyen, T. H., & Hoang, T. N. H. G. (2025). Investigating the Promises and Perils of Generative AI in EFL Learning in Higher Education: A Literature Review. *AsiaCALL Online Journal*, *16*(1), 1–15. DOI: 10.54855/acoj.251611

Nguyen, T. T., & Tran, M. H. (2025). Evaluating the Effectiveness of AI-Powered Mental Health Chatbots in College Settings. *Journal of Mental Health Technology*, *12*(1), 89–102. DOI: 10.1016/j.jmht.2025.01.007

Niazai, H., & Monib, W. K. (2025). AI for Personalized Learning in Medical Education. In Martínez Asanza, D. (Ed.), *Teaching in the Age of Medical Technology* (pp. 91–122). IGI Global Scientific Publishing., DOI: 10.4018/979-8-3373-1519-5.ch004

O'Neil, C. (2016). *Weapons of math destruction: How big data increases inequality and threatens democracy*. Crown Publishing Group.

Obermeyer, Z., Powers, B., Vogeli, C., & Mullainathan, S. (2019). Dissecting racial bias in an algorithm used to manage the health of populations. *Science, 366*(6464), 447–453. DOI: 10.1126/science.aax2342 PMID: 31649194

Okoli, C. S. A., & Yekini, A. (2023). Implied jurisdiction agreements in international commercial contracts: A global comparative perspective. *Journal of Private International Law, 19*(3), 321–361. DOI: 10.1080/17441048.2023.2294615

Olujimi, P. A., & Ade-Ibijola, A. (2023). NLP techniques for automating responses to customer queries: A systematic review. *Discover Artificial Intelligence, 3*(1), 20. DOI: 10.1007/s44163-023-00065-5

Ormiston, H. E., Nygaard, M. A., & Apgar, S. (2022). A Systematic Review of Secondary Traumatic Stress and Compassion Fatigue in Teachers. *School Mental Health, 14*(4), 802–817. DOI: 10.1007/s12310-022-09525-2 PMID: 35694002

Ouadoud, M., Rida, N., & Chafiq, T. (2021). Overview of E-learning Platforms for Teaching and Learning. *Int. J. Recent Contributions Eng. Sci. IT, 9*(1), 50–70.

Özdere, M. (2025). AI in Academic Writing: Assessing the Effectiveness, Grading Consistency, and Student Perspectives of ChatGPT and You.com for EFL Students. *International Journal of Technology in Education, 8*(1), 123–154. DOI: 10.46328/ijte.1001

Padovano, A., & Cardamone, M. (2024). Towards human-AI collaboration in the competency-based curriculum development process: The case of industrial engineering and management education. *Computers and Education: Artificial Intelligence, 7*, 100256. DOI: 10.1016/j.caeai.2024.100256

Page, L. C., & Gehlbach, H. (2017). How an artificially intelligent virtual assistant helps students navigate the road to college. *AERA Open, 3*(4), 1–12.

Pane, J. F., Steiner, E. D., Baird, M. D., & Hamilton, L. S. (2017). *Informing Progress: Insights on Personalized Learning Implementation and Effects*. RAND Corporation.

Parker, L., Halter, V., Karliychuk, T., & Grundy, Q. (2019). How private is your mental health app data? An empirical study of mental health app privacy policies and practices. *International Journal of Law and Psychiatry*, *64*, 198–204. DOI: 10.1016/j.ijlp.2019.04.002 PMID: 31122630

Parveen, K., Tran, P. Q. B., Alghamdi, A. A., Namaziandost, E., Aslam, S., & Xiaowei, T. (2022). Identifying the Leadership Challenges of K-12 Public Schools During COVID-19 Disruption: A Systematic Literature Review. *Frontiers in Psychology*, *13*. Advance online publication. DOI: 10.3389/fpsyg.2022.875646 PMID: 35432078

Patel, R., & Kumar, S. (2024). Conversational AI and Student Well-being: A Systematic Review. *Journal of Educational Psychology*, *116*(3), 123–138. DOI: 10.1037/edu0000756

Pavunraj, D., Mathan Kumar, A., & Anbumaheshwari, K. (2025). *AI in Personalized Treatment Planning*., DOI: 10.4018/979-8-3373-1275-0.ch006

Pedro, F., Subosa, M., Rivas, A., & Valverde, P. (2019). Artificial intelligence in education: Challenges and opportunities for sustainable development.

Peyton, K., Unnikrishnan, S., & Mulligan, B. (2025). A review of university chatbots for student support: FAQs and beyond. *Discover Education*, *4*(1), 21. DOI: 10.1007/s44217-025-00397-7

Piaget, J. (1971). *Science of Education and the Psychology of the Child*. Viking Press.

Picard, R. W. (2010). Affective computing: From laughter to IEEE. *IEEE Transactions on Affective Computing*, *1*(1), 11–17.

Pilav, S., De Backer, K., Easter, A., Silverio, S. A., Sundaresh, S., Roberts, S., & Howard, L. M. (2022). A qualitative study of minority ethnic women's experiences of access to and engagement with perinatal mental health care. *BMC Pregnancy and Childbirth*, *22*(1), 421. DOI: 10.1186/s12884-022-04698-9 PMID: 35585579

Pillai, A. S., & Tedesco, R. (2023). *Machine Learning and Deep Learning in Natural Language Processing*. CRC Press., DOI: 10.1201/9781003296126

Ping, Q., Niu, F., Thattai, G., Chengottusseriyil, J., Gao, Q., Reganti, A., Rajagopal, P., Tur, G., Hakkani-Tür, D., & Nataraja, P. (2020). Interactive Teaching for Conversational AI. *ArXiv*, abs/2012.00958.

Pinto, A. M., Bazzoli, A., & Mercedes, J. (2024). Mental health and lifestyle health behaviors among commuter college students. *Cogent Mental Health*, *3*(1), 1–25. DOI: 10.1080/28324765.2024.2436432 PMID: 38550624

Pisriwati, S. A., Hardi, Y., & Siswanto, D. H. (2024). Enhancing organizational development through principal leadership to improve teacher and staff work discipline. *Journal of Organizational and Human Resource Development Strategies*, *1*(01), 52–62.

Poleto, T., Nepomuceno, T. C. C., de Carvalho, V. D. H., Friaes, L. C. B. de O., de Oliveira, R. C. P., & Figueiredo, C. J. J. (2023). Information Security Applications in Smart Cities: A Bibliometric Analysis of Emerging Research. *Future Internet*, *15*(12), 393. DOI: 10.3390/fi15120393

Ponnuviji, N. P., Murugan, P., Esakkiammal, S., Kumar, S., Vishal, K. S., & Meenakshi, S. (2024, March). AI-Powered Business Intelligence for Transforming Finance and Education. In *2024 2nd International Conference on Disruptive Technologies (ICDT)* (pp. 1287-1291). IEEE.

Ponnuviji, N. P., Sumaiya Begum, A., Gnanasekaran, T., Rajendiran, M., & Shenbaga Ezhil, S. (2023, April). Leveraging Random Forest for Intelligent IoT Systems in Industrial Environments. In *International Conference on Internet of Things* (pp. 46-57). Cham: Springer Nature Switzerland.

Pradeep, E., Mukherjee, S. K., Selvakumar, P., Koppaka, A. K., Chandel, P. S., & Vats, C. (2025). Empowering Social Media Users With Ethical AI. In Chakraborty, S. (Ed.), *Ethical AI Solutions for Addressing Social Media Influence and Hate Speech* (pp. 91–118). IGI Global Scientific Publishing., DOI: 10.4018/979-8-3693-9904-0.ch005

Priyadharshini, S. I., Irene, D. S., Beulah, J. R., & Ponnuviji, N. P. (2025). Enhancing real-time health monitoring with hybrid recurrent long short-term tyrannosaurus search for menstrual cups. *Biomedical Signal Processing and Control, 100*, 107065.

Quach, S., Thaichon, P., Martin, K. D., Weaven, S., & Palmatier, R. W. (2022). Digital technologies: Tensions in privacy and data. *Journal of the Academy of Marketing Science*, *50*(6), 1299–1323. DOI: 10.1007/s11747-022-00845-y PMID: 35281634

Quaquebeke, N. V., & Gerpott, F. H. (2023). The Now, New, and Next of Digital Leadership: How Artificial Intelligence (AI) Will Take Over and Change Leadership as We Know It. *Journal of Leadership &amp. Organization Studies*, *30*(3), 265–275. DOI: 10.1177/15480518231181731

Quijada, M. A. (2021). My Mental Health Struggle in Academia: What I Wish All Business School Faculty, Students, and Administration Knew. *Journal of Management Education*, *45*(1), 19–42. DOI: 10.1177/1052562920958433

Rahman, H. (2025). The Ethical Dimensions of Digital Interactions. In *Digital Citizenship and Building a Responsible Online Presence* (pp. 123–164). IGI Global., DOI: 10.4018/979-8-3693-6675-2.ch005

Rahman, M. A., Emon, M. M. H., Khan, T., & Siam, S. A. J. (2024). Measuring the Influence of Brand Image on Consumer Behavioral Intentions by using AI: Exploring the Mediating Role of Trust. *2024 IEEE International Conference on Computing, Applications and Systems (COMPAS)*, 1–7. https://doi.org/DOI: 10.1109/COMPAS60761.2024.10796396

Ranjitha, P. K., Selvakumar, P., Anute, N., Manjunath, T., Sureshkrishna, G., & Pougajendy, S. (2025). Transportation Challenges In Islands Tourism. In Hassan, V. (Ed.), *Navigating Mass Tourism to Island Destinations: Preservation and Cultural Heritage Challenges* (pp. 287–312). IGI Global Scientific Publishing., DOI: 10.4018/979-8-3693-9107-5.ch011

Ravarini, A., Canavesi, A., & Passerini, K. (2024). From Users to Allies: Exploring Educator and Generative AI Roles in Shaping the Future of Higher Education [Conference paper]. *International Conference on Higher Education Advances*, 312-319. https://doi.org/DOI: 10.4995/HEAd24.2024.17345

Reamer, F. G. (2018). Artificial Intelligence in social work: Emerging ethical challenges. *Social Work*, *63*(3), 233–242. DOI: 10.1093/sw/swy019

Reddy, B. A., Nayak, U. A., Srinivasan, S., Angela Jean Mary, E., Chauhan, A., & Rajagopal, R. (2025). Sentiment and Emotion Analysis Using Machine Learning Techniques. In *Exploring Psychology, Social Innovation and Advanced Applications of Machine Learning* (pp. 173–190). IGI Global. https://doi.org/DOI: 10.4018/979-8-3693-6910-4.ch009

Robbins, R., Krebs, P., Rapoport, D. M., Jean-Louis, G., & Duncan, D. T. (2021). Examining the Effects of COVID-19 on Sleep, Mental Health, and Technology Use Among Adults in the United States: Cross-sectional Survey. *JMIR Mental Health*, *8*(1), e22857.

Rodriguez, L., & Smith, J. A. (2023). Chatbots as a Tool for Promoting Student Mental Health: A Case Study. *Educational Technology Research and Development*, *71*(4), 789–805. DOI: 10.1007/s11423-023-10123-4

Rogers, C. R. (1961). *On Becoming a Person: A Therapist's View of Psychotherapy*. Houghton Mifflin.

Roll, I., & Wylie, R. (2016). Evolution and revolution in artificial intelligence in education. *International Journal of Artificial Intelligence in Education*, *26*(2), 582–599.

Rong, K., Ling, Y., Yang, T., & Huang, C. (2025). Cross-border data transfer: Patterns and discrepancies. *Journal of International Business Policy*, *8*(1), 10–32. DOI: 10.1057/s42214-025-00209-7

Ruan, S., Jiang, L., Xu, Q., Liu, Z., Davis, G., Brunskill, E., & Landay, J. (2021). EnglishBot: An AI-Powered Conversational System for Second Language Learning. *Proceedings of the 26th International Conference on Intelligent User Interfaces*. https://doi.org/DOI: 10.1145/3397481.3450648

Russell, S., & Norvig, P. (2021). *Artificial Intelligence: A modern approach* (4th ed.). Pearson.

Sakaue, J., & Yamanaka, T. (2025, March). Enhancing English proficiency through AI conversations: The impact of ChatGPT on TOEIC and Speechace performance in a project-based learning context. *English Language Teaching*, *18*(3), 1–70.

Salam, U. (2024). The Integration of ChatGPT in English for Foreign Language Course: Elevating AI Writing Assistant Acceptance. *Computers in The Schools*, •••, 1–21. DOI: 10.1080/07380569.2024.2446239

Sanfilippo, M. R., Apthorpe, N., Brehm, K., & Shvartzshnaider, Y. (2023). Privacy governance not included: Analysis of third parties in learning management systems. *Information and Learning Science*, *124*(9/10), 326–348. DOI: 10.1108/ILS-04-2023-0033

Santhini, C., Ruba, M., Sakthi Priya, V., & Hemalatha, R. (2025). Intercultural communication and assessment practices in the integration of AI with education. In *Generative AI approaches to sustainable development in higher education*. IGI Global.

Saputra, F. (2021). Leadership, Communication, and Work Motivation in Determining the Success of Professional Organizations. *Journal of Law. Politic and Humanities*, *1*(2), 59–70. DOI: 10.38035/jlph.v1i2.54

Sarfaraj, G. K., Adhvaryu, R., & Jha, A. K. (2025). A REVIEW ON INTELLIGENT TUTORING SYSTEMS: Enhancing Learning with Conversational AI. *Indian Scientific Journal Of Research In Engineering And Management*, *09*(01), 1–9. DOI: 10.55041/ijsrem40649

Schiff, D. (2022). Education for AI, not AI for education: The role of education and ethics in national AI policy strategies. *International Journal of Artificial Intelligence in Education*, *32*(3), 527–563.

Schiff, D. (2022). Education for AI, not AI for Education: The Role of Education and Ethics in National AI Policy Strategies. *International Journal of Artificial Intelligence in Education*, *32*(3), 527–563. DOI: 10.1007/s40593-021-00270-2

Schmitz, M. L., Antonietti, C., Consoli, T., Cattaneo, A., Gonon, P., & Petko, D. (2023). Transformational leadership for technology integration in schools: Empowering teachers to use technology in a more demanding way. *Computers & Education*, *204*, 104880.

Seo, K., Tang, J., Roll, I., Fels, S., & Yoon, D. (2021). The impact of artificial intelligence on learner–instructor interaction in online learning. *International Journal of Educational Technology in Higher Education*, *18*(1), 54. DOI: 10.1186/s41239-021-00292-9 PMID: 34778540

Serban, I. V., Lowe, R., Henderson, P., Charlin, L., & Pineau, J. (2018). A survey of available corpora for building data-driven dialogue systems. *Dialogue & Discourse*, *9*(1), 1–49.

Settles, B., & Meeder, B. (2016). A trainable spaced repetition model for language learning. In *Proceedings of the 54th Annual Meeting of the Association for Computational Linguistics (*Volume 1*: Long Papers)* (pp. 1848–1858).

Shahzad, M. F., Xu, S., Liu, H., & Zahid, H. (2025). Generative Artificial Intelligence (ChatGPT-4) and Social Media Impact on Academic Performance and Psychological Well-Being in China's Higher Education [Article]. *European Journal of Education*, *60*(1), e12835. Advance online publication. DOI: 10.1111/ejed.12835

Sharma, S. K., Dixit, R. J., Rai, D., & Mall, S. (2024). Artificial intelligence and machine learning in smart education. In *Infrastructure Possibilities and Human-Centered Approaches With Industry 5.0* (pp. 86–106). IGI Global., DOI: 10.4018/979-8-3693-0782-3.ch006

Shende, A. D., Tekade, S. A., Deshmukh, A. A., Tembhurkar, S. P., & Selvakumar, P. (2025). Water Quality Monitoring and Control With AI. In Ruiz-Vanoye, J., & Díaz-Parra, O. (Eds.), *Smart Water Technology for Sustainable Management in Modern Cities* (pp. 51–80). IGI Global Scientific Publishing., DOI: 10.4018/979-8-3693-8074-1.ch003

Shimizu, I., Kasai, H., Shikino, K., Araki, N., Takahashi, Z., Onodera, M., Kimura, Y., Tsukamoto, T., Yamauchi, K., Asahina, M., Ito, S., & Kawakami, E. (2023). Developing Medical Education Curriculum Reform Strategies to Address the Impact of Generative AI: Qualitative Study. *JMIR Medical Education*, *9*. Advance online publication. DOI: 10.2196/53466 PMID: 38032695

Shneiderman, B. (2020). Bridging the Gap Between Ethics and Practice. *ACM Transactions on Interactive Intelligent Systems*, *10*(4), 1–31. DOI: 10.1145/3419764

Shore, J. H., Yellowlees, P., Caudill, R., Johnston, B., Turvey, C., Mishkind, M. C., & Hilty, D. M. (2018). Best practices in videoconferencing-based telemental health. *Telemedicine Journal and e-Health*, *24*(11), 827–832. DOI: 10.1089/tmj.2018.0237 PMID: 30358514

Shtayyat, A., Gawanmeh, A., & Mashaleh, A. (2025). *Risk Analysis of AI Integration in Educational Systems*., DOI: 10.4018/979-8-3373-0832-6.ch017

Siemens, G., & Long, P. (2011). Penetrating the fog: Analytics in learning and education. *EDUCAUSE Review*, *46*(5), 30–32.

Singh, A., & Kaur, P. (2023). AI Chatbots and Student Mental Health: An Indian Perspective. *Asian Journal of Psychiatry*, *65*, 102789. DOI: 10.1016/j.ajp.2023.102789

Singh, B., & Kaunert, C. (2024). *Augmented Reality and Virtual Reality Modules for Mindfulness*., DOI: 10.4018/979-8-3693-1123-3.ch007

Singh, O. (2023). Artificial Intelligence in the Era of ChatGPT—Opportunities and Challenges in Mental Health Care. *Indian Journal of Psychiatry, 65*(3), 297–298. DOI: 10.4103/indianjpsychiatry.indianjpsychiatry_123_23:contentReference[oaicite:29]{index=29} PMID: 37204980

Sleeman, D., & Brown, J. S. (1982). *Intelligent Tutoring Systems*. Academic Press.

Sterrett, W., & Richardson, J. W. (2020). Supporting Professional Development through Digital Principal Leadership. *Journal of Organizational and Educational Leadership*, *5*(2), 1–19. https://www.proquest.com/scholarly-journals/supporting-professional-development-through/docview/2430112403/se-2

Stige, Å., Zamani, E. D., Mikalef, P., & Zhu, Y. (2024). Artificial intelligence (AI) for user experience (UX) design: A systematic literature review and future research agenda. *Information Technology & People*, *37*(6), 2324–2352. DOI: 10.1108/ITP-07-2022-0519

Stone, A. (2023). Student Perceptions of Academic Integrity: A Qualitative Study of Understanding, Consequences, and Impact. *Journal of Academic Ethics*, *21*(3), 357–375. DOI: 10.1007/s10805-022-09461-5 PMID: 36466717

Subramanian, M., Portia, R., Mishra, B. R., & Selvakumar, P. P. V., R., & T. C., M. (2025). Assessment and Evaluation in Personalized STEAM Education. In N. Son (Ed.), *Integrating Personalized Learning Methods Into STEAM Education* (pp. 103-122). IGI Global Scientific Publishing. https://doi.org/DOI: 10.4018/979-8-3693-7718-5.ch005

Subramanian, Y. R., & Rajendran, R. (2024). *Transforming Healthcare: The Convergence of IoT and AI* (pp. 357–394). https://doi.org/DOI: 10.1007/978-3-031-65022-2_20

Sule, M.-J., Zennaro, M., & Thomas, G. (2021). Cybersecurity through the lens of Digital Identity and Data Protection: Issues and Trends. *Technology in Society*, *67*, 101734. DOI: 10.1016/j.techsoc.2021.101734

Suleski, T., Ahmed, M., Yang, W., & Wang, E. (2023). A review of multi-factor authentication in the Internet of Healthcare Things. *Digital Health*, *9*. Advance online publication. DOI: 10.1177/20552076231177144 PMID: 37252257

Sun, C., Major, L., Daltry, R., Moustafa, N., & Friedberg, A. (2024). Teacher-AI Collaboration in Content Recommendation for Digital Personalised Learning among Pre-primary Learners in Kenya [Conference paper]. *L@S 2024 - Proceedings of the 11th ACM Conference on Learning @ Scale*, 346-350. https://doi.org/DOI: 10.1145/3657604.3664662

Sunandar, E., Purnama, A., Arribathi, A. H., Yusuf, D. A., & Daeli, O. P. M. (2024). Strategies and Consequences of AI-Enhanced Predictive Models for Early Identification of Students at Risk [Conference paper]. *2024 3rd International Conference on Creative Communication and Innovative Technology, ICCIT 2024*. https://doi.org/DOI: 10.1109/ICCIT62134.2024.10701122

Supriatna, N., & Zulganef, Z. (2023). The Influence of Innovation Leadership on Employee Performance. *International Journal of Business, Economics, and Social Development*, *4*(1), 20–24. DOI: 10.46336/ijbesd.v4i1.365

Susnjak, T., Ramaswami, G. S., & Mathrani, A. (2022). Learning analytics dashboard: A tool for providing actionable insights to learners. *International Journal of Educational Technology in Higher Education*, *19*(1), 12. DOI: 10.1186/s41239-021-00313-7 PMID: 35194560

Swan, B. A., Febres-Cordero, S., Steiger, L., Lisenby, A., Getz, T., Hudson, J., Cole, K., Branch, R., McDermott, C., Fugate, K., & Giordano, N. A. (2025). Feasibility and acceptability of incorporating artificial intelligence into simulation education [Article]. *Clinical Simulation in Nursing*, *104*, 101739. Advance online publication. DOI: 10.1016/j.ecns.2025.101739

Tambyah, S. K. (Ed.). (2022). *Student Growth and Development in New Higher Education Learning Spaces: Student-centred Learning in Singapore*. Taylor & Francis.

Tang, X. (2025). L2 Writing with AI: Perceptions and Engagement of EFL Learners in China. *English Language Teaching*, *18*(2), 68. DOI: 10.5539/elt.v18n2p68

Theodore, S. J., Jr., Lodhi, A. R., Upadhyay, P., & Yadav, S. P. (2025). Augmenting Mental Healthcare Using Artificial Intelligence Advancements. In *Demystifying the Role of Natural Language Processing (NLP) in Mental Health* (pp. 127–144). IGI Global. https://doi.org/DOI: 10.4018/979-8-3693-4203-9.ch008

Topol, E. (2019). *Deep medicine: How artificial Intelligence can make healthcare human again*. Basic Books.

Torous, J., Myrick, K. J., Rauseo-Ricupero, N., & Firth, J. (2020). Digital mental health and COVID-19: Using technology today to accelerate the curve on access and quality tomorrow. *JMIR Mental Health*, *7*(3), e18848. PMID: 32213476

Torous, J., & Wykes, T. (2020). Opportunities From the Coronavirus Disease 2019 Pandemic for Transforming Psychiatric Care With Telehealth. *JAMA Psychiatry*, *77*(12), 1205–1206. PMID: 32391857

Tulaskar, R., & Turunen, M. (2022). What students want? Experiences, challenges, and engagement during Emergency Remote Learning amidst COVID-19 crisis. *Education and Information Technologies*, *27*(1), 551–587. DOI: 10.1007/s10639-021-10747-1 PMID: 34690527

Tychola, K. A., Vrochidou, E., & Papakostas, G. A. (2024). *Emotional Learning Analytics in Education*., DOI: 10.4018/979-8-3693-2663-3.ch004

Uwosomah, E. E., & Dooly, M. (2025). It Is Not the Huge Enemy: Preservice Teachers' Evolving Perspectives on AI. *Education Sciences*, *15*(2), 152. DOI: 10.3390/educsci15020152

Vaidyam, A. N., Wisniewski, H., Halamka, J. D., Kashavan, M. S., & Torous, J. B. (2019). Chatbots and conversational agents in mental health: A review of the psychiatric landscape. *Canadian Journal of Psychiatry*, *64*(7), 456–464. DOI: 10.1177/0706743719828977 PMID: 30897957

Vaiyapuri, S., Kadam, P., Chandrasekharuni, G., Oliveira, I. S., Senthilkumaran, S., Salim, A., Patel, K., de Almeida Gonçalves Sachett, J., & Pucca, M. B. (2023). Multifaceted community health education programs as powerful tools to mitigate snakebite-induced deaths, disabilities, and socioeconomic burden. *Toxicon: X*, *17*, 100147. DOI: 10.1016/j.toxcx.2022.100147 PMID: 36632238

Van Brummelen, J., Heng, T., & Tabunshchyk, V. (2020). Teaching Tech to Talk: K-12 Conversational Artificial Intelligence Literacy Curriculum and Development Tools., 15655-15663. https://doi.org/.DOI: 10.1609/aaai.v35i17.17844

VanLehn, K. (2011). The relative effectiveness of human tutoring, intelligent tutoring systems, and other tutoring systems. *Educational Psychologist*, *46*(4), 197–221.

Vayena, E., Blasimme, A., & Cohen, I. G. (2018). Machine learning in medicine: Addressing ethical challenges. *PLoS Medicine*, *15*(11), e1002689. DOI: 10.1371/journal.pmed.1002689 PMID: 30399149

Vayyala, R. (2025). Data Lineage. In *Data Governance, DevSecOps, and Advancements in Modern Software* (pp. 73–98). IGI Global., DOI: 10.4018/979-8-3373-0365-9.ch004

Venter, I., Cranfield, D., Blignaut, R., Achi, S., & Tick, A. (2024). Conversational AI in Higher Education: Opportunities, Challenges, and Ethical Considerations. *2024 IEEE 28th International Conference on Intelligent Engineering Systems (INES)*, 000195-000202. https://doi.org/ DOI: 10.1109/INES63318.2024.10629104

Vygotsky, L. S. (1978). *Mind in Society: The Development of Higher Psychological Processes*. Harvard University Press.

Wang, T., Bruckman, A. S., & Yang, D. (2025). The Practice of Online Peer Counseling and the Potential for AI-Powered Support Tools. *Proceedings of the ACM on Human-Computer Interaction*, *9*(2), 1–33. DOI: 10.1145/3711089

Wang, X., & Liu, Y. (2025). The Use of Conversational Agents for Mental Health Support in Higher Education: A Review. *International Journal of Human-Computer Interaction*, *41*(1), 1–15. DOI: 10.1080/10447318.2025.1001234

Wang, Y., Wang, Y., Crace, K., & Zhang, Y. (2025). Understanding Attitudes and Trust of Generative AI Chatbots for Social Anxiety Support. *Proceedings of the 2025 CHI Conference on Human Factors in Computing Systems*, 1–21. https://doi.org/DOI: 10.1145/3706598.3714286

Williams, R., Ali, S., Devasia, N., DiPaola, D., Hong, J., Kaputsos, S. P., Jordan, B., & Breazeal, C. (2023). AI + Ethics Curricula for Middle School Youth: Lessons Learned from Three Project-Based Curricula. *International Journal of Artificial Intelligence in Education*, *33*(2), 325–383. DOI: 10.1007/s40593-022-00298-y PMID: 35935456

Winkler, R., & Söllner, M. (2018). Unleashing the potential of chatbots in education: A state-of-the-art analysis. In *Academy of Management Annual Meeting Proceedings.*

Woldegiorgis, E. T., & Chiramba, O. (2025). Access and success in higher education: Fostering resilience in historically disadvantaged students in South Africa. *Journal of Applied Research in Higher Education*, *17*(2), 759–771. DOI: 10.1108/JARHE-05-2023-0217

World Health Organization. (2022). Mental health and COVID-19: Early evidence of the pandemic's impact. https://www.who.int/publications/i/item/9789240055672

Xie, X. (2023). Influence of AI-driven Inquiry Teaching on Learning Outcomes. *International Journal of Emerging Technologies in Learning*, *18*, 59–70. DOI: 10.3991/ijet.v18i23.45473

Yadav, M., Kanwal, P., & Luu, T. M. N. (2024). *Overcoming Imposter Syndrome.*, DOI: 10.4018/979-8-3693-3144-6.ch004

Yadav, R., Huzooree, G., Yadav, M., & Gangodawilage, D. S. K. (2025). Generative AI for personalized learning content creation. In *Transformative AI Practices for Personalized Learning Strategies* (pp. 107–130). IGI Global., DOI: 10.4018/979-8-3693-8744-3.ch005

Yadav, S. (2025). Leveraging AI to Enhance Teaching and Learning in Education. In *Optimizing Research Techniques and Learning Strategies With Digital Technologies* (pp. 211–238). IGI Global., DOI: 10.4018/979-8-3693-7863-2.ch008

Yambal, S., & Waykar, Y. A. (2025). *Future of Education Using Adaptive AI*. Intelligent Systems, and Ethical Challenges., DOI: 10.4018/979-8-3693-6527-4.ch006

Yang, H. (2025). Harnessing generative AI: Exploring its impact on cognitive engagement, emotional engagement, learning retention, reward sensitivity, and motivation through reinforcement theory [Article]. *Learning and Motivation*, *90*, 102136. Advance online publication. DOI: 10.1016/j.lmot.2025.102136

Yang, H., & Rui, Y. (2025). Transforming EFL students' engagement: How AI-enhanced environments bridge emotional health challenges like depression and anxiety [Article]. *Acta Psychologica*, *257*, 105104. Advance online publication. DOI: 10.1016/j.actpsy.2025.105104 PMID: 40413880

Yang, J., Buechele, S., Natori, A., & Kay, J. (2022). Conversational agents in education: A systematic review. *Computers and Education: Artificial Intelligence*, *3*, 100066.

Ye, Q., & Hu, H. (2020). *Local Differential Privacy: Tools*. Challenges, and Opportunities., DOI: 10.1007/978-981-15-3281-8_2

Zawacki-Richter, O., Marín, V. I., Bond, M., & Gouverneur, F. (2019). Systematic review of research on artificial intelligence applications in higher education – Where are the educators? *International Journal of Educational Technology in Higher Education*, *16*(1), 39.

Zhai, C., Wibowo, S., & Li, L. D. (2024). The effects of over-reliance on AI dialogue systems on students' cognitive abilities: A systematic review. *Smart Learning Environments, 11*(1), 28. DOI: 10.1186/s40561-024-00316-7

Zhang, M., & Crosthwaite, P. (2025). More human than human? Differences in lexis and collocation within academic essays produced by ChatGPT-3.5 and human L2 writers. *International Review of Applied Linguistics in Language Teaching*. Advance online publication. DOI: 10.1515/iral-2024-0196

Zhao, X. (2022). Leveraging Artificial Intelligence (AI) Technology for English Writing: Introducing Wordtune as a Digital Writing Assistant for EFL Writers. *RELC Journal, 54*, 890–894. DOI: 10.1177/00336882221094089

Zhao, Y., Yusof, S. M., Hou, M., & Li, Z. (2024). How Can Generative Artificial Intelligence help Teachers in Early Childhood Education with their Teaching? Analyses from the Perspective of Teaching Methods. *International Journal of Academic Research in Progressive Education and Development, 13*(1). Advance online publication. DOI: 10.6007/ijarped/v13-i1/20958

Zhao, Y., Zhao, M., & Shi, F. (2023). Integrating Moral Education and Educational Information Technology: A Strategic Approach to Enhance Rural Teacher Training in Universities. *Journal of the Knowledge Economy, 15*(3), 15053–15093. DOI: 10.1007/s13132-023-01693-z

Zhou, X., Snoswell, C. L., Harding, L. E., Bambling, M., Edirippulige, S., Bai, X., & Smith, A. C. (2019). The Role of Telehealth in Reducing the Mental Health Burden From COVID-19. *Telemedicine Journal and e-Health, 26*(4), 377–379. PMID: 32202977

Zimmerle, J. C. (2021). Safe, Sound, and Private: Promoting Data Protection for Students. *Computers in the Schools, 38*(1), 1–18. DOI: 10.1080/07380569.2021.1882203

About the Contributors

Suha Khalil Assayed holds a Ph.D. in Computer Science from The British University in Dubai, UAE, specializing in Artificial Intelligence and Deep Learning. With over two decades of experience in the higher education sector, she has developed deep expertise in machine learning, natural language processing (NLP), and neural network architectures, focusing on innovative AI applications that enhance educational outcomes. Dr. Assayed's research bridges theory and practice, emphasizing the design and deployment of AI-driven tools, including generative AI models, for personalized student advising and support. Her scholarly contributions encompass pioneering work on AI integration in education, intelligent chatbots, and adaptive learning systems, with publications in leading journals and conferences. Passionate about advancing smart education, she explores how emerging technologies can create more inclusive and effective learning environments.

***

Abu Bakar Abdul Hamid chose academia as his profession in 1992, beginning as a lecturer and later rising to a Professor of Marketing and Supply Chain Management. He holds a BBA and an MBA from Northrop University (USA) and a PhD from the University of Derby, UK. He has demonstrated an excellent record of teaching and supervision for more than 25 years in the academic field, at both undergraduate and postgraduate levels. Above all, his achievement in graduating more than 35 PhD candidates proves his ability, capability, and passion in postgraduate supervisions. He has also produced impactful research and publications which directly strengthen his expertise in his area of interest. In particular, he has published more than 300 articles in competitive international journals, proceedings, books, and book chapters. He also managed to secure several competitive national grants and consultancies for various projects. Such commitment is truly a landmark of an academician. His accolades, academic recognition, and leadership demonstrate his level of professorship. His notable contributions are recognized locally and internationally, as proven by the multiple invitations he has received to be an invited speaker, reviewer, editor in journals, external assessor, and internal or external examiner. With such calibre, he has much to contribute to any academic institution in the world.

Sana Alsayed is an Assistant Professor of Psychological Counseling at Philadelphia University, Jordan. She has published several articles exploring the intersections of artificial intelligence, psychology, and emotions. Her research reflects an interdisciplinary approach to understanding human behavior and emotional well-being. Alongside her academic role, she serves as Library Director and Information Resources Manager at the university. Through her dual positions, she contributes to both educational development and applied research.

Areej Khalil Assayed is an educator, academic leader, and trainer with over 25 years of experience in the field of education. She is the Head of the English Department and Humanities at Jordan International Schools (JIS) and a PhD candidate in Educational Leadership and Curriculum at Westcliff University, California, USA. Holding an MA in Linguistics and a BA in English Language and Literature, she has extensive expertise in curriculum development, instructional innovation, and teacher professional development. Her work integrates modern pedagogical approaches such as cooperative learning, multiple intelligences, and critical thinking, and she has conducted inspections for private schools in Jordan in collaboration with Accreditation International (AI). Her career reflects a strong commitment to advancing educational quality, fostering professional growth, and promoting the holistic development of learners.

Abid Aziz is serving as a Trustee on the Board of Uttara University Trust in Bangladesh. He has a BSc in Business from Birkbeck College, University of London, United Kingdom, as well as an MBA and an MS in Economics. His work towards smart tech deployment and dissemination, digitization of majority or the administrative business processes, integration of Ai into academics and Smart Campus transition, future-proofing Uttara University with digital transformation is the first of its kind in the country that has been setting benchmarks, fostering innovation, ensuring efficiency, and generating socioeconomic impact within the community. He has a robust research background with expertise in corporate strategy as well. Mr Aziz had previously served as the Director of the Fintech Research Group and is presently steering the Office of the Future, leading the transformation project in partnership with top industries. This project team is actively working on improving the tech-led academic experience, which is at par with global forces.

Nabid Aziz is a Doctoral Researcher at the University of Hull in the East Riding of Yorkshire, located in the United Kingdom. Additionally, in Bangladesh he has been serving as an Assistant Professor at Gopalganj Science and Technology University (formerly BSMRSTU) and as a member of the governing body of Uttara University he heads it's Planning and Development Committee ensuring growth of the institutions. His work in academia and educational administration is concentrated on the areas such as inclusive technology deployment, campus infrastructure and capacity building, faculty development, internationalisation and business innovation. With a long term association with the education sector, he continues to contribute towards institutional sustainability.

Yamini B is an faculty member in the Department of Networking and Communications at SRM Institute of Science and Technology, Kattankulathur. Her academic and research interests focus on emerging trends in networking, communication technologies, and related domains. She is dedicated to fostering innovation, academic excellence, and student skill development in her field.

Ferdi Çelik is a researcher specializing in English as a foreign language (EFL) teaching. With a keen focus on language acquisition, pedagogy, and innovative teaching methodologies, he explores ways to enhance language learning effectiveness. His work delves into curriculum development, assessment strategies, and the integration of technology in language education. Passionate about advancing the field, Ferdi contributes through research, publications, and active engagement in the academic community.

Most. Sharmin Ara Chowdhury is a research practitioner with a strong focus on key areas such as Artificial Intelligence, strategic innovation, management information systems, and sustainability. Her research explores the intersection of emerging technologies and organizational strategy. By aligning innovation with practical needs, she addresses real-world challenges through applied and impactful research. Sharmin's work bridges academic theory and professional practice, making significant contributions to the evolving landscape of digital transformation and sustainable development.

D. Senthil Kumar is an Assistant Professor in the Department of Computer Science and Engineering (Cyber Security) at R.M.K. College of Engineering and Technology. He is actively involved in teaching and guiding students in cybersecurity and digital forensics. His areas of interest include network security, ethical hacking, and secure system design.

|Volkan Duran - Contributing Author|Curriculum an instruction

Md Mehedi Hasan Emon is a research practitioner in Business and Management, with specialized in Supply Chain Management, Digital Transformation, Marketing, Information Systems, and Educational Technology (Edutech). His work bridges a diverse range of domains including Artificial Intelligence in Business, Human-Computer Interaction, Cognitive Behaviour, E-commerce, and Smart Logistics. His research extensively explores the integration of emerging technologies in business ecosystems focusing on AI-driven innovation, behavioral responses to technology adoption, and digital marketing strategies. He has also contributed significantly to sustainability-focused fields such as GreenTech, Green Finance, Renewable Energy, and Blockchain-enabled financial innovation. Additionally, his work in Smart Cities and IoT adoption emphasizes the importance of user trust, security, and operational efficiency. Emon has authored numerous peer-reviewed publications on topics including AI adoption intention, supply chain visibility, digital learning acceptance, and crisis-resilient supply chains. Many of his studies adopt behavioral and cognitive perspectives to understand how professionals and consumers interact with technology highlighting the psychological and user-centric aspects of digital transformation. He has participated in several research initiatives funded by the University Grants Commission of Bangladesh and the European Union. His work aligns closely with the United Nations Sustainable Development Goals (SDGs), particularly in areas such as poverty reduction, access to quality education, clean and affordable energy, inclusive economic growth, sustainable industrialization, responsible consumption, climate resilience, and ocean sustainability. His work also reflects a commitment to reducing inequalities and fostering international partnerships for sustainable development. In addition to his research contributions, he serves as a peer reviewer for several high-impact academic journals and is widely recognized for promoting academic rigor and ethical scholarship. As a prolific author, he continues to shape the discourse on sustainability, innovation, and digital advancement through his research, writing, and knowledge dissemination.

Shilpa Gaidhani is an Assistant Professor in the MBA Department at Balaji Institute of Management and Human Resource Development, Sri Balaji University, Pune. She holds over 9 years of teaching experience, specializing in management education for MBA students. Dr. Gaidhani has published more than 10 research papers in reputed national and international journals, reflecting her active engagement in academic research and scholarship.

Prashant Kalshetti is a Professor and Head of the Department of BBA at Dr. D. Y. Patil Vidyapeeth's Global Business School and Research Centre, Pune. With a strong academic background and extensive experience in business education, he is known for his contributions to curriculum development, student mentorship, and academic leadership. Dr. Kalshetti is deeply committed to nurturing future business leaders through a blend of theoretical knowledge and practical exposure. His areas of expertise include business strategy, entrepreneurship, and management education, and he actively participates in academic research and institutional growth initiatives.

Shaista Md. Mumtaz Khan is an Assistant Professor in the Department of MBA at Datta Meghe Institute of Management Studies, Nagpur, Maharashtra. With over 15 years of teaching experience in management education, she brings a strong academic foundation and a passion for student development. She is currently pursuing her Ph.D., further deepening her expertise in the field.

Ruba M completed her Master's Degree in VLSI Design and she received her Bachelor's Degree in Electronics and Communication Engineering, Anna University, Chennai. She currently works as an assistant professor at Velalar College of Engineering and Technology. She has published 4 papers in international journals (SCOPUS) and presented 19 papers in national & international conferences. Her current research areas are VLSI Design and the Internet of Things (IoT).

Dinesh M G is a faculty member at EASA College of Engineering and Technology, Coimbatore, Tamil Nadu. He is actively engaged in teaching and research in the fields of computer science and emerging technologies. His academic interests include machine learning, data analytics, and cloud computing.

T.C. Manjunath was born on 6th February 1967. He did his BE from RV College of Engg. in 1989, ME in Robotics & Automation from LD College of Engg. in 1992 with First Rank and PhD in Systems & Control Engg. from IIT Bombay in the year 2007. He is currently working as the Dean Research R D and as Professor in the Dept. of Computer Science & Engineering with specialization in IoT, Cyber Security & Blockchain Technology in Rajarajeswari College of Engineering, Bengaluru, Karnataka. He has completed B.E. Degree from R.V. College of Engg., M.E. Govt.'s LD College of Engg., Gujarat Univ., Ahmedabad in First Rank and Ph.D. in Systems and Control Engineering from the Indian Institute of Technology Bombay IIT Bombay He has got a teaching academic, research and administrative experience of more than 35+ years 10 years as Principal, 8 years as HoD rest as faculty and has published more than 1200+ research papers in various national & international journals and conferences, with 175+ patents, 25 book-chapters, 25 awards and also published 25 text books in various field of science, engineering and technology, completed projects worth Rs. 9 Crores till date apart from guiding 10 PhD scholars. He is a member of 30 Professional Society Chapters and is a fellow of IE, IETE, AMIEE and a chartered engineer. He got the best research scholar award in 2006 in IIT Bombay amongst all the research scholars of the institute. He has got 10 awards in academics and research activities.

Daniel Kwalipo Mbangula is currently employed as a lecturer in the Faculty of Applied Educational Sciences at the University of Namibia, Namibia. He currently holds a PhD in Education from the University of Namibia. A Masters' degree from Midland State University, Zimbabwe. With over 15 years' experience in the education sector, he has been able to contribute and improve the learning environment in Namibia through series of school based projects. His research interests are on social science related field with key focus on the Education sector. Daniel Kwalipo Mbangula has published in different peer reviewed journals and book chapters in different areas.

Gokuldhev M is a Professor in the Department of Computer Science and Engineering (Data Science) at Vel Tech Rangarajan Dr. Sagunthala R&D Institute of Science and Technology, Avadi, Chennai. He specializes in data science, artificial intelligence, and advanced computing technologies. His work focuses on research, innovation, and guiding students in cutting-edge technological domains.

Girija P is a dedicated faculty member in the Department of Information Technology at Panimalar Engineering College, Chennai. With a strong academic and research background, she is actively involved in guiding students and contributing to advancements in the field of IT. Her areas of interest include data analytics, software engineering, and emerging computing technologies.

P. Selvakumar is currently an Associate Professor in the Department of Science and Humanities at Nehru Institute of Technology, Coimbatore,

Tamil Nadu, India. Prior to joining Nehru Institute of Technology, he held positions as an Assistant Professor in the Department of Science and Humanities various engineering colleges in Coimbatore, Tamil Nadu, India, spanning from 2011 to 2023. Dr.P. Selvakumar's academic and research interests lie primarily in the field of phytochemistry. He has made significant contributions to his field, with an impressive record that includes 30 journal publications, 12 patents, and 20 conference papers. Additionally, he has organized 5 seminars and conferences, further demonstrating his commitment to academic and scientific exchange. Throughout his career, Dr. P.Selvakumar has been recognized for his dedication and excellence in teaching, having been honored with several awards, including the Best Teacher Awards. He holds a prominent position in the academic community, contributing actively to research.

R.Devi is a distinguished professional over 9 years of teaching experience. She holds a B.E degree in Computer Science and Engineering from Anna University affiliated college in Chennai. M.E degree in Computer Science and Engineering from R.M.K Engineering College affiliated to Anna University, Chennai. She is also pursing her Ph.D at Anna University, Chennai. Her academic career started in 2016. She is successfully travelling into her ninth year of teaching. Her career reflects a strong dedication to both teaching and research in the field of Computer Science and Engineering making her a valuable asset in academia. She has already started her initial work in writing books and she is interested to do them further in future. She also has a hobby of listening to songs as well as writing anthology and publishing it. Already two of her anthology got published and one of her solo book is yet to be published.

Md. Adnan Rahman is an Associate Professor of Digital Marketing and MIS at Uttara University, Dhaka, Bangladesh. Additionally, he is the Director of the Office of Brand & Communication and Public Relations of this university. Dr. Adnan is a postdoctoral researcher at Infrastructure University Kuala Lumpur (IUKL), Malaysia. Dr. Adnan holds a PhD in Marketing from Putra Business School (AACSB-Accredited), UPM, Malaysia; an MSc in MIS; and an MA in IHRM from the University of Bedfordshire, United Kingdom.

Chandra Rajesh is an Assistant Professor in the Department of Computer Science and Engineering at Vel Tech Multi Tech Dr. Rangarajan Dr. Sankunthala Engineering College, Avadi, Chennai. He is dedicated to teaching and mentoring students in emerging areas of computer science. His academic interests include software development, machine learning, and data science.

Mohit Sharma is a research scholar at the Institute of Management Studies and Research, Maharshi Dayanand University, Rohtak, Haryana, India. His research focuses on the dynamic relationship between brand image and purchase intentions, particularly in the context of brand extensions within the FMCG sector. He has co-authored several scholarly works and continues to contribute to the academic community. Mohit can be reached at mohitattri.rs.imsar@mdurohtak.ac.in

Zerin Tasnim is an Assistant Professor of Supply Chain Management at North South University, Dhaka, Bangladesh, where she also serves as the Course Coordinator for the MBA program. She holds a PhD in Management from Putra Business School, Universiti Putra Malaysia (UPM), and a BSc in Mechanical Engineering from Bangladesh University of Engineering and Technology (BUET). Dr. Tasnim brings an interdisciplinary academic background and a global research perspective to her work, with research interests spanning digital supply chains, healthcare logistics, and sustainable and green operations.

Shanmugapriya V is an Assistant Professor in the Department of Information Technology at Jeppiaar Institute of Technology, Tamil Nadu. She is involved in teaching, mentoring, and research in core areas of IT. Her academic interests include cloud computing, web technologies, and software engineering

Index

A

C

D

E

T

www.ingramcontent.com/pod-product-compliance
Ingram Content Group UK Ltd.
Pitfield, Milton Keynes, MK11 3LW, UK
UKHW050947290926
15470UKWH00005B/1680

9 798337 333168